Missouri River

Mississippi River

Arkansas River

Fe

Red River

TEXAS

Hidalgo Treaty 1848.

• Austin   New Orleans •
• San Antonio
                • Galveston

G U L F   O F   M E X I C O

• Matamoros

• Zacatecas
        Tampico •
Tabasco •
  • Guanajuato   Mérida •
    Querétaro •   Jicaltepec •   YUCATÁN
                              Campeche •   PENINSULA
Mexico City • Jalapa •
        •   Veracruz •
    Puebla • Orizaba •
              • Minatilán
    Oaxaca •   Tehuantepec •

jrb-77

The French Experience in Mexico, 1821–1861

The French Experience in Mexico, 1821–1861:

A History of Constant Misunderstanding

by Nancy Nichols Barker

The University of North Carolina Press
Chapel Hill

© 1979 The University of North Carolina Press
All rights reserved
Manufactured in the United States of America
Library of Congress Catalog Card Number 78-12935
ISBN 0-8078-1339-7

Library of Congress Cataloging in Publication Data

Barker, Nancy Nichols.
  The French experience in Mexico, 1821–1861.

  Bibliography: p.
  Includes index.
  1. France—Foreign relations—Mexico. 2. Mexico—
Foreign relations—France. 3. France—Foreign rela-
tions—19th century. I. Title.
DC59.8.M6B37   327'.44'072   78-12935
ISBN 0-8078-1339-7

To My Husband
Stephen Barker
Again and Always

Contents

Illustrations

Preface

It is small exaggeration to say that Franco-Mexican relations in the nineteenth century have been known only as they pertain to the expedition of Napoleon III that placed the Archduke Ferdinand Maximilian on his ill-fated throne. This intervention of the 1860s has called into existence an enormous body of literature both popular and scholarly. Its sheer volume is attested by the publication by Martín Quirarte in 1970 of an entire book on the historiography of the Maxmilian affair that cites nearly three hundred works without even touching on periodical material.[1]

Through the years I have myself been a worker of this seam from the time when, in my doctoral dissertation, I first encountered the Mexican expedition through the eyes of the Empress Eugénie, wife of Napoleon III. Yet the more I read of this literature, the more I realized that it (my own included) was too limited in one way or another to give adequate, reasonable explanations for the French intervention. Inevitably the emperor appeared as a dreamer (or schemer) who foolishly launched his country on a futile (and/or sinister) adventure that he should have recognized as folly from the start. But the emperor was in fact no fool. He was an intelligent, widely read man who was benevolently disposed toward Mexico. Why should he have blundered so badly?

The problem with most of the studies of the intervention is the narrowness of their focus. Usually they are confined to diplomatic history and to the decade of the 1860s with no more than flashbacks to the events of the War of the Reform in the late 1850s. Studies of Franco-Mexican relations in the years between 1821, when Mexico achieved its independence, and the Napoleonic intervention are virtually nonexistent. Much of the period was virgin territory without track or trace of a scholarly predecessor when I began to explore it. The few books or articles that exist are devoted to very short periods

1. *Historiografía sobre el imperio de Maximiliano.*

of time, such as those on the "Pastry War" of 1838–39 or the diplomatic study by William Spence Robertson, *France and Latin-American
Independence*, on French relations with all of the Latin American republics in the 1820s.

Moreover, virtually all of the books on the Maximilian affair (even
if written by a citizen of the United States) have been written from
either a distinctly European or a distinctly Mexican viewpoint. The
European-oriented authors frequently displayed a woeful ignorance
of Mexican history. Their Mexican counterparts were no better
grounded in their knowledge of the French scene. Not infrequently
during the course of my research, I encountered French scholars
working on the Napoleonic expedition who could not read Spanish
and who saw no need to do so. On the other hand, it was not rare to
meet with Mexican researchers who never used French sources and
who were unable to distinguish between the Bourbon, Orleanist,
and Bonaparte regimes. To them all French rulers were alike. This
state of affairs is largely explained by Quirarte's conclusion, "No
European historian has ever been able to analyze with the necessary
critical depth the riches of Mexican documentation related to the
empire. For our part we must also confess that no Mexican historian
has been able to plumb with any thoroughness the European and
American archives necessary for a knowledge of the French intervention and the Second Empire."[2]

This study attempts to broaden and deepen our knowledge of
French policies and attitudes toward Mexico by going back to the
1820s, moving methodically forward from there, and using a wide
variety of materials, published and unpublished, on both sides of the
Atlantic. It proceeds from the convictions that (1) the earlier, ignored
decades deserve investigation in their own right and (2) a knowledge
of their history is essential to understanding of the intervention of the
1860s. As luck would have it, I was well situated both academically
and geographically to undertake this kind of endeavor. As a specialist
in ninteenth-century French history I was accustomed to going to
Europe for my sources and familiar with such great repositories as
the Archives of the Ministry of French Foreign Affairs and the Austrian Haus-, Hof-, und Staatsarchiv. In Paris I came across the archives of the Mexican Embassy, an abundant treasure that has been
all but ignored. As a resident of Texas I was close to Mexico and,

2. Ibid., pp. 113–14.

even more important as it turned out, to the rich resources of the Nettie Lee Benson Latin American Collection of the University of Texas and the help of its learned staff. While I can have no hope that the resulting book has escaped the pitfalls of prejudice, conscious or unconscious, of its author, or that its coverage is anywhere near complete, I can at least say that the research is not limited to European sources. The book is French-oriented only in that its subject (deliberately so) is the French experience in Mexico, not vice versa. My aim has been to build, or to begin to build, a kind of scholarly bridge between the Old World and the New. Doubtless, critics will soon inform me if I have in part succeeded or if I have instead splashed down somewhere in between.

I have also tried to move outside the confines of diplomacy wherein virtually all of the existing scholarly works on France and Mexico are to be found. While diplomatic history is undeniably important to the knowledge of Franco-Mexican relations and constitutes a large part of this volume, it cannot tell the whole story. The attitudes and personalities (*mentalités*) of the French needed to be analyzed to see how they bore upon French behavior and reception in Mexico. French economic interests in Mexico deserved more consideration than they have received. Much needed to be found out about French subjects living in Mexico, who have indeed been the forgotten men, even though the intervention of the 1860s was taken, ostensibly at least, for the protection of their persons and properties. Who were these French? How many of them were they? (Here I needed the quantitative method.) How did they make a living? Were they remarkably trouble-prone or litigious? Were they somehow different from other foreigners resident in Mexico? These are some of the questions I was able to answer as I made the acquaintance of the French colony of urban little men in Mexico and in them uncovered an important generator of intervention. I found, moreover, that at times the interplay between the more or less constant economic and social factors and the changing scene of public policy and private intrigue yielded *conjonctures* of vital significance. If the result of these efforts is scarcely history in the manner of the *Annales* school, it nevertheless yields a French experience in Mexico wider than conventional diplomatic history would allow.

During the many years of research and preparation of material for this book I have incurred debts of gratitude to many individuals and institutions for their help. In France I owe much to Maurice Degros,

Conservateur en chef, and to Georges Dethan, Directeur de la bibliothèque, of the Archives of the French Foreign Ministry, and to their
staff, for facilitating my work over a number of years. I am equally
grateful to Silvio Zavala Vallado, Mexican Ambassador to France,
and to his staff, who went beyond the call of duty in permitting me
to forage at will in the embassy archives, even though the embassy is
not (or was not when I was there) equipped with a public reading
room and my presence underfoot caused no little inconvenience. I
also wish to thank my good friend Maurice Paz, Avocat à la Cour de
Paris honoraire, who shared with me the fruits of his own remarkable research on Alphonse Dubois de Saligny and who has done so
much in many ways to foster my work. The mayors of the towns of
Bellême and Saint Martin-du-Vieux-Bellême in Normandy (where
Dubois de Saligny lived in retirement and died), Denis Durand and
the Count of Romanet, graciously supplied me with local lore and
documents illuminating the furtive career of the French agent.

On this side of the ocean I am especially indebted to Nettie Lee
Benson, for many years Director of the Latin American Collection
(that now bears her name) and Professor of History at the University
of Texas. For years she has done her best to guide me into the
labyrinth of nineteenth-century Mexican history. She has read much
of my work and offered valuable suggestions for its improvement. A
number of the themes in this book were born in a graduate seminar
on France and Mexico that we conducted jointly (to my great benefit)
some years ago. To her should go most of the credit for what expertise in Mexican history I may possess. May she not be held accountable for my failings. I also wish to thank Jorge Flores Díaz, Jefe del
Departamento del Archiv Histórico de la Secretaría de Relaciones
Exteriores (Mexico, D.F.) for permission to work in that archive and
to his staff for their helpfulness and courtesy in facilitating my research.

Institutional help has been forthcoming in the form of grants from
the American Society of Learned Studies and the University Research
Institute of the University of Texas and also, from the last, in the
form of two leaves of absence that permitted me periods of uninter-
rupted research. Quotations of crown copyright records in the Public Record Office appear by permission of the Controller of Her
Majesty's Stationery Office. The editors of *French Historical Studies*,
The Journal of Modern History, *The Southwestern Historical Quarterly*,
and *Hispanic American Historical Review* have given permission to

quotc parts of my articles previously published in those journals.

Nor can I forget the many colleagues and friends who have come to my aid in various ways: Lynn M. Case, my mentor at the University of Pennsylvania, who is never too busy to help a former student; David Pinkney, Professor of History at the University of Washington and former editor of *French Historical Studies*, who read this manuscript in its entirety and offered constructive criticism, and saved me from not a few blunders; Warren Spencer, Professor of History at the University of Georgia; Laura Gutíerrez, present Director of the Nettie Lee Benson Latin American Collection; Llerena Friend, Professor Emeritus at the University of Texas; Joe B. Frantz, Walter Prescott Webb Professor of History at Texas and former Director of the Texas State Historical Association; Tuffly Ellis, its present Director; James R. Buchanan, who did the map work; Ona Kay Stephenson, who skillfully typed the manuscript; and many others. Finally and above all, I am indebted to the apparently inexhaustible (but much tried) support and patience of my husband, Stephen Barker, to whom I am once again happy to dedicate my work.

Nancy Nichols Barker
Austin, Texas

The French Experience in Mexico, 1821–1861

A MEXICAN VIEW OF THE FRENCH

Y[our] E[xcellency] will be aware that love of glory and the desire of conquest have always been and are to this day characteristic of this people [the French]. —Mangino to Mexican foreign minister, 1848

A FRENCH VIEW OF THE MEXICANS

[The Mexicans] would be the most despicable of all the people on earth if they were not the most ignorant and the most frivolous. —Gabriac to French foreign minister, 1857

1

Before Recognition:
Bourbon Ambivalence (1821–1830)

[France is a] versatile, vain, rich and powerful nation; she desires to have relations with us, but on her own terms, and our policy must attempt to bring her to yield to the imperious voice of justice.—Rocafuerte to the Mexican foreign minister, 11 April 1826

France, Spain, and Mexico: The French Dilemma

Unquestionably it was unfortunate for the future of Franco-Mexican relations that Mexico achieved its independence from Spain while France was under the rule of the Bourbon monarchy. Louis XVIII, King of France, was a blood relation of King Ferdinand VII of Spain. The two monarchies had been allied ever since Louis XIV had placed his grandson on the Spanish throne in 1700. The Bourbon Family Compact of 1761, declaring that whosoever attacked one crown attacked the other, had given formal expression to their united defense of their possessions.[1] According to its terms, the monarchs could call on each other in perpetuity for military and naval aid. The ensuing revolutionary and Napoleonic upheavals, during which the Bourbons in both countries lost their thrones, had interrupted this supposedly permanent arrangement and had lent a strong impetus to the movement for independence in Mexico. In 1814 the traditional alliance between France and Spain was revived with the Bourbon restorations in the persons of Louis and Ferdinand. Under the rule of Louis, France could be expected to deny recognition of Mexican independence as long as Spain still claimed possession of her colony.

Louis had additional reason to oppose the revolt in Mexico. As a Bourbon, as king "by the grace of God," he personified the principle of legitimacy. The younger brother of the unfortunate Louis XVI, decapitated in the French Revolution, he had spent twenty-two years of his life in exile before ascending the throne. He and his family had seen and suffered enough from revolution to oppose it from the heart wherever it occurred.

Yet to oppose the revolt in principle was one thing; to combat it in practice was another. Soon after Louis began his rule the separatist movement in Mexico had achieved such undeniable importance that it could no longer be ignored. In February 1821 Augustín de Iturbide published at Iguala a plan of independence that was accepted by his army. By this project Mexico was to become an independent monarchy under a prince of the Spanish ruling dynasty. Louis was enough of a realist to recognize the limits of the possible. After a generation of foreign and civil wars on the Continent, France was impoverished and deeply divided in its body politic. Even had the king been so inclined, he was in no position to lead a crusade across the Atlantic to restore Mexico to colonial status. Even as early as 1821 there is evidence that his government was beginning to recognize the irreversibility of the revolutionary movement in Latin America and the necessity of adjusting to it.[2]

Moreover, an independent Mexico appeared to offer commercial opportunities that France could ill afford to pass up. The French loss of much of their colonial empire in the eighteenth century and the subsequent revolutionary and Napoleonic wars had spelled disaster for French commerce. During the prolonged hostilities the British navy had swept the French merchant marine from the seas. French Atlantic ports and Marseilles had become economic deserts. Under the Bourbon restoration French merchants, overjoyed with the return of peace, looked "with avidity" to the former Spanish colonies as outlets for their exports to remake their fortunes.[3] While under Spanish rule these countries had been prohibited from direct trade with Europe. French trade with them had amounted to a trickle, conducted indirectly through Cádiz. Newly independent, they appeared to offer limitless compensation for French colonial losses in Haiti and Louisiana. The French government could promote and protect this nascent trade by establishing French agents and consuls in Mexico and negotiating a treaty of commerce. On the other hand, if Louis held aloof and declined all intercourse with the rebellious colony, as principle dictated, he would have to stand by helplessly while other maritime powers, especially his archrival, England, forestalled French traders in these new markets. The Mexicans could be expected to discriminate against French merchandise and merchants and perhaps to exclude them from the country altogether. Few French merchants would dare to enter so risky a commerce. France had already lost out too many times in maritime competition with England deliberately to deny herself entrance to this vast new market.

Yet what was to be done? The well-known obstinacy and short-sightedness of Ferdinand offered little hope that he would accept the Plan of Iguala and preserve some tie with Mexico. Moreover, a revolutionary outbreak in Spain in 1820, led by Rafael de Riego, was gaining strength and posing a real threat to his throne. After he had been compelled to proclaim adherence to the liberal constitution of 1812, which he abhorred, he had appealed to Louis for armed intervention in his behalf. In April 1823 a French army under the Duke of Angoulême, nephew of Louis, crossed the Pyrenees and quelled the uprising with little difficulty. On Ferdinand's urging it remained in occupation until 1828. Louis's action in the Iberian peninsula served further to restrict French freedom in the New World. He could not move in the direction of recognition of Mexico, still claimed by Spain, while his troops were protecting the Spanish throne in Madrid. At the same time, he incurred the ill will of Mexico and risked reprisals against his commerce. The Mexican government took the position that by maintaining troops in Spain, France was liberating Spanish ones that could be used to reconquer Mexico.[4]

A "Monarchical Emancipation"?

To the French government, the best way out of this dilemma appeared to be the creation of a Spanish appanage in Mexico. If Ferdinand could be persuaded to place an infante on a Mexican throne, the principle of legitimacy would be left intact. At the same time France would be free to establish diplomatic relations with the new monarchy and to promote her trade.[5] The solution was the more attractive as it was judged easy of attainment. European statesmen were virtually unanimous during most of the nineteenth century in believing that Mexico could offer little resistance to their forces. The Duke of Wellington, whose military judgment certainly was among the best in Europe, did not doubt that even Argentina, the most stable of all the former Spanish colonies, could be recovered by Spain with ten thousand men in a matter of weeks.[6] Mexico was thought to be an easier target, since Cuba was available as an operating base. If only

Mexico were emancipated from Spain, the French ambassador in London, Prince Polignac, told George Canning, "a Spanish prince at Havana with five or six thousand men would soon be on the throne of Montezuma."[7]

In promoting a monarchy in Mexico at this time Louis had no idea of making a French colony out of Mexico or of sending out an immediate member of his family. The painful shortage of princes in the French Bourbon line would have precluded such action even had he entertained it.[8] Unable to sire children himself, the king depended on the Count of Artois, his younger brother, and the future Charles X, to continue the line. But of Artois's two sons, one, Angoulême, was likewise afflicted with the intermittent Bourbon curse of sterility and the other, the Duke of Berry, had been assassinated in 1820 while apparently without a male heir. When seven months later the widow gave birth to a son, the so-called Miracle Child became the sole hope of the continuation of the line. Angoulême was the only French Bourbon of an appropriate age to rule in Mexico but, owing to the advanced age of his father, he could assume that in the not-too-distant future he would ascend the throne of France. It was unthinkable that he should embark on an adventure overseas.

Throughout the 1820s the French government repeatedly advised Ferdinand to furnish a prince for Mexico, becoming most insistent during the years 1823 and 1824. The Ultras, led by Artois, were then on the ascendant, partly because of the advancing senility of Louis. They strongly desired to intervene in Spanish America if possible. When French troops entered Spain in 1823, Count Jean-Baptiste Guillaume Joseph Villèle, chief minister of the king, outlined in detail to Angoulême a plan by which France would supply the Spaniards ships, money, and troops (very few) thought to be sufficient to create appanages in Mexico, Peru, and Argentina.[9] If the infantes should not find the natives submissive to their rule, it mattered little, wrote Villèle. "They would at least find realms that could easily be subjugated by the aid of our navy and our credit." France would bear this expense and effort in "anticipation of the commercial advantages that those sacrifices would assure her in the future."[10]

Villèle's project could not have gone into immediate operation, since the French fleet was concentrated off Cádiz and was required for the blockade of the Spanish coast. After the fall of Cádiz in October 1823 the scheme was taken up again and, according to Viscount François Auguste René Chateaubriand, the romantic literary genius then occupying the Foreign Ministry, "pushed very far."[11] The presence of Angoulême and the French army in Spain could be relied upon to overcome the resistance of the captive Ferdinand. The "monarchical emancipation" of Mexico "and other former Spanish colonies," wrote Chateaubriand, "would have brought France to the pinnacle of prosperity and glory."[12]

Still, these plans came to nothing. George Canning, British foreign secretary, learned of the bruited intervention. Determined not to permit France to reassert her presence in the New World, he forcefully expressed the British displeasure and elicited from Polignac a formal statement of abjurement.[13] Not long thereafter Chateaubriand lost the confidence of Louis and was abruptly dismissed. Of his monarchical designs in the New World he later wrote, "Such was the last vision of my mature years: I believed myself in America, and I woke up in Europe."[14]

Visionary as these plans now appear, they did not seem so to contemporaries. They probably came closer to realization in the early 1820s than at any other time until the abortive intervention of Louis Napoleon in the 1860s. Little ideological objection could then be made, since the Mexicans themselves, to all appearances, desired a monarchical form of government. Prior to independence more than one plan for the creation of monarchies in Mexico had been proposed to the Spanish king.[15] The Plan of Iguala of 1821 had called for a European prince. When Iturbide failed to obtain an infante, he had sent a delegation to Vienna to offer the crown to Archduke Charles Louis, Austrian general and field marshal.[16] Subsequently, Iturbide used the plan to place a Mexican crown on his own head. European statesmen then, as later, took it for granted that a monarchy was a necessity for *les races latines*. Mexico had been under the rule of viceroys for centuries. It did not promulgate a republican constitution until 1824. Few republics then existed in the world, and those that did were regarded in ruling European circles as pernicious examples to be avoided rather than emulated. The very word *republic* brought back the still-fresh memories of the Reign of Terror and the bloody civil war of the French Revolution. Nor was the potential opposition of the United States to the introduction of a European prince in Mexico considered a deterrent. No European government as yet attached any importance to the Monroe Doctrine, for the material strength was still lacking to make it respected.[17] Finally, early nineteenth-century diplomats could not have been expected to see anything inherently unrealistic in submission of Mexico to a foreign prince. The Congress of Vienna had only just finished moving kings about the map of Europe as though they were pieces on a chessboard, and ensuing decades saw many a prince accept a foreign crown at the dictation of the powers. It seemed only natural for the new and weak Mexican state to turn to "the enlightenment"[18] of Europe for its guidance.

That the monarchical solution was not given a trial at this time was owing, on the face of it, to Ferdinand's refusal to admit the fait accompli of Mexican independence and his fear that the infantes might act too independently.[19] Other powers ruled by legitimist monarchs—Austria, for example—declined to furnish princes to a state still claimed by its sovereign.[20] On the other hand, Ferdinand, dependent on the French army for his throne, surely could have been "persuaded" to cooperate had the French government been truly determined on a Mexican intervention. Why did France hold back, when the Ultras were keen on the project and when the general climate of opinion favored a monarchy? The French documents concerning Mexico in this early period are formal and offer little enlightenment on government thinking. But the real reason for her inaction, or at least a principal one, must inevitably have lain in her postwar exhaustion and her centuries-old rivalry with England. The expedition into Spain had cost a terrible effort. Even Chateaubriand was acutely aware of the dangers of a crusade in the name of legitimacy that might entail another contest with the British navy. "It is easy to . . . enunciate legitimist principles," he wrote the French ambassador in Madrid in 1823, "but when it is a matter of equipping vessels and of spending two hundred millions, as we did, in order to send one hundred thousand soldiers into action [in Spain], very little ardor is displayed." If France were to uphold Ferdinand's sovereignty in the New World, he continued, France would be left alone on the field, "and we would lose our treasure, our fleets, and our colonies without any recourse."[21] Obviously, France could not risk a war with England over Mexico. When Canning voiced his formal opposition to French deployment of force in support of an infante, and when England recognized Mexican independence in December 1824, the most auspicious moment for intervention had passed.

The Declarations of May 1827

While this flirtation with the infantes was going on, the French government was simultaneously moving timidly toward encouragement of a nascent French trade with Mexico and establishment of contacts with its leaders. During the French military action in the Iberian peninsula, French naval forces in the Antilles were instructed to regard colonial ships as nonbelligerents and to take no action against them.[22] As early as 1822 the government had declared its willingness to admit Mexican ships in French ports if they kept their flags furled. Although this decision was a mere gesture, as no Mexican ship had yet appeared nor could be expected in the forseeable future, it was, to the Mexicans, an encouraging departure from legitimist principles.[23] In 1823 the French government sent out a special agent, one Lieutenant Samouel, in order to enter into relations with Mexico's political leaders and to offer French mediation in a reconciliation with Spain. Although Samouel's mission yielded no tangible result, it brought the French agent into personal contact with prominent Mexicans, among them Lucas Alamán, distinguished conservative statesman, one of the chief personages on the Mexican political scene until his death in 1853.[24] Working still farther out of the straitjacket of the Spanish alliance, Villèle in 1824 received a Mexican emissary, Tomás Murphy, as "confidential agent" in Paris with the mission of promoting and regulating trade between the two countries.[25]

When Artois succeeded Louis as Charles X in the same year, he made no change in this pragmatic policy despite his leadership of the Ultra Right and his well-advertised doctrinaire rigidity. Probably he realized that the irreversibility of Mexico's separation from Spain was nearly impossible to deny. The promulgation of a federal, republican constitution by a Mexican congress in 1824, recognition of the new state by England late in the same year, and the capitulation of the Spanish garrison at San Juan de Ulúa in November 1825 gave the Mexican nationality an undeniable substantiality. Charles permitted the establishment of Mexican agents in the Atlantic ports of Bordeaux, Le Havre, and Nantes, and on the Mediterranean at Marseilles. As a further token of goodwill he announced that Mexican ships might henceforth fly their flags while in French ports.[26] Of more substance was the dispatch in 1826 of a salaried agent, Alexandre Martin, to Mexico as "Inspector of French Commerce" with permission to appoint other French agents (unsalaried) in Mexican cities as he thought appropriate.[27] Serving as the counterpart of Murphy in Paris, who was given a corresponding title, he was viewed by the Mexican government, eager to sign a treaty with France, as a forerunner of French consuls and agents of diplomatic rank.

In permitting these overtures the French government was reacting, however hesitantly, to the remarkable spurt in French trade with Mexico in the mid-1820s and to mounting pressure from leaders in commerce and industry. The surrender of the Spanish garrison at San Juan de Ulúa in 1825 had reopened the port of Veracruz, Mexico's major Gulf port. French merchandise, which had previously entered the country mostly in small coastal vessels from the United States via Tampico, whose harbor was too shallow to admit deep draft vessels, could subsequently be shipped directly to Veracruz in French bottoms.[28] According to the French newspaper Le Constitutionnel, French exports to all of Spanish America in 1824 had amounted to a mere one million francs. By 1826 the total value of French annual exports to Mexico alone soared to some twelve million francs.[29] Although these figures must be regarded as the roughest of estimates, given the existence of an already notorious contraband trade and the arbitrary values attributed to French goods, they are undeniable evidence of an important expansion.

The balance of this trade was heavily favorable to France. It was carried on in French ships with the value of French exports exceeding her imports from Mexico at a rate of ten to one for the years 1825 to 1827.[30] For French merchants Mexico was an outlet for textiles, wines and brandies, paper, and fancy goods (articles de Paris). In return they bought but small amounts of mahogany, pepper, coffee, vanilla, cochineal, and other exotic raw materials.

During this time the chambers of commerce of the Atlantic ports and Marseilles had often petitioned the government for the exchange of consuls and a treaty of commerce with Mexico. By June 1826 Murphy believed that their arguments had made a definite impression on Villèle.[31] Bordeaux in particular took the lead in pressing the government on the path toward recognition of Mexico. The city had suffered most grievously during the long war with England in the late eighteenth and early nineteenth centuries and in the 1820s was experiencing a feverish revival of activity. Isaac Balguerie, enterprising shipowner in Bordeaux, wrote to the members of the chamber of commerce in 1821, "[Mexico and] the vast continent of South America offers to our commerce and to our merchant navy a fine compensation for all our colonial losses if we know how to avail ourselves of it."[32] The merchants of Bordeaux possessed some advantages in entering this market. As a result of its geographic position, Bordeaux had taken the lead in the earlier indirect trade with colonial Mexico via Cádiz and had some already established contacts with Spanish wholesale houses. After independence, many Spaniards fled Mexico, and numbers of them chose Bordeaux as their port of refuge. The capital they had brought with them had contributed to the economic revival.[33] Bordeaux was, moreover, royalist by sympathy and enjoyed considerable political influence under the Bourbon monarchy. Bordelais merchants could hope to attain their economic renaissance through their officials in the government: such men as Joachim Lainé, member of the Chamber of Deputies in 1815, minister of the interior in 1818, made peer by the king in 1823; Baron Pierre-Barthélemy Portal, minister of the navy and colonies; and Elie Gautier, shipowner and member of the Chamber from 1827 to 1830. Royalists in politics, they were laissez-faire liberals in economics and opposed the protectionist policy of the government with its system of high external tariffs.[34]

They were fighting an uphill battle. In economic theory as well as in political principle, under the Bourbon monarchy the cards were stacked against the friends of Mexico. The government was rigidly mercantilist in its international commercial policy, a reflection of the interests of the large landholders and industrialists who dominated the electorate and hence the Chamber. Crushing tariffs on wheat, iron, and textiles protected French agricultural and industiral products, while a "closed colonial system" prohibited the former Spanish colonies from trading with the remnants of the French empire in the Antilles. Again, the ambivalence of the Bourbon monarchy revealed itself. Although it wished to sell as much as possible, the monarchy erected tariff walls that, inevitably and predictably, provoked reprisals against their merchandise and in the long run led to commercial stagnation.

Not surprisingly, the economic liberals interested in the New World markets were unable to persuade the government to take the next logical step in the encouragement of trade with Mexico: diplomatic recognition of the new republic and the establishment of a legation and consulates. The scruples of the king, the power of the Ultra faction, and the continuation of French military occupation of the Iberian peninsula remained as solid roadblocks in their path. Threats by the Mexican government to raise the already high duties on French wines, brandies, and textiles and to close Mexican ports to French ships produced little effect. Villèle, when urged by Murphy to interpret the exchange of commercial agents as de facto recognition or to negotiate a treaty, invariably replied that France could not "precipitate things."[35]

This state of affairs was most unsatisfactory to Mexico, whose goal was diplomatic recognition. This act would not only establish more firmly the fact of its independence but would serve as proof that France had broken with Spain and would desist from attempts to subjugate Mexico by force. Moreover, because the Mexicans regarded France as the "most respected nation" in Europe, they expected other powers to follow the French example. Finally, recognition could be expected to increase the flow of trade between the two countries. And although Mexico bought much more than she sold in that trade, its government collected at least one-fourth (and often more) the value of French exports in customs duties, which constituted a major source of revenue for its insolvent treasury.[36]

Perhaps the impasse might have lasted indefinitely had not Sebastián Camacho, Mexican foreign minister, appeared in London and in December 1826 signed a Treaty of Friendship, Commerce, and Navigation with the British foreign secretary.[37] Fearing that this treaty would enable British merchants to forestall the French in Mexico, Villèle and Baron Maxence de Damas, foreign minister, agreed to receive Camacho in the spring of 1827, although they held out no promise of immediate recognition. Camacho, however, declared that he bore specific instructions from his government to negotiate a treaty and, on his arrival in Paris, immediately presented his arguments for French recognition and threatened to discriminate against or even to prohibit French commerce if France continued to hold out.[38]

In reply, Villèle again adduced the Family Compact as the insurmountable obstacle to recognition. However, he acknowledged the irreversibility of Mexican independence and declared that France would sign treaties with the former Spanish colonies as soon as her armies had evacuated the Iberian peninsula. He also pledged the word of his government not to give aid to Spain against the Americas. Privately, Villèle regretted the intransigence of Charles that prevented his saying more, for he saw that by withholding recognition France was creating a false position for herself in Mexico.[39]

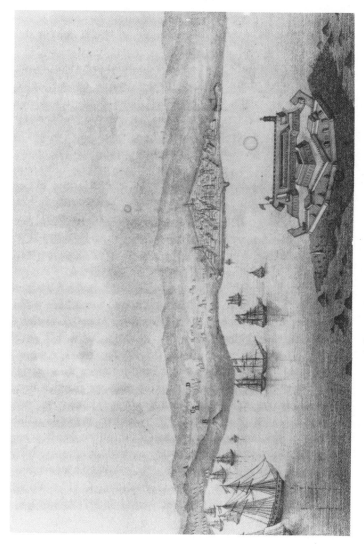

*The Gulf coast at Veracruz with the
fortress of San Juan de Ulúa in the foreground*

Lucas Alamán, Mexican statesman
and proponent of monarchy in Mexico

Since both negotiators desired to escape from the status quo, they arrived at an ingenious substitute for a treaty: they would sign a "convention or document" with all of the provisions of a treaty, but they would call it something else. Thus came into existence the Declarations of 8 May 1827, which were to regulate Franco-Mexican commerce on a basis of reciprocity.[40] Although the Declarations did not confer recognition of Mexican independence, by their terms each country promised the other the right of the most favored nation in levying duties on merchandise and tonnage. Each would send and receive consuls for the protection and fostering of trade. French merchants in Mexico and Mexican merchants in France were assured liberty and security in the conduct of their business, although they were prohibited from engaging in coastal trade (an attempt to discourage the smuggling in Gulf ports). The French in Mexico and the Mexicans in France were to be subject to the laws and statutes of the country in which they were residing but exempt from military service and forced loans. Upon the signature of the Declarations by the two foreign ministers, their provisions were to be considered provisionally obligatory until January 1830 (and even thereafter) unless one or the other party gave six months' notice to reject them.

Camacho returned to London well pleased with his "triumph," as Murphy called it. If it were recalled, wrote Murphy, that the French government had preferred the status quo, was by principle opposed to the "cause" of the American republics, and was little influenced by public opinion, the Declarations must be considered a great success for Mexico.[41] Those remarks were true enough, at least so far as Charles was concerned, and the Mexican's success seemed to augur well for the development of closer and more friendly relations between the two countries. That the reverse was unfortunately true came about through circumstances beyond his control or ability to predict.

The Early French in Mexico

The separation of Mexico from Spain had opened a new frontier to French subjects. For centuries Spain had followed a formal policy of exclusion of foreigners from her colonies in the New World. Mexico and the other Latin American countries were virtually *terrae incognitae* in France. Except for the accounts of the rare travelers with special permission, such as the celebrated Alexander von Humboldt and his French companion, the naturalist Aimé Bonpland, in the late eighteenth century, the French had few sources of reliable information. "The interior geography [of Mexico] is imperfectly known in Europe," Damas wrote Martin in 1827, "and the information that you provide . . . can only be very useful."[42] Martin and other French agents or representatives in Mexico in the 1820s and 1830s were always instructed to travel as extensively as possible and to report minutely on all that they saw.

Yet the Spanish policy of exclusion had never been perfectly enforced, sometimes by accident, sometimes by design. After Louis XIV placed his grandson on the throne of Spain in 1700, the Spanish government had occasionally even encouraged the entry into Mexico of especially skilled and/or educated French.[43] French engineers, for example, had reconstructed the fortress of San Juan de Ulúa in the eighteenth century. Other French had entered Mexico via New Orleans, notably in the period immediately after the French sale of Lousiana to the United States in 1803.[44] Still others had originally lived in French departments near the Pyrenees. They had emigrated to Spain, had learned the Spanish language, and had subsequently managed to slip into Mexico illegally, where they passed as Spaniards. In 1828 after the Mexican republic expelled the Spaniards from its territory, Martin was startled at the number of these Hispanicized French who, seeking his support in resisting expulsion, assured him "in good Spanish that they had never ceased to be good French subjects."[45] Recent research in the Archivo General de la Nación Mexicana has established that some eight hundred French heads of families resided in Mexico between 1700 and 1820.[46] Since this list contained no children and only five women, one can assume that the total French population must have been much larger.

Yet despite these not inconsiderable exceptions to the Spanish rule of exclusion of foreigners, the French could not have been a visible presence on the Mexican scene before independence. If they were often tolerated, they were not protected. They had no legation or consulate to which they might appeal in case of trouble. Also, since many of them had "slipped in," they sought to disguise their nationality and remained undetected by officialdom. Not until the arrival of Martin in the Mexican capital in 1826 and the establishment of French commercial agents in Veracruz and Tampico were the French in Mexico assured the right of entering, leaving, or residing in Mexican territory. By 1827, reported Martin, the French were treated on a basis of equality, in theory at least, with the English and the North Americans, although the diplomatic representatives of those powers preceded Martin in matters of protocol.[47]

A substantial growth in the number of French in Mexico seems to have begun in the 1820s. Only the roughest estimate of this trend is possible, owing to the absence of a reliable Mexican census of the period and to the sketchiness of French efforts to keep track of their subjects.[48] Late in 1827 Martin, who by then held the title of consul, reported that French subjects were living in Texas, Oaxaca, Sonora, and California and were in need of at least two additional consulates for their protection: one at Tepic to oversee agencies at San Blas, Mazatlán, and Guaymas; and another at Tampico for Tamaulipas and Texas. These would be in addition to the then existing consulates at Xalapa and Veracruz and the consulate general established in the spring of 1827 in the capital. Early in 1827 the Mexican government was so displeased at the number of "soldiers . . . and adventurers" coming to Mexico from France that it instructed its agents in France to deny passports to French subjects unless they possessed a trade or some occupation enabling them to make a living.[49]

So far as can now be known, Martin seems not to have tried to count the heads of his compatriots. His successor, Adrien Cochelet, however, ordered the opening of registers in at least three cities (the capital, Veracruz, and Tampico) in 1829 and reported that by December 1831 they showed the signatures of 678 French subjects.[50] Since these were all heads of families (even if single), they signified the presence of a much larger group, although precisely how much larger is difficult to say. If one assigns an average, admittedly arbitrary, of 3 persons to a family, these 678 would denote a colony of some 2,000 individuals. To these should be added at least some of the 500 to 600 French subjects who arrived in successive boatloads from 1829 through 1831 at Coatzacoalcos in the Isthmus of Tehuantepec in an unsuccessful attempt to establish an agricultural colony. Many of these colonists went to Veracruz (where they may have figured on Cochelet's register), and others returned to France as soon as possible. But a number of them found employment elsewhere and remained in Mexico.[51]

These early French emigrants seem to have been a restive and trouble-prone lot. "France has not sent to Mexico the flower of its population," groaned Martin, "and they [the French] make more noise than all the other foreigners put together."[52] Many, he wrote, were miscreants, bankrupts fleeing their creditors, or unemployed old soldiers unable to adjust to peace. Cochelet, who arrived in Mexico in 1829, was likewise poorly impressed with the caliber of his compatriots. Leaving their homes as a result of business failures, he wrote, they brought to the Mexican capital their grudges and their ill humor.[53] Some tried to pose as martyrs of political repression in France and were hostile to Cochelet, the representative of the king. In Tehuantepec they were no better, he believed, for there many were artists, writers, men of bad repute, "lost in debt." All too few were "sturdy laborers" accustomed to hard work on the land.[54] This view was later corroborated by two of the colonists themselves, who published accounts of their experiences, and by the sponsor of the unfortunate colony, Gabriel Laisné de Villevêque. Mathieu de Fossey, one of the colonists and son of a landowner in Burgundy, agreed that the Tehuantepec settlers were poorly chosen and lacked the skills necessary to earn a living from virgin land. Another, M. A. Brissot, son of the Girondin republican leader of the French Revolution, described many of the men in his boatload as "fashionable idlers," others as students, jewelers, and assorted odd types. Few seem to have had either capital or practical knowledge of agriculture. Villevêque was harsher in his judgment, summing them up as "do nothings" and "drunks" who brought their misfortunes on themselves.[55]

Although these accounts are much too sketchy to permit sound generalization, and Villevêque's in particular must be suspected of attempted self-justification, the indigence attributed to the colonists should occasion no surprise. The emigration to Mexico in the 1820s seems a natural reflection of the economic and social miseries of life under the Bourbon regime during the slow and painful readjustment to a peacetime economy. With French borders returned roughly to those of the Old Regime, the enormous Napoleonic bureaucracy had been dismantled and the army drastically reduced. The revival of the economy was too feeble to absorb all those seeking jobs. The young found themselves blocked by officeholders and professional men of the previous generation. Although the number of emigrants was not large enough to affect the contours of the French population as a whole, they seem to have been expressing the troubles of their times with their feet.[56]

Notwithstanding the scoffing of Cochelet, some left France at least in part for political reasons. Although Louis XVIII had in general eschewed retaliation against republicans and Bonapartists, many were profoundly disillusioned by the return of the Bourbons. Mexico, in revolt against Spain, inevitably attracted the interest and sympathy of the French Left of one kind or another. Jean Arago, for example, brother of the celebrated astronomer, went to Mexico in 1818 to serve with General Francisco Javier Mina to fight for Mexican independence. He took an active part in subsequent revolutions until his death in 1837, always on the side that he believed opposed reaction.[57] Adrien Woll, another soldier of fortune, also came to Mexico with the Mina expedition, although he later moved away from the Mexican Left.[58] Young Brissot, republican like his father, left for ideological as well as economic reasons. A French-speaking Italian, M. A. Beltrami, who had served Napoleon in Italy, went to Mexico in 1824 hoping to taste the promised freedoms of the New World.[59] M. Giordan, French director of the colony at Coatzacoalcos, planned not only to pay his debts but also to found a commune according to the principles laid down by utopian socialist François Fourier. The conventional Martin found Giordan's ideas so fantastic as to befit better an inmate of Charenton (French insane asylum) than a director of an agricultural colony.[60] Other politically motivated émigrés could be cited.

Once in Mexico, these types, complained Martin, clustered about the legation of the American minister, Joel Poinsett. They embarrassed the representative of the king by their support of the leftist Yorkino party and their rude and insulting remarks about the Bourbon government.[61] Almost without exception, subsequent representatives of France were to make similar complaints. French radicals, although they could not be precisely counted, were early and constantly a visible and vocal part of the French presence in Mexico.

How did the French in Mexico earn their living? Although evidence for this period is fragmentary, what documentation exists reveals that they soon played a prominent role in the commercial life of the cities, to which they came out of economic necessity. The urban dwelling pattern is perceptible even before 1820.[62] The French were never able to establish a position of importance in the mining industry, which was monopolized by the British.[63] Nor could they take up farming or ranching unless they came in organized groups such as the colonists at Coatzacoalcos, who were promised land from *empresarios* with grants from the government. According to Mexican law, individual foreigners could not possess real estate without giving up their nationality and the protection of their legation.

It was in retail trade that the French found their forte. According to tradition, this trend began in 1821 when three brothers, Arnaud by name, spinners of silk, left their Alpine village (Department of Basses-Alpes) in the valley of Barcelonnette to establish a retail clothing shop in the Mexican capital. They apparently settled down to work in earnest and, unlike the miscreants of whom French officials complained, achieved a reputation for diligence, thrift, and business acumen. They were presently followed by so many of their former neighbors, eager to emulate their success, that the "Barcelonnettes" allegedly came to monopolize retail trade all over Mexico. Although the number of French from the Basses-Alpes has been much exaggerated by antiquarian accounts, there can be no doubt of the early prominence of the French as urban little men engaged in trade. They appear to have moved into the vacancies created by the emigration of many Spaniards after independence and especially after their expulsion from the republic in 1828. By 1831, noted the French foreign minister with satisfaction, French subjects had achieved "an incontestable superiority" over their remaining Creole competitors and "by their intelligence and activity" had virtually excluded other foreign nationals from the practice of retail trade.[64]

Mounting Aggravations and Grievances

Although Charles had approved the Declarations of May 1827 regulating commercial relations with Mexico, his aversion to republicanism remained unchanged. In large and small ways he and many of his ministers demonstrated their disdain for the new state. The official contacts with the Mexicans had an inauspicious beginning. Tomás Murphy, Jr., who succeeded his father as commercial agent in 1827, found himself roundly snubbed. Before being received in the Foreign Ministry, usually by some "lesser functionary," he was obliged to wait in the public antechamber, rather than in that reserved for the diplomatic corps. His notes went unanswered or elicited replies of an insulting impersonality.[65]

The French government was little more generous in choice of its agents to go to Mexico. Martin, its first representative, was a man of mediocre talents who had always occupied subordinate positions. Although conscientious and hardworking, he was, by his own admission, lacking in the education and intelligence necessary to analyze the political and economic currents flowing past him. Ill-paid and lacking private wealth, he cut a poor figure in Mexican society. His successor, Cochelet, had served as intendant in Illyria and prefect of the Department of the Meuse under Napoleon, but had risen only to the rank of consul under the Bourbons. Like Martin, he was not wealthy.[66] Moreover, both Martin and Cochelet held the rank of mere consuls in Mexico after 1827, although, in accordance with the precedents set in Buenos Aires and Lima, the post in the capital called for a consul general. Since the king was unwilling to pay the salary of an agent higher than consul in Mexico, Martin and, later, Cochelet were named as titular holders of consulates at Tampico, Xalapa, or Veracruz, although they actually resided in the capital and were the *gérants* ("directors") of the consulate general, which lacked a titulary. Meanwhile, unpaid ("honorary") vice-consuls, who were French merchants, directed the consulates of Xalapa and the two coastal cities, whose titularies were in the capital. This jugglery not only was intensely irritating to the Mexican government, but also seemed another indication of the French low esteem of Mexican independence and its secret ill will.[67]

The Bourbon monarchy was equally as niggardly in its naval policy toward Mexico. Although France then possessed naval stations in the Antilles and in Cuba, the ministers of the navy and commanders of those stations were reluctant to show the French flag with any regularity or for any length of time on a coast regarded as one of the most dangerous in the world. In the winter strong and sudden gales from the north and in summer the dreaded *vomito negro* endangered ships and crews. These perils were real enough, but they might have been to some degree surmounted by a rearrangement of priorities that permitted more frequent relief of vessels in dangerous areas, as was the British practice. Instead, Martin and Cochelet called in vain for the regular appearance of French warships off the coast as an indication of French support for their claims and grievances and of interest in the welfare of the colony. The sporadic appearances of French ships, sometimes after an absence of over a year, undoubtedly did more harm than good to Franco-Mexican relations, as they then aroused consternation and distrust. On the other hand, during the long periods of their absence the Mexican government tended to believe that French agents lacked the confidence of their government and paid less heed to their complaints.[68]

Nor was the French government willing to go to much expense or effort to assure regular and secure passage of mail, passengers, merchandise, and specie between the two countries. Until 1827 no regulated communication with Mexico existed. Persons desiring such service were obliged to use British packet ships, armed corvettes that left Falmouth on a monthly schedule. Since the French royal navy possessed no ships appropriate to such duty and the government was unwilling to construct them, the king turned instead to the merchant navy. In July 1827 the government signed a contract with the house of Elie Gautier and Company in Bordeaux establishing a monthly service with Veracruz. In return for a small subvention, Gautier's vessels were to carry, in addition to merchandise, correspondence to and from the French representatives in Mexico and dispatches to French naval stations en route.[69]

The first of these merchant-vessels-turned-packet-ships arrived in Veracruz late in August 1827. Its performance proved immediately unsatisfactory, just as that of its successors. Laden with cargo, they were slow sailors, averaging fifty days per crossing, while the British packets, carrying only letters, passengers, and specie, covered the distance from Falmouth in some thirty-one days.[70] The departures and arrivals of the French ships were too erratic for erstwhile customers to rely upon. Martin was gravely hindered in his mission by the long delay, often amounting to six to eight months, between the dispatch of his report and the reception of the corresponding instructions that were, needless to say, usually inappropriate to the situation as it had meanwhile developed. Hazards of nature such as storms or calms were only partly responsible for the unreliability of the service. The major problem lay in its unprofitability. Since the costs of a single crossing amounted to some forty-six thousand francs,[71] the government subvention of five thousand was too meager to compensate for the required regularity of departures. Rather than sail with holds half full, the captains, after casting off lines on schedule in Bordeaux, waited downstream, often for weeks, for the arrival of additional cargo.[72] Despite these problems the Bourbon government declined to initiate a line of military packets like those of the British. In 1829, when the house of Gautier declined to renew its contract, the government turned to still another commercial house that continued the same type of deficient service.[73]

Meanwhile in Mexico, clashes between the two nationalities increased as the French extended their presence. Undeniably a certain degree of xenophobia was responsible for much of the violence. Unsophisticated *campesinos* were instinctively hostile to these unfamiliar faces. In their inability to distinguish between foreigners of any kind, they variously labeled the French "los godames," "Ingles," or Jews, whom they abhorred as infidels.[74] Typical of the many incidents of Mexican attacks on the persons and property of the French is the following, reported by Cochelet in 1829:

M. Tremontel, French subject, owner of a sugar refinery, was returning last Sunday with his wife and nephews from a dinner with one of his compatriots. They were all on horseback according to the usage of the

country and were proceeding tranquilly toward their establishment by the
suburb that led to it. They were soon assailed by some of those hideous and
hostile common people known here by the name of *léperos*, who hailed
them [the French] as Spanish and English. It is thus that all foreigners are
called. They replied that they were French and very christian French at that.
No matter, they must be killed, said the women. A large gathering of
several hundred individuals formed, some soldiers and civil guardsmen
always ready to mix in seditious crowds swelling their numbers; and our
nationals, having been forced to dismount, were made the butt of the most
outrageous mistreatment and received various wounds. One of them drew
his pistols that everyone habitually carries in this country and made out to
intimidate the populace, but during the struggle the gun went off and the
bullet hit one of the *léperos* in the nose.[75]

If this account is evidence of popular hostility to foreigners, it is
also, in its style of expression, an unconscious manifestation of French
attitudes and prejudices that must have exacerbated the difficulties of
their reception. Coming from a nation whose cultural superiority
had been acknowledged for centuries, they tended to see themselves
as torchbearers of civilization into barbarian darkness. Often they
viewed the Mexican scene with a contempt untempered by recognition of the problems besetting an emerging nation or, for that matter,
of the revolutionary trauma from which France herself was then
struggling to recover. The same clichés may be found repeatedly in
French contemporary accounts. Mexican laws were never obeyed,
the Mexican "government" never governed. All judges were corrupt, all officials were venal. A good example is the following excerpt from a report by Cochelet in 1829:

The cement of social order is lacking in Mexico; laws are not obeyed. Justice
is . . . shameless. It absolves the guilty and weighs all its arrests in the
amount of gold that it receives. . . . The customs are of an unparalleled
venality. . . . The army is undisciplined. The officer is a strutting peacock in
peace and a coward in combat. The sober and patient soldier could show
some quality if better led but, a pillager by nature, he sees service in arms
only as a means of stealing with impunity. Religion is nothing but hollow
rites. The priests are shameless in their habits and avid to enrich themselves.
. . . The Indian shows on his face the mark of his former servitude. He is
docile and timid. He offered no resistance to the Spanish conquest. . . . The
Mexican Creole is vain of his origins. . . . He adores distinctions and honors.
. . . His indolent habits, his depraved tastes, and his habitual vices prevent
him from comprehending ideas of independence, liberty, and equality. He
would like the power that position and honors would bring him if he could
obtain it without effort and as a way of flattering his intolerable vanity.[76]

In Paris such reports tended to be accepted uncritically. In response to Cochelet's disquisition, the foreign minister acknowledged the "painful" situation in Mexico, "the unparalleled outrages practiced against foreigners and especially the French," and bemoaned the "passions and venemous prejudices of a blind multitude."[77]

French attitudes toward the Mexicans inevitably affected the manner in which they negotiated with the government. A French foreign minister would warn his representative in Mexico of the faults in the Mexican character that could be expected to impede his mission and how to overcome them. "Suffice it to say," ran one such lecture, "[the Mexican] possesses the habits of delay and procrastination, the spirit of craftiness and chicanery, the penchant for contending the most equitable claims, and a deviousness that enables him to evade the consequences of his actions." Therefore the agent must at the outset adopt a tone of "resolution and firmness" and show himself "inflexible" on all matters of importance. Only in that manner, concluded the foreign minister, could the French agent hope "to have his rights respected and to obtain satisfaction."[78] Such views and such tactics boded little good for the future of Franco-Mexican relations.

Even had the French been better disposed toward Mexico, they, as well as all foreigners, were endangered in the revolutionary turmoil of the late 1820s. In civil war, wrote Martin, "We will infallibly be the first victims. The people hate us: Already there are cries of 'Death to the Foreigners.'"[79] His fears were not unfounded. When the forces of the government failed to defeat the revolution led by Vicente Guerrero early in December 1828, street fighting broke out in the capital. The populace used the opportunity presented by the disorder to pillage and to burn the Parian, a vast bazaar, well guarded under normal conditions, in which was concentrated the majority of the commercial houses of the capital. Previously the almost exclusive domain of the Spaniards, by this time the Parian sheltered the places of business of foreigners and Mexicans who had in part replaced them. The destruction spread to the neighboring streets, where the shops of seven French retailers were completely destroyed.[80] The French government held the Mexican government responsible for the damages to French subjects and instructed Martin and later Cochelet to estimate their amounts as generously as possible and to insist on reparation. The ensuing debate, as one Mexican ministry after another eluded payment, was to envenom Franco-Mexican relations for over a decade.

Not only the French colony in Mexico but also French trade with Mexico soon became a breeding ground of disputes. By the late 1820s the new markets were proving far more difficult to exploit and far less rewarding than had been anticipated. Even in the best years an absence of navigable rivers, bad roads, and poorly sheltered harbors meant slow and costly transport. French exports, which had reached 13.6 million francs in 1827, fell off abruptly to 7.8 and 7.7 millions in 1828 and 1829.[81] The French government tended to blame this decline on the failure of Mexico to observe the terms of the Declarations of 1827 in general and on the high rates of the Mexican tariff in particular. The government pointed out that the Mexican tariff of 1827, while placing high duties on virtually all goods, discriminated sharply against French products and thus violated the French right to treatment of the most favored nation. By this tariff French brandies, the equivalent of which no other country could produce, were taxed at 160 percent of their value. Wines were taxed more than 260 percent. The duty on French cotton cloth was nearly double that on textiles from other countries, and the inequities were even more pronounced for fancy goods and shawls.[82] Many Mexicans believed that the high tariffs were a mistake and that lower duties, by encouraging more imports, would in the long run yield more revenue. Yet the plight of the Mexican treasury was too desperate for the government to be able to forego the immediate returns from the customs duties, which were the principal source of income to pay its army and bureaucracy. In its penury the Mexican government was trapped in a policy from which it could not easily escape.

Another unfortunate offshoot of the high tariffs was the abundant practice of smuggling. "It is painful to be obliged to confess," wrote Cochelet in January 1830, "that contraband, trickery, bribery, usury, etc. form the principal bases of this commerce [French trade with Mexico]."[83] Smuggling not only led to conflicts with Mexican officialdom and new grievances, but also harmed French export trade as a whole. The consignee of merchandise in Mexico [the French wholesaler] passed back to the shipper in France the cost of the customs duties even when they had in fact been evaded. The consignee then sold the contraband goods to retailers at the same high price he would have charged had the duties been legally paid. The upshot was discouragement of shippers in France and spectacular profits by a handful of French wholesalers in Mexico. These illicit profits realized by a few unscrupulous merchants in turn stiffened the resistance of the Mexicans to pay reparations of any kind to French merchants, since they were convinced, or said they were, that the whole business of claims was a speculation from which the French turned fortunes.[84]

Toward Gunboat Diplomacy

After the triumph of Guerrero and the Yorkino party early in 1829, relations between the two countries deteriorated markedly. The Bourbon government viewed the men of the new Mexican regime as demagogues at the beck and call of the American minister, as "Jacobins," and "men of '93," i.e., radicals who had presided over the Reign of Terror during the French Revolution.[85] Their victory, especially since it had been accompanied by the destruction of the Parian, overcame any inclination the French government might have had to grant diplomatic recognition, even though by the end of 1828 France had at last withdrawn its troops from Spain.[86] Charles and his government were themselves moving farther to the Right as they strove on the domestic political scene to surmount the liberal challenge to the royal prerogative. In August 1829 the king appointed Prince Polignac, one of the most unbending of the Ultras, as foreign minister. The ideological gap between France and Mexico became an unbridgeable ravine. Polignac pointedly insulted Murphy. Receiving him infrequently, he refused to give Murphy his proper title, lectured him on the expulsion of the Spanish, and did not have even the courtesy to ask him to be seated. Murphy correctly understood that recognition was more remote than it had ever been.[87]

Indeed, the king and Polignac had never given up the cherished project of the establishment of a monarchy in Mexico and did not cease to work through random agents for that realization. Although these efforts always failed and in any case were little more than trial balloons, they deepened the already profound Mexican distrust of French intentions. In 1828 a mission entrusted to Charles Bresson, secretary of the French legation in Washington, to prepare the way in Colombia and Mexico for an Orleanist prince, aroused so strong a reaction from the Mexican government that Cochelet feared reprisals against the French in Mexico and found his own position badly compromised.[88] Bresson was recalled before he had even arrived on the Mexican scene. Another monarchist scheme that acquired notoriety arose from a conversation between Laisné de Villevêque and Polignac in September 1829. They had discussed the desirability of

French annexation of the Duchy of Parma in Italy and of compensation of its ruler, Bourbon Prince Luis, with a Mexican crown. Although Polignac had not then seriously contemplated implementation of the plan, Villevêque instructed his son, Athanase, whom he had placed in Mexico as vice-consul in Acapulco, to go to the capital to seek monarchist support for the prince. Young Villevêque followed his instructions only too zealously and soon reported that he had lined up a strong array of supporters, notably among them Lorenzo de Zavala, former minister of finances.[89] Even though nothing came of the scheme, it provided another black mark on the Bourbon record.

The relations between the two countries and the position of the French in Mexico became particularly critical in August and early autumn of 1829 when Spain made a last attempt to subjugate Mexico by force of arms. By unfortunate coincidence, just as the Spanish expedition was preparing to descend on Tampico, the French navy chose this moment to make one of its rare appearances on the Mexican coast. Not just one but three French men-of-war anchored at Sacrificios, in sight of Veracruz. Cochelet, whose appeals for a regular patrol of the coast had heretofore fallen on deaf ears in Paris, was aghast at this inopportune apparition. How could he ever convince the Mexican government that the French ships had appeared independently and were not cooperating with Spain? The effect on the public was deplorable, he reported, and the defiance of the government extreme. "I must not conceal from Your Excellency the fact that we are approaching the moment of crisis in which the natural antipathy of the Mexicans for foreigners could be fatal to the subjects of His Majesty."[90] Fortunately, the commander of the vessels, M. Le Coupé, whose instructions obliged him merely to supply moral support to French claims, had the good sense to understand the untimeliness of his arrival.[91] He prudently withdrew. Even so, the Mexicans continued to suspect that his appearance had been meant as at least a gesture of support of Spain's attempted reconquest.

Another subject of bitter debate that arose from the Spanish invasion was governmental imposition of forced loans on French commercial houses. Short on funds to finance the resistance at Tampico, the Mexican government on 18 August decreed a forced loan of $2,894,849. Several states followed with decrees of their own. The sums were allotted arbitrarily and apparently capriciously among foreign commercial houses and a few Mexican ones that did not enjoy the favor of the government. Cochelet immediately protested these loans, citing Article 9 of the Declarations of 1827 as proof of French exemption. He was immediately rebuffed. Other foreigners, he was told, even the British who had recognized Mexico and had signed a treaty with the republic, were paying the sums levied on them. Why should French subjects, whose ruler treated Mexico with disdain, be given preferential treatment? Cochelet himself was conscious of the near hopelessness of his cause and the weakness of his argument. He had come to realize the falseness of the French position in Mexico and had frequently urged the government to regularize it by granting diplomatic recognition. Moreover, he very much feared that French citizens might be subject to far worse exactions and harassment and even to expulsion should he persist in his resistance. To ride out the emergency and still obey orders of his own government, which, he knew, would insist on execution of the terms of the Declarations, he made various arrangements with his compatriots by which groups of them proffered lump sums to the government in return for bonds that could be used in payment of customs duties. By such subterfuges he managed to placate the Mexican government and still maintain the fiction that the Declarations had not been violated.[92]

Nonetheless, in the last months of Bourbon rule, the refusal of the Mexican government to abide by the terms of the Declarations became the main point of conflict between the two countries. The Mexicans not only levied forced loans on French subjects but also declined to remove the discriminatory provisions in the tariff. Noting that neither the French king nor the Mexican legislature had ratified the Declarations, the Mexicans declared them invalid. The Guerrero government had turned against Camacho, who had signed the instrument, and had dismissed him in disgrace.[93]

From a legal standpoint the Mexican government was in the wrong. According to the text of the Declarations they became valid at the moment the signatures of the plenipotentiaries were affixed and required no additional action by either government. Yet in repudiating them the Mexicans believed that moral right lay on their side. They had seen the agreement as tantamount to recognition or at the very least as a tacit promise that recognition would not be long delayed. When instead the king passed over the Declarations in silence in his speech opening the French Chambers and continued to treat the republic with contempt, the Mexican government felt that it had been misled. With the touchy pride of an emerging nation, unsure of its identity and conscious of its material inferiority to the French monarchy, it vowed not to be treated "like Berbers or Algerians" whom the French were preparing to roll over in North Africa.[94] Although in 1827 the Mexican government had greeted the signing of the Declarations with joy, it had begun to realize that it had granted France virtually everything she could wish in Mexico (most-favored-nation treatment, exemption from forced loans and military service, and, implicitly, the right of her subjects to engage in retail trade) and that Mexico had received little or nothing in return.[95] To be sure, these terms were reciprocal, and the French government was observing them carefully.[96] Yet since Mexican exports to France were usually only approximately one-tenth the value of French exports to Mexico, and since few Mexicans resided or traded in France, the terms availed Mexico little. The Declarations were, in fact, more generous than any of Mexico's existing treaties with other countries and conceded more than France was ever able to obtain in subsequent decades in the nineteenth century.

To repair what it regarded as a past mistake and to induce France to grant recognition, the Mexican Chamber decided early in 1830 to adopt successive measures of reprisal against French trade and French subjects resident in Mexico. Beginning with raises in tariff rates on goods from all countries that had not recognized Mexican independence (a measure obviously aimed at France), the Chamber progressed to the prohibition of French subjects from engaging in retail trade.[97] Finally, in a stormy session of 9 February in which the president of the Chamber denounced the Bourbon monarchy and called its former agent, Martin, a spy, the body voted to require foreign wholesalers and retailers whose governments had not signed treaties with Mexico to close shop immediately and to repair to the coast within a period of ninety days.[98]

Now it was French pride that was wounded. Cochelet was astounded at the impudence of the Mexicans. How could this "venal Chamber" with "the most absurd ideas" in an ignorant country like Mexico presume to defy the will of France? His past moderation forgotten, he could now see no alternative to coercion, or at least a show of force. After the prohibition of retail trade was voted, he wrote to the French foreign minister, "It is of the highest importance, Sir, that His Excellency the Minister of the Navy give the most positive orders to the station of the Island of Cuba, which might better be called the Mexican station, to cruise frequently between Tampico and Campeche." In his correspondence with the Mexican government, he continued, he did not hesitate to employ both entreaties and threats, but they became useless unless backed up by force. Nor should France hesitate to show her might, for while Mexico dares to defy all foreign powers, "there is no nation more easy to subjugate, be it by money, be it by several well-acclimated and disciplined regiments."[99]

The reaction of the king and his ministers was as strong as Cochelet could have wished. Although the government was in serious political trouble in France and on the verge of launching an expedition to Algiers, it decided immediately to blockade the coasts of Mexico and to "demand" both complete observance of the Declarations and payment of reparations for the sack of the Parian. The honor of France as well as the national interest, wrote Polignac, required her to defend her subjects "by all possible means and to renounce a policy of moderation and temporization that is henceforward without object."[100]

The dangerous moment had arrived. That it did not lead immediately to hostilities was due only to the overthrow of Guerrero by the conservative faction of Anastasio Bustamante in January. Lucas Alamán, who returned as foreign minister, prevailed upon the Senate to reject the rash retaliatory measures voted by the Chamber.[101] Yet the change in government yielded no more than a reprieve and did not remove the fundamental causes of trouble between the two countries. France was more determined than ever to withhold recognition and to insist on Mexican observance of the Declarations. Mexico under Alamán and Bustamante refused to grant France the rights of the most favored nation unless Mexican independence were recognized.[102]

As the reign of Charles numbered its last days, the two nations were fast heading toward a collision. In Mexico several fresh "outrages" pushed Cochelet beyond the limits of his endurance. Late in 1829 a French merchant vessel, the Bonne Laure, had been pillaged by Mexican customs officials while lying off the coast of Yucatán taking on a cargo of wood.[103] Before Cochelet could obtain a promise of compensation, he learned that his vice-consul in Veracruz, Félix Carrère, had gotten into a brawl with Mexican officials, who arrested him amidst great publicity and put him in jail. Although Cochelet obtained Carrère's release, he was unable to elicit further satisfaction or to calm the excitement of the public over the incident.[104] In its wake several Mexican hotheads seized a French ship captain and carried him bodily from his ship. Just as Cochelet was claiming reparation from Alamán for this new offense, he received instructions from Paris ordering him to insist "in the most formal and categorical manner" upon total execution of the Declarations and immediate payment of reparations for the sack of the Parian.[105]

The crisis was at hand. If France still withheld recognition, Alamán decided to close Mexican ports to all French merchandise.[106] He declined even to discuss the Declarations or reparations with Cochelet on the grounds that they constituted a diplomatic question outside the province of a mere consul. Cochelet, exasperated by what he regarded as a series of snubs, could see no alternative to the deployment of force. Recapitulating his grievances to Polignac, he concluded, "For it is by the law of the cannon that we must teach these new people the law of nations and respect for flags."[107]

Fortunately for the maintenance of peace between the two countries, the king and Polignac had fallen to revolution before Cochelet's inflammatory report arrived in Paris. In retrospect it appears virtually certain that only the overthrow of the Bourbon monarchy in July 1830 prevented the departure of a French naval expedition and the outbreak of the first Franco-Mexican war.

2
Recognition and After:
Orleanist Vacillation

Foreign commerce will prosper [in Mexico] only if it can find in the peacefulness of the country and in the protection of a strong government that security that is its first need.—French foreign minister to Deffaudis, 26 August 1833

Imitation of the institutions of the United States has been fatal for Mexico.—Deffaudis to Broglie, 15 July 1833

The Decision to Recognize

Although the July Revolution in France had no connection either in its origin or in its consummation with the republics of the New World, it proved to be an unexpected windfall for them. The overthrow of the Bourbons released France from the fetters of the Family Compact and removed the chief ideological obstacle to French recognition of the former Spanish colonies. The French government, with a new cast of players, had the opportunity to sponge the slate clean and begin afresh.

The new king, Louis Philippe, former Duke of Orleans, was a member of the cadet branch of the Bourbon line and had blood as blue as that of Charles X. But he professed himself a believer in republican government and was sympathetic to the cause of the Latin American republics. In his youth he had borne arms briefly for the first French republic and had later traveled in the United States during his years in exile. Now as symbols of his obedience to the mandate of the people, he adopted the title "King of the French" and replaced the white flag of the Bourbons with the revolutionary tricolor. Like the regimes of the former Spanish colonies, he and his government were the product of revolt against legitimate authority. He could not in principle deny them admission to the family of nations without destroying the validity of his own claim to recognition by the European powers as the legal ruler of France.

From the very beginning of Orleanist rule there was little doubt that France would extend diplomatic recognition to Mexico. The question was when and on what terms? According to the usual method of procedure in the diplomatic world, the senior government informed the junior one of its willingness to establish relations and to negotiate a treaty of friendship, commerce, and navigation. As a rule, the first article of the treaty proclaimed the act of recognition. The remaining articles regulated trade and commerce between the two countries and stipulated the rights and privileges of the nationals of each country when residing in the other. This procedure would not be without drawbacks for Mexico. Because diplomats and documents would have to cross and recross the Atlantic and then be subject to the scrutiny of the Mexican Congress, the negotiation might stretch out over months, perhaps years. And in drawing up the treaty France would undoubtedly regard her act of recognition as a favor for which a quid pro quo in the form of privileges for her commerce and subjects would be expected.

Therefore, in the wake of the revolution the friends of Mexico, both French and Mexican, began to press the French government to omit these formalities and instead to grant immediate, unconditional recognition. "All the elements are favorable," reported Murphy to Alamán. "The men who are in authority today in this country are precisely those who have pleaded our cause and whose friendship I have cultivated."[1] He was joined in his efforts by Manuel Eduardo de Gorostiza, Mexican minister plenipotentiary in London, who, when he learned of the revolution, immediately crossed the channel. "In diplomacy," wrote Gorostiza from Paris, " . . . it is all in knowing when the time is right and in taking advantage of it."[2]

What made the moment peculiarly "right" for Mexico was, ironically, the precarious position of the Orleanist monarchy in the early weeks of its existence. Public demonstrations, strikes, and other ominous evidences of civil discontent threatened at any moment to topple the new throne. This situation meant that the king was dependent for the continuation of his authority on the loyalty and activity of the National Guard, which was the key to public order. And the commanding general of the National Guard was none other than the

Marquis of Lafayette, most famous of all of the "friends of the Americans," who was eager to do still another good turn for the New World republics. His great name and revolutionary fame had gone far to induce the Parisians to accept Louis Philippe in the critical days of late July as "the best of republics" and as their sovereign. Now for a few months Lafayette was in possession of a power base that made him a potential rival to the king himself.[3]

As a member of the Chamber of Deputies under the Bourbons, Lafayette had often spoken out in favor of recognition of the Latin American republics. He was firmly convinced that all of France's problems with Mexico had their roots in monarchist intrigues in the courts of Madrid and Paris. Once these intrigues had ceased and Mexico had been duly accepted into the family of nations, he had declared, "tranquillity of commerce will be reborn."[4] In the summer of 1830 the old general was well aware of the leverage he could exert and determined to make his voice heard while he could be sure of an attentive audience. "One of my first concerns," he wrote Murphy later, "was to speak to this object [recognition of Mexico] to M. [Count Louis Mathieu] Molé, minister of foreign affairs; I availed myself of the new circumstances in which we were situated to engage him to admit no delay [granting] this recognition."[5]

In bringing off what amounted almost to a coup, Lafayette apparently encountered little resistance from the king, who, so far as existing evidence shows, played only a passive role. Confronted with widespread civil disorder in France, Legitimist conspiracies, and an international crisis provoked by revolution in Belgium, the ruler must have considered the republics of the New World of small importance and given them little of his thought. Yet, as Lafayette understood, Louis Philippe could but yield, both as a matter of principle and because of his need of the general's presence at the head of the National Guard.

The professionals in the Foreign Ministry disapproved of Lafayette's plan of action. It was not that they opposed recognition on principle. The head of the commercial division, Baron Antoine Deffaudis, believed strongly in the existence of a large, untapped market for French exports in Mexico and had written a memorandum the preceding August recommending prompt recognition of Mexico, Peru, Bolivia, and La Plata.[6] For Deffaudis, however, recognition was to be accompanied by a treaty conferring commercial privileges on French subjects and trade and settling the question of indemnities claimed by the French since 1828. The foreign minister, Molé, was equally reluctant to rush into recognition. Although he had joined the liberal opposition to Charles X in the late 1820s, as an aristocrat and former cabinet minister of the Bourbons, he was not inclined to bestow free gifts on republics out of ideological fervor. He was far more interested in obtaining the seal of approval on his government from the legitimate monarchies of Austria, Russia, and Spain, and in Europe was playing down the alleged liberalism of the new regime.[7] Moreover, he had been irritated recently by the importunities of Murphy. The Mexican had ill-advisedly accompanied his pleas for recognition with a sudden and unsubstantiated claim for compensation by France for property lost over eight years previously on a vessel seized and detained by a French warship.[8] The whole incident smacked of a trumped-up claim to offset French claims for the sack of the Parian and had forewarned Molé of probable difficulties in future negotiations with the Mexicans.

Yet the resistance of the Foreign Ministry was unequal to the pressure exerted by Lafayette. After his conversation with the general, Molé had forwarded an official proposal to the king requesting authorization to inform the governments of Mexico, Peru, Chile, La Plata, and Colombia of French readiness to recognize those governments and of its desire to negotiate with them.[9] Having obtained the king's endorsement, Lafayette moved his operation to the floor of the Chamber where he arranged to interrogate Molé in order to oblige him to make public the government's intention. This carefully orchestrated performance went off faultlessly on 4 September.[10] On the heels of this victory, Lafayette and a handful of other liberals in the Chamber pressed for the outright declaration of "recognition in principle" without waiting for negotiation of treaties. Again they succeeded with little difficulty. On 30 September Molé wrote officially to Murphy in Paris and to Cochelet in Mexico that he was instructed by the king to state that the French government, "recognizing in principle the independence of the United Mexican States," was ready to negotiate with them a treaty of friendship, commerce, and navigation.[11]

By this dispatch the Orleanist government presented without delay and without condition the prize so long sought in vain by Mexico. As Deffaudis later ruefully explained the decision, "At that time there were in the French parliament great friends of the Americans, powerfully influential, which the government believed it needed. . . . They had their way."[12]

Plus Ça Change, Plus C'est la Même Chose

The news of the July Revolution and the overthrow of the Bourbons did not reach Mexico until late in September. It was received by French subjects, according to Cochelet, with "a most pronounced outburst of enthusiasm." In the capital French retailers did a brisk business in hastily manufactured red-white-and-blue cockades for the hats of patriots, who shouted "Long live liberty" and "Long live the republic" in the streets.[13] In Veracruz the French publicly celebrated the "glorious event," saluted the tricolor run up on a French packet ship, and drew up a subscription list to aid the "victims of the immortal days of July 1830." Both Cochelet and Carrère hastened to assure the new regime of their loyalty and their liberal credentials.[14]

These rejoicings were in sharp contrast to the dour reception given the news of the revolution by the Mexican government. Considering the state of Franco-Mexican relations in July 1830, one might have expected Alamán and Bustamante to have viewed any change in the French government as desirable. But no. Stronger than their dislike of the rule of Charles X was their horror of revolution. When notified officially of the advent of Louis Philippe, Lucas Alamán clearly articulated his scorn for the events of July in France with his remark, "His Excellency [Vice-President Bustamante], like all Mexicans, has noticed with pleasure that this triumph of the nation *has not so far been accompanied by the criminal acts or those aberrations so common as to be inevitable in popular movements.*"[15] Nor was Bustamante more gracious in acknowledging the diplomatic recognition of Mexico by the new regime. Instead of the effusions of gratitude expected by the French, Bustamante in his speech to the Chambers on New Year's Day announced first of all the recognition of Mexico by the "Empire of Brazil." Almost as an afterthought, he added, "France has done likewise" and passed immediately to other matters.[16] His laconism and his placement of France behind an American nation had all the earmarks of a calculated insult.

Oddly enough, the ideological positions of the two countries had now temporarily reversed thesmelves. To Alamán (who Cochelet believed wrote Bustamante's speech), Louis Philippe was a crowned

Jacobin, impious, radical, and unpredictable because he was in the leading strings of the "mob." His reign might very well lead to republicanism of a most detestable sort. All in all, Alamán found the king a dangerous example to other countries. To lessen the likelihood of contagion, he ordered the Mexican press to record the events of July in France and the act of diplomatic recognition as starkly and unobtrusively as possible. No public celebrations, such as had attended earlier recognition by the United States and England, were permitted.[17] Later in January, as if to drive home his ill will, Alamán told Cochelet that Mexico refused to acknowledge responsibility for damages to the Parian and again denied the validity of the Declarations. Far worse, he proposed a surtax on goods imported from countries without signed treaties with Mexico. This measure was aimed so pointedly at France that Cochelet lodged a formal protest.[18] By way of explaining Alamán's attitude, Cochelet noted that in addition to ideology, the Mexican was motivated by anglophilism arising from his financial connection with British mining companies. Perhaps, thought Cochelet, Alamán had hoped to draw closer to England and had been disconcerted by the French olive branch. Others believed that Alamán had secretly desired to provoke a rupture with France to prompt a European intervention and introduction of a monarchy. The advent of Louis Philippe had foiled his monarchist plot.[19] However it may have been, for Alamán's motives must remain speculative, the refusal of the Mexican government to come halfway to meet the French gesture was immediate proof that Franco-Mexican problems would not at once evaporate, as Lafayette had naively believed, once the fact of Mexico's independence had been acknowledged.

Yet even if Mexico had responded with more grace, it is doubtful that subsequent difficulties would have been averted. Despite its precipitate decision to recognize the republic, the Orleanist monarchy showed neither an inclination to display a more generous spirit toward Mexico nor an interest in an active pursuit of its mercantile interests in the New World. In its relations with Mexico, as in much else, the July Monarchy was to retain more than it discarded of Bourbon practice.

The celebrants of the July Revolution were soon to learn the truth of the French expression "plus ça change, plus c'est la même chose" (the more things change, the more it's the same thing). The revolution had made no substantial change in French infrastructures. The charter of the Bourbons continued in effect with only minor revisions. The suffrage had been broadened by less than a hundred thousand voters. The epithet "bourgeois" so frequently applied to the Orleanist regime then and since is misleading if interpreted to mean a government directed by or for a new class of capitalist entrepreneurs. If many new men did appear in the ministry, chambers, courts, and local governments, they were of very similar social background to those whom they replaced. The men who took control of the ministries and chambers came very rarely from commerce or industry. Many were intellectuals and members of liberal professions. Officeholders and proprietors again predominated. Their economic policies, continuing to reflect the interests of landholders and traditional industrialists, were rigidly protectionist.[20] Bordeaux, for example, suffered some of the worst years of its post-1815 economic life in the wake of the so-called bourgeois revolution.[21]

The Orleanist monarchy did not inaugurate an activist policy in the New World for many other reasons as well. The Belgian crisis, on the very doorstep of France, preoccupied the French ministry through much of the decade of the 1830s and made heavy demands on the French treasury. French troops bombarded and captured Antwerp late in 1832. Not until 1839 did the Dutch king acknowledge his defeat and recognize the neutrality and independence of the Belgian state. Other revolutionary outbreaks in the early 1830s, Anglo-French controversies, and the vexatious "Eastern Question" took priority over the Latin American republics. The two foreign ministers succeeding Molé—Horace Sébastiani de la Porta, a Napoleonic general who held office in 1831 and 1832, and the Duke of Broglie, his successor in 1833 and 1834—evinced but slight interest in Mexico. Usually they left Mexican affairs to subordinates in the department and only at rare intervals sent out instructions to its legation there.

During these years Mexico lost a number of its most influential friends in France. The first to leave the scene was Lafayette. When the government successfully weathered the civil disorders of December 1830, he lost his indispensability. Late that same month the king found a way to maneuver him into resignation and virtual political retirement.[22] Lafayette was followed in 1831 by Villevêque, who lost his seat in the Chamber in the March elections, owing to the scandal that had arisen over his Tehuantepec colony. The unsavory financial details that came to light and the well-publicized plight of the colonists aroused public disgust.[23] He never again appeared in the Chamber of Deputies. A third old friend of the Americans, the liberal Bordelais, Lainé, failed rapidly in health and seldom appeared in the Chamber of Peers after 1831.[24]

Unfortunately, the Mexican government failed to offset these losses with a strong diplomatic representation in Paris. Instead, during much of the decade of the 1830s it tried to use its legation as a convenient post of honorable exile for its political enemies. When the nominee declined to accept this thinly disguised punishment, the government left its affairs in the hands of chargés d'affaires insufficiently prestigious to command respect in the French Foreign Ministry. In 1830, when French recognition was bruited, Bustamante had offered the post to his arch-enemy, Manuel Gómez Pedraza, exiled since 1829, as a means of preventing his return to Mexico. But the former Mexican president scornfully rejected the "honor" when he learned that Bustamante had intervened directly to block his disembarkation at Veracruz in October 1830.[25] Until 1834 Murphy, Jr., and another chargé d'affaires, Fernando Mangino, served as caretakers of the legation. In that year Lorenzo de Zavala arrived as the first Mexican minister plenipotentiary. He too was a political exile, sent abroad by Valentín Gómez Farías and Antonio López de Santa Anna to remove him from the Mexican scene. Lacking the confidence of his government, his mission was of pedestrian quality. He was necessarily condemned to almost total inactivity since his instructions did not permit him to entertain issues of any importance between the two countries.[26] After his recall in 1835, the legation remained in the hands of a chargé d'affaires until 1837.

After French recognition of Mexico, the first serious business between the two countries was the negotiation of a treaty of friendship, navigation, and commerce. Parleys got under way early in 1831 and culminated with surprising swiftness, all things considered, in a signed treaty on 31 March.[27] Yet the resulting instrument was anything but satisfactory to France. As Molé had predicted, once the French had given away their major asset, i.e., recognition, they were unable to exact many of the privileges they desired for their subjects and their commerce. Their bargaining position was not enhanced by the mediocrity of their negotiators. Sébastiani had placed the burden of it on Martin, the former Bourbon commercial agent, who displayed no more acumen in this assignment than in his mission in Mexico. His colleague, P. L. Bartholomé, member of the Chamber of Deputies, was a specialist in tariffs, not diplomacy. Neither the one nor the other was able to profit from the knowledgeable advice on the terms of the treaty supplied by Cochelet. They yielded point after point to the experienced Gorostiza, who had been entrusted with the Mexican side of the negotiation.[28]

The treaty of 1831 was much less favorable to French interests than the earlier Declarations. Although it granted the French in Mexico treatment of the most favored nation and freedom of religious practice, the agreement fell woefully short on guarantees of rights and privileges essential to the nascent colony of merchants and craftsmen. The guarantee of the right of practice of retail trade was an absolute necessity, but the article granting it was so qualified as to permit harassment of French retailers or even closing of their shops by local authorities. Nor were the French exempt from forced loans or other contributions that were levied on Mexican citizens as well. The phraseology of the clause on exemption from military service was likewise of suspicious subtlety, as was that permitting (with many restrictions) the practice of coastal trade, i.e., the right of a French vessel to take on cargo in more than one port on the Mexican coast. Yet this right too was a necessity for French merchantmen lest, after discharging their cargoes at Veracruz, they be required to recross the Atlantic with nearly empty holds. Moreover, the concession by Mexico of freedom of religious practice was of little value, given the prevalence of Roman Catholicism in both countries and the absence of religious controversy between them. Finally, the treaty afforded not the slightest satisfaction to French claims to compensation for the sack of the Parian and other injuries. Gorostiza had successfully separated this question from negotiation of the treaty. Instead, the French had to be content with a useless "Declaration" by Gorostiza made after the signing of the treaty that "he did not doubt" the willingness of his government to bring this question "to a prompt and felicitous conclusion."[29]

Although Sébastiani had taken no part in the negotiation, he was aware of the deficiencies of the treaty; but after some hesitation and with the consent of the king, he decided to send it to Mexico for ratification. At least it had the merit, he thought, of being so much less favorable to France than the Declarations of 1827 that it would be a convincing proof of French goodwill and could not possibly be rejected by the Mexican Congress.[30] Fortunately for him, he did not need to seek the approval of the French Chambers, which, according to the French Charter, were not empowered to accept or reject treaties.

Only the king's signature would be required to validate the treaty when it was returned to Paris for the final exchange of ratifications. Meanwhile, in expectation of its immediate acceptance, Sébastiani recalled Cochelet and appointed an interim chargé d'affaires to Mexico to serve until a minister plenipotentiary could take his place.

The French government had not long to wait before learning how badly it had misjudged the reception that Mexico would give the treaty. Before the new chargé d'affaires could arrive at his post the Mexican Congress in December 1831 rejected it, almost in toto. Cochelet, who knew something of the fate of treaties in Mexico, could have forewarned his superiors, at least to some extent. He knew, for example, that the article granting freedom of religious practice would be sure to be struck down, because it was in fact a violation of the Mexican constitution. Gorostiza had become so Europeanized by his long residence abroad that he apparently had lost touch with the laws of his own country. But the religious issue was scarcely a fundamental one and could be easily circumvented. Far more serious were the other objections raised by the Mexican Congress to the terms of the treaty. Professing a desire to discourage the immigration of fortune hunters into Mexico, the Congress refused to guarantee the right to practice retail trade to the French under any circumstances, not even to those who came out with their families or to those who married Mexican citizens. In order to suppress smuggling, it threw out the article permitting coastal trade on a limited basis and declared its total prohibition. Finally, it wished to narrow even further access of French consuls to Mexican cities so that consuls from the United States would be unable to cite French consulates as precedents and thus demand the right to set up in Matamoros on the Rio Grande and foment revolution there.[31]

In rejecting the French treaty, the Mexican Congress could claim with justice that it had not singled out France for discriminatory treatment. It had also recently obstructed ratification of treaties with the United States, the Hanseatic cities, and Prussia. Delays, rejections, and renegotiations were to be expected in treating with Mexico. After five years of parleys the United States still had no ratified treaty with Mexico. England had needed three years and as many treaties before obtaining a complete ratification, and the resulting document proved a breeding ground of controversy. It conceded "freedom of conscience" rather than freedom of religious worship. It was ambiguous on the right of practice of retail trade. Exemption from forced loans, granted to British subjects in the English text, was partly denied them in its Spanish counterpart by a nuance of language unnoticed by British negotiators at the time. At no time and with no nation had the Mexican republic explicitly given up its right to levy forced loans on foreigners or to withdraw the practice of retail trade.[32]

Cochelet was nonetheless profoundly discouraged as he prepared to leave his post. Here was the second agreement with France to be rejected even though it, like the first, had been negotiated on the orders of the Mexican foreign minister and signed by his plenipotentiary in France. He feared that Congress harbored a special animus against France and would never approve a treaty with her. On all sides, he reported, representatives were saying, "At the slightest infraction they [the French] will pick a quarrel with us, blockade and bombard our ports. Look what France has done in Algiers and Lisbon."[33]

Baron Gros and the Mexican Revolution of 1832

The stalemate between the two countries was broken in January 1832 by a *pronunciamiento* in Mexico that inaugurated over a year of political upheaval and led to the removal of the conservatives from office in 1833. At first the French welcomed this revolution, since it promised to relieve them of what they regarded as the systematic hostility of Alamán and Bustamante.[34] Yet they were soon to learn that civil disorder was more destructive to their interests than even the calculated slights of conservative statesmen.

The revolution was only a month old when the new French chargé d'affaires, Baron Jean-Baptiste Louis Gros, arrived in the Mexican capital. It was his first experience in the New World, his previous service having been limited to a stint as attaché in Lisbon from 1823 to 1828 and a later special mission to Egypt and Greece. He owed his present appointment not to his professional qualifications, for he had never before directed a legation, but to his position vis-à-vis the royal family. This was indeed unique. His father, secretary to the Duchess of Bourbon, sister of Louis Philippe's father, had been rewarded for his loyalty with the hand of the duchess's illegitimate daughter. The chargé d'affaires was thus a blood relation of the Orleanist family and second cousin of the King of the French.[35]

Gros's inexperience probably mattered little under the circumstances. At least he was fluent in Spanish, and his title, aristocratic bearing, and personal fortune assured him a respectful reception. Most of the difficulties that he was to encounter were neither of his making nor in his control.

Gros's instructions were of little use to him by the time of his arrival except as the most general guide to French objectives. They informed him that French interests in Mexico were "principally if not uniquely" commercial and adjured him to remain completely detached from Mexican political activity while cultivating "the seeds of union and prosperity that exist between the two countries."[36] This was sound advice at any time, no doubt. But Sébastiani, author of the instructions, had very little conception of the difficulties to be encountered in treating with Mexico. He not only failed to anticipate Mexican rejection of the French treaty but expected Gros by himself to repair its deficiencies. Thus Gros was ordered to obtain from the Mexican government explicit exemption of French subjects from all forced loans and admission of Mexican liability for damages suffered by foreigners in civil disorder.

The political turmoil into which Gros was dropped made pursuit of any of these goals virtually impossible. How could Gros cultivate the seeds of friendship between France and Mexico when Alamán, alarmed and preoccupied with the spreading revolution, declined even to discuss relations with France until internal order had been restored?[37] How could he remain neutral himself and assure the neutrality of his compatriots when the government embarked on a press campaign that blamed foreigners, especially the French, as instigators of rebellion and incited the Mexican masses against them? The French were accused not only of lending military and financial aid to the enemy but also of reviling the Holy Sacrament, violating Mexican womanhood, and a host of other repellant crimes. "Mexicans: open your eyes," exhorted one government newspaper. "This war has been incited by foreigners so that we will always need them . . . and be dependent on them for commerce. . . . By taking up arms against us they want to make us their slaves."[38]

These accusations contained just enough truth in them to prove an embarrassment. Gros and the British chargé d'affaires, Richard Pakenham, admitted that most foreigners welcomed the revolution in the belief that they would fare better if the conservatives were evicted from office.[39] Santa Anna, principal military motor of the revolt, operating from his base in Manga de Clavo near Veracruz, had undeniably attracted the open support of many French subjects. Carrère was his personal friend and was suspected by Gros of stepping outside the path of official neutrality.[40] Of the foreigners who had enrolled in his army, some twenty were French. Gros assured Alamán that by taking up arms these French had deprived themselves of the protection of their legation. Unmollified, Alamán replied that if the French in Veracruz did not wish to come to harm during the conflict, they had best remove themselves from the country.[41] Finally, Gros was additionally embarrassed by the conduct of the French navy, which had chosen this moment to make another of its unpredictable appearances off Veracruz. In addition to the man-of-war *Héroine*, on which Gros had arrived in February, a corvette and a brig were patrolling offshore and were naturally objects of suspicion.[42]

Most frustrating of all to Gros was the plight of French commerce, the promotion of which, according to his instructions, should be his primary aim. Yet as the civil war widened and intensified, trade was increasingly paralyzed, for reasons that Gros was powerless to combat. By 1833 there were in Mexico at least 21 French wholesalers and 438 retailers, employing approximately 650 other French subjects, not counting the many French artisans who sold the work of their hands in their own shops.[43] In 1831 these enterprises had consumed some 16.9 million francs of French merchandise. In 1832 they purchased only 9.7 millions from France, largely because of the effect of civil war.[44] The reports of Gros and his vice-consuls chronicled the woes of the merchants during these months even though they escaped for the most part actual pillage or other physical damage. "The position of our wholesalers at Veracruz is extremely unfortunate," wrote Gros in one of his first reports.[45] Santa Anna was pocketing the customs duties that constituted the principal source of revenue of the central government. Bustamante declared the port closed to commerce, a decree that in itself was meaningless, since Mexico had no ships to enforce it; but it meant that merchants who paid the duties to Santa Anna were liable for repayment or other penalties for goods that traveled into the interior. Gros realized that these duties would soon give rise to sizable claims by French merchants. After only a month in Mexico he was already convinced that France would be obliged to resort to a blockade of the coast to obtain justice for her subjects.[46]

By May communications between the capital and Veracruz were cut. Because *conductas* (mule trains bearing specie) could not pass from the interior, merchants in Veracruz were unable to pay the duties demanded by Santa Anna. In the capital the government, feeling the pinch from loss of the customs duties, raised four hundred thousand dollars from merchants by threatening them with expulsion if they did not subscribe to the loan. The following autumn the government levied two additional forced loans on foreign merchants, eliciting formal protests from Pakenham and Gros.[47] In Tampico, wrote the French vice-consul, commerce was ruined. "Whether the end of the revolution comes sooner or later, commerce will be a good long while in recuperation and confidence can be restored only [by] a period of public tranquillity."[48] As the year drew to a close and the army of Santa Anna began a siege of the capital, Gros feared for the very lives of his compatriots. The government was once again propagating hatred of foreigners, and in the wake of this propaganda Gros reported the harassment or molestation of several French subjects. Meanwhile, he had been unable even to begin discussion of the tariff or of past claims with either Alamán or his successor in the Foreign Ministry, F. Fagoaga.[49]

During these months of travail Gros received scant support from his government in Paris, whose eyes were, as usual, focused elsewhere. The warships at Veracruz that Gros found on his arrival did not remain to lend support to the demarches of the legation. The *Héroine* had returned immediately to Brest after delivering Gros to his post. Of the remaining two, one cracked up on the reefs at Tuxpan in May; the other departed Veracruz in August.[50] Five months were to pass before another warship appeared. In vain did Gros appeal to the minister of the navy for reinforcement of the Gulf station. Preoccupied by the impending crisis in Holland, the navy was concentrating rather than dispersing its fleet. "It is impossible," wrote the naval minister, "to add to the number of ships in commission beyond the limits fixed by the budget of my department."[51]

Nor did the government devote much time or intelligence to the negotiation of a second commercial treaty. Sébastiani again delegated the duty to subordinates, this time to Jean-Baptiste Roux de la Rochelle, who had represented France in the United States, and Charles David, who had served briefly as commercial agent in Mexico between the missions of Martin and Cochelet. The Mexican plenipotentiary was again Gorostiza. At first the French negotiators heeded the shrewd advice of Gros to defer the conclusion of a treaty until the end of the military contest between the Bustamante government and

Santa Anna. Better terms almost certainly could be obtained should the revolting Yorkinos emerge the victors.[52] Unfortunately, this prudent resolve was undermined by a French ministerial crisis in October 1832 and the resignation of Sébastiani from office. Only four days after the Foreign Ministry changed hands and before the new minister, the Duke of Broglie, could settle into office, the treaty was signed.[53] It was a signal victory for Gorostiza. Of those provisions regarded by Gros as indispensable to French interests, only one, and that perhaps the least important, was obtained: exemption of French subjects from military service. The vital guarantee of the right to practice retail trade was given away in its entirety, Mexico being, according to the treaty, at "entire liberty to regulate this commerce by its legislation, as it judges useful to its own citizens." As for taxes and forced loans, the French were again to be subject to all requisitions imposed on Mexican nationals. France also gave up the right to engage in coastal trade, although one clause might be construed to permit her ships to stop at more than one Mexican port under certain circumstances. The article on religion replaced the freedom of worship of the first treaty with an ambiguous statement that French subjects professing a religion other than Catholic would not be harassed on account of it. In return for these concessions, the French negotiators obtained nothing more than general assurances of adherence to the principles of free trade and the right of ships in distress to protection.

When this treaty arrived in Mexico late in December 1832, Gros, nearing the end of his interim appointment, was much disappointed. The Yorkinos had just captured the capital and placed Gómez Pedraza in the presidency. The new men in the government, reported Gros, were much more favorable to foreign commerce and industry than had been Bustamante and Alamán and would have consented to better terms.[54] Gros believed a treaty essential to French interests in a country as unstable as Mexico. Even though the Yorkinos were now in the saddle, the future was uncertain. Gómez Pedraza would remain in office only until 1 April. Gros had little trust in Santa Anna as his successor. The revival of commerce was feeble and slow. The French were without naval protection, and the merchants were grumbling that their government had abandoned them. "The situation is not reassuring," he concluded, "and everyone seems to believe in future revolutions."[55]

The Early Mission of Baron Deffaudis: A Display of Moderation

For its first minister plenipotentiary to Mexico the Foreign Ministry reached into its commercial division to name Baron Deffaudis. No doubt it could have made a more tactful choice. Deffaudis was known to the Mexicans as the servant of Charles X and partial author of the greatly regretted Declarations. Murphy had been wont to refer to him as "that functionary" who gave him cold reception on the occasions of his visits to the department.[56] Nor was Deffaudis an experienced diplomat. His only previous career service outside the bureaucracy had been two years as consul in Stettin under the First Empire. He had never before traveled outside Europe.[57]

Yet Deffaudis did not lack assets for his post. An economist with seventeen years' experience in the commercial division, no one knew better than he the facts of French commerce with Mexico. Although his Spanish was less than fluent, he had at least a reading knowledge of the language and also the assistance of Gros, who was to remain as first secretary of the legation. His birth and fortune were not the equal of his subordinate, but his title of baron (awarded him by Charles X) and his rank of minister plenipotentiary and envoy extraordinary lent him prestige. Moreover, he brought to his mission a real sense of dedication. Believing in the unlimited potential of the market in Mexico for French exports, he felt called upon to develop it.[58] He had a clear idea of what was needed: the establishment of additional consulates in Mexican ports, the inauguration of a line of military packet ships between Bordeaux and Veracruz, the negotiation of a treaty favorable to French commerce, and above all the reinforcement of the Gulf station to insure the regular presence of the French flag off Veracruz.[59]

Attainment of his goal implied a direction and a consistency in French policy toward Mexico so far conspicuous only by their absence. Yet Deffaudis was sure that such an expenditure of time and money would more than pay off. Properly cultivated, he was convinced, the Mexican market could rank second only to the United States in the New World and as high as fourth among all nations as a consumer of French products.[60]

Another asset possessed by Deffaudis, especially valuable in a country like Mexico, was his genuine disinterest in politics. It was true that he believed that the Mexicans were ill-suited to republicanism and federalism, but he was totally disinclined to involve himself in partisan struggles and would treat with any party that was in office. In France he had proved his adaptability by serving successively the Bonapartes, the Bourbons, and the Orleanists. In Mexico, although his personal friends came to be among the "aristocrats," he was pleased upon his arrival to have to deal with the Yorkinos. "Although not always scrupulous in their financial dealings," he reported, "they [the Yorkinos] are favorably disposed toward foreigners, especially the French, . . . and realize that their industry is needed to prod the Mexicans out of the lethargic state in which they languish." [61]

When he assumed his duties in February 1833 his first aim was to convince the Mexicans of his goodwill and to earn their confidence. He planned to emphasize the positive aspects of Franco-Mexican relations while creating an atmosphere of cordiality. Thus, he would eschew presentation of old claims and play down or ignore minor grievances, while bringing the Mexicans around to policies more favorable to French trade. For nearly two years, by adhering to this program of action he managed a display of moderation and avoided an open clash with the Mexican government.

The obstacles in his way were formidable. In Mexico he never knew from one week to another with what government he would be treating. Throughout much of 1833 Santa Anna, playing an ambiguous game, appeared intermittently and unpredictably in the capital to take over the executive authority from Vice-President Gómez Farías. From April to September in 1834 the general assumed dictatorial powers, turning away from his former partisans and toward the "priest party" for his support. When he retired he left the government in the hands of the conservatives. During these two years Deffaudis had to negotiate with five successive foreign ministers.

This game of musical chairs was accompanied by eruptions of civil disorder. One of its by-products was the levying of another forced loan on Mexican and foreign merchants in August 1833, this time by the state of Veracruz. Although the sums demanded of the French were negligible when partitioned among them, the principle was important. Repeated compliance with such decrees might serve as precedents that could commit the French to payment of much larger sums in the future. [62]

During the summer of 1833 even the forces of nature appeared to ally against Deffaudis. Cholera, which had devastated Paris in 1831, struck Tampico and Campeche and spread to the capital. In August

1833 Deffaudis reported that the plague had taken a toll of twelve thousand in Mexico City alone and, although abating, was still claiming some three hundred victims daily. In Atencingo in the state of Puebla, late in the same month, panic-stricken *campesinos*, believing that the foreigners had poisoned the water supply and brought on the disease, set upon and assassinated five French subjects.[63]

Through all these troubles Deffaudis maintained his equanimity. In the question of the forced loans he did not hesitate to mitigate the severity of his instructions, which bade him hark back to the Declarations of 1827 and insist on exemption of French subjects from all loans as a matter of principle.[64] Such intransigence would have closed the door to all negotiation. He knew that the Mexicans would never accept the validity of the Declarations, which he himself recognized as beyond redemption. Moreover, he believed the French government was on dubious ground in invoking a question of principle. France herself had subjected foreigners to a special levy in 1815 in the wake of the Napoleonic wars, as even Broglie admitted.[65] Nor could France claim for her subjects the right of the most favored nation in demanding exemption from all forced loans, because the British government had recently come around to agreeing to the taxation of its subjects if the levies were imposed upon Mexican citizens as well.

Deffaudis's solution was a compromise. For the loans levied by the federal government in 1832 he accepted as satisfactory the emission of bonds applicable to payment of 40 percent of the customs duties to those French merchants who had complied with the decree. In the case of the Veracruz levy he filed claim to compensation for the French who had paid it, on the grounds that its purpose was political: the raising of money to combat the enemies of the government in the civil war.[66] In this manner he avoided a showdown with the Mexican government over small sums of money but did not explicitly admit the liability of French subjects to forced loans in general.

He was equally flexible in other issues of relative insignificance. When the Mexican government asked foreigners to contribute to the formation of a civil guard to keep the public peace in the capital, Deffaudis accepted the request as a reasonable one even as his British colleague was strongly protesting it.[67] Not even the cholera and the attendant assassinations at Atencingo broke in on his serenity. The disease itself, he assured Broglie, was not the real *cholera morbus* that had struck Europe earlier but a mere "cholérine" that would not faze a Frenchman.[68] It should by no means deter shippers in France from dispatching their merchantmen as usual. As for the assassinations in Atencingo, they were, of course, deplorable. He submitted a note to the Mexican Foreign Ministry asking exemplary punishment of the perpetrators and publication in the official newspaper of an article designed to discourage future attacks of this type. Yet he could not bring himself to share Broglie's sense of outrage at the event and readily accepted the Mexican promise of "full and complete justice." After all, he reminded Broglie, similar attacks on foreigners had occurred in Europe, even in Paris, during the epidemic of 1831.[69]

Always he sought to avoid a confrontation that would place France in a position of choosing between deployment of force or a humiliating retreat. It was not that he doubted the ease with which France could bring Mexico to heel should she so desire. As a civilian with no military experience, he could readily believe that by an attack on the fortress of San Juan de Ulúa France could defeat Mexico with a single warship and "in a matter of hours." But he advised against such action, which would be certain to invite retaliation against French subjects in the interior. "They [the French] would certainly be massacred. . . . Such is the powerful consideration that must prevent us . . . from carrying matters to extremes."[70]

While Deffaudis was managing to stay on speaking terms with the Mexican government, he was less successful in bringing his own government to adopt the measures he believed necessary to the development of its interests. The French navy failed him from the first. He had been in residence only a few weeks when he learned that a French warship had arrived at Veracruz and departed without establishing communication with the legation. Deffaudis was indignant. How could French captains, when they did occasionally appear in the Gulf, support the French minister in Mexico if they refused to remain long enough to notify the legation of their arrival and receive a reply? He dismissed the perils of the coast as mere pretexts for their swift departures. In his opinion French sailors disliked Veracruz because it offered little in the way of entertainment and obliged them to eschew hard drink as a protection against yellow fever.[71]

Yet his protests failed to make a dent in the French Ministry of the Navy, where they were not popular. For reasons of economy and overextension the navy not only refused to reinforce the Gulf station but, in mid-decade, suppressed it altogether. The base in Martinique, over two thousand miles distant from Veracruz, became the nearest source of naval protection for the French in Mexico. Since it too was not at full strength, consisting as a rule of no more than a frigate and a corvette, appearances of French warships in the Gulf became even less frequent than in the last years of Bourbon rule.[72]

The government was likewise deaf to Deffaudis's pleas for a line of military packet ships. Holding that the commercial importance of the Mexican market did not justify the expense of such an operation, it simply continued the meager subvention of the Bourbons of commercial service out of Bordeaux. This service was proving ever more unsatisfactory. The house of Balguerie that had taken over Gautier's contract with the government fell on hard times in the *mauvais temps économique* of the early 1830s and cut all possible corners to effect economies.[73] In 1835, convinced by Deffaudis's ceaseless complaints of the worthlessness of the commercial line, the government allowed its contract with Balguerie to lapse and, substituting for it neither another commercial service nor the naval packets, left France without any regular maritime communication with Veracruz. To Deffaudis this decision smacked of improvidence. Together with the infrequent appearance of French warships it would lead the Mexicans to believe that France was indifferent to her interests and subjects in Mexico and would not sustain the representations of its legations.[74]

The government was scarcely more receptive to Deffaudis's recommendations to expand the consular network. Upon recognition of Mexico the foreign minister had brought an end to the false position of the Bourbon agents by the establishment of consulates at Veracruz and Tampico and a chancellery in the capital to assist the legation in consular duties. But he refused Deffaudis's request for three subsidized agencies on the west coast (at Guaymas, Mazatlán, and Acapulco), directing instead that, if established, they be operated by resident French merchants serving at their own expense. On the Gulf the government likewise drew the line at Deffaudis's plea for three consulates. It replied with the establishment of a consulate of the first class at Veracruz (the classification affected the amount of salary paid the consul), one of the second class at Campeche, and demotion of the consulate at Tampico to an agency directed by an honorary (unsalaried) vice-consul. Again Deffaudis was disappointed with the government's parsimony. Unsalaried agents had neither the time nor the incentive to perform their consular duties, he complained; as a rule, they corresponded with him only to submit their resignations. He remained convinced that the inadequacy of consular protection greatly impeded the development of French trade.[75]

Most vexing of all for Deffaudis in the early years of his mission was the question of a commercial treaty; here he had to contend not only with Parisian penury and indifference, but also with the byzantine intricacies of Mexican politics. He was thoroughly dissatisfied with the treaty of 1832, which had arrived in Mexico for ratification shortly before he took over the legation.[76] His private fear was that the Mexican Congress would hasten to ratify it and that Broglie would have no plausible reason for rejecting it.

It came as a positive relief to him that the Mexican Congress "reverted to type" and out of sheer "amour propre" late in 1833 foiled Gorostiza's efforts to obtain total ratification.[77] After splitting hairs over grammatical constructions, the Congress finally fell upon and exorcized Article 6, which gave French subjects the right to appeal to the Mexican minister of finances if they disagreed with the valuations assigned their merchandise. It ratified all the rest. Yet Deffaudis deemed what amounted to a victory for him too slender to be reported to Paris. After all, the rejected article was of minor importance. Broglie might well feel honor bound to accept the remainder of the treaty that, with its disastrous limitations on the right to practice retail trade, would hamper French commerce in Mexico for years to come. Therefore, he took it on himself early in 1834 to negotiate what he called a "Provisional Convention" providing that, pending the ratification of a definitive treaty, France and Mexico would be accorded the rights of the most favored nation. The Mexican foreign minister, Lombardo, agreed in February to accept such an instrument.[78] By July, after many delays and vexations due to the kaleidoscopic Mexican political scene, Deffaudis obtained the formal approval of Santa Anna, then in possession of a virtual dictatorship.[79] Only after this achievement did Deffaudis inform the French foreign minister of the incomplete ratification of the French treaty the previous year and of his negotiation of a provisional agreement. He recommended acceptance of his convention in order to provide a breathing space for renegotiation of a treaty more favorable to French interests.

Now it was the turn of French political convulsions to hinder his efforts. In the spring of 1834 the adversaries of Broglie (who were numerous and included even the king) were able to force his departure from office. It was the beginning of a long ministerial crisis that was not resolved until March 1835.[80] In the ensuing confusion and changes of foreign ministers, Deffaudis's convention and the treaty of 1832 were totally lost from sight. Deffaudis waited in vain for approval of his initiative and authorization to negotiate a third treaty. Not until September 1835 did the foreign minister, once again Broglie, even note the lacuna in its instructions and promise to take the matter into consideration.[81] By then it was far too late. The reservoir of goodwill that Deffaudis had endeavored so patiently to build up had been drained dry; profitable resumption of treaty negotiation was out of the question.

The End of Détente

By the spring of 1835 the conservatives in Mexico (the Centralists, as they came to be called) had returned to office. Santa Anna having retired to Manga de Clavo, the Mexican Congress refused to recognize the right of the liberal vice-president, Gómez Farías, to the executive power and instead named General Miguel Barragán as president ad interim. The foreign minister was José María Gutiérrez de Estrada, known to be one of the "most honorable and richest men in Mexico," and also one of the most reactionary.[82] The new minister of war, General José María Tornel, despite the French origin of his family, was notoriously ill-disposed to French commerce. This administration, dependent on the "aristocracy and the clergy" and "fundamentally hostile to foreigners" (Deffaudis's opinions) could be expected to place all possible obstacles in the path of the development of French industry and commerce.[83]

Friction first surfaced in an issue whose very triviality was significant. In February 1835 Gutiérrez de Estrada and the Mexican Congress suddenly rejected both the partially ratified treaty of 1832 and Deffaudis's Provisional Convention of 1834. The only reason given was that in these instruments Mexico had not been granted the "Alternative," i.e., the courtesy of placing the name of Mexico and its president before that of France and its king in the Spanish text of the treaty. It was true, as the Mexicans pointed out, that Mexican treaties with England and the United States gave precedence to Mexico in the Spanish text. But Mexico had never before raised this question of etiquette with France. A review of Mexico's pacts with France revealed that, apparently by chance, the Declarations had granted the Alternative while the treaties of 1831 and 1832 had not. Deffaudis believed that Gutiérrez was going out of his way to find a new subject of controversy between the two countries.[84]

By this time Deffaudis's patience was beginning to wear thin. He reacted strongly to what he saw as Mexican vanity. "France," he lectured Gutiérrez de Estrada, "by reason of her antiquity that, so to say, is lost in the dim mists of time, has had from the days of old been so honored in its conventions with almost all of the powers of the world." The Mexican, disliking to be taught by a minister representing a regime less than five years of age, retorted that Mexico too was a "Nation of Antiquity."[85] The ensuing battle of pens, published in the Mexican press, served only to demonstrate the pettishness of the authors and to embitter their relationship.

This opéra bouffe was still playing when problems of more substance appeared. In March Gutiérrez de Estrada proposed to Congress a "Law on Foreigners" that would, if passed, deny foreigners the right to claim indemnities for damages incurrred in Mexican political disturbances. Given the ever-present threat of revolution in Mexico, Deffaudis believed this law would deal a crippling blow to the growing French colony of artisans and merchants. Foreigners would be "fleeced at will" and at the mercy of "every big and little thief in the Republic."[86] Even if they were willing to adopt Mexican nationality they would gain nothing, because Mexican citizens were usually denied compensation for such damages.

Both Deffaudis and Pakenham believed the proposed law was contrary to the Law of Nations and submitted formal protests. They were on sufficiently strong ground. In England the common law obliged the parish or district where the damage occurred to indemnify the aggrieved party, be he foreign or British born.[87] In France after the Revolution of 1830 the French Commission on Damages had authorized payments in excess of eight hundred thousand dollars for compensation to individuals, regardless of nationality, who had suffered losses during the July days.[88] The largest single category of claims recognized had been those for losses from pillage or accidental destruction. Moreover, France had signed a treaty with the United States in 1831 that obligated her to pay indemnities to American shippers damaged in the Napoleonic wars.

Perhaps as a result of Deffaudis's and Pakenham's protests, the Mexican Congress adjourned in May without passing the offensive law. But it refused to admit either the correctness of the two diplomats' arguments or the liability of Mexico for damages suffered in civil disorder. Deffaudis was well aware that the administration was determined to deny the validity of all French claims.[89]

The evident hostility of the "aristocratic party," as Deffaudis styled it, caused him deliberately to change his "system of negotiation." Earlier he had been willing to let old grievances lie and to try to prevent new ones from arising in the hope of concluding a treaty and of obtaining the removal of surtaxes on French commerce. Now he decided to fix on each and every conceivable grievance as it arose, to submit claims for indemnities, and at the same time to revive older claims against Mexico.[90]

His subsequent correspondence in 1835 shows that he was as good as his word. In March he submitted claims for compensation for a French packet ship, the *Petite Louise*, damaged during a spring revolt of the Veracruz garrison. At the same time he protested the expulsion from Mexico of a M. Gallix, owner of a wax factory in Tehuantepec. Deffaudis regarded Gallix's case as especially serious, because the Mexican government had made no specific charge against him. If the Mexican government believed it could expel French subjects at will without showing cause, none of them would have an instant's security. He also revived and presented for the first time during his mission the claims of the victims of the sack of the Parian in 1828 and reminded the Mexicans that the assassins of the French at Atencingo in 1833 were as yet unpunished. During the summer he protested the seizure of a French merchant ship charged with smuggling and presented claims for indemnities for French subjects deprived of the practice of retail trade in Sonora by state decree. In all these claims, needless to add, he obtained no satisfaction whatsoever except for the trifling sum of two hundred dollars paid by the governor of Veracruz for damages to the *Petite Louise*.[91]

With a single exception, the reaction of the French government to Deffaudis's change of policy was its habitual silence. The Gallix case, however, struck a nerve. It appeared to be a good test case to establish the right of French subjects to compensation for grievances. Broglie, again foreign minister, wrote the usually ignored Mexican chargé d'affaires in Paris demanding Gallix's immediate return to Tehuantepec and full compensation for his losses. To Deffaudis he sent instructions to demand reparation of all damages suffered by French subjects and "in case of necessity the right to exact them by force."[92]

Broglie's threat did little more than to demonstrate that Franco-Mexican relations had returned to the familiar state of ill-humored contentiousness. The Mexican government was impressed only to the extent of permitting Gallix to return to Tehuantepec; but it denied him compensation and threatened to report Deffaudis to Paris for "impertinent behavior." [93]

After five years the government of Louis Philippe could scarcely be proud of its record of relations with Mexico. France still had no treaty with Mexico, her volume of exports was diminishing rather than increasing, her merchandise was discriminated against by Mexican tariffs, and her subjects were not even assured the rights of the most favored nation. The French navy, stationed at far-off Martinique, came but rarely to Mexican shores. The Bordeaux packet ships had ceased to function, and nothing replaced them. Despite its act of recognition, the Orleanist monarchy had enjoyed no more, and in some cases less, success than the Bourbons in fostering its interests in Mexico.

3
Gunboat Diplomacy:
The "Pastry War"

What these people [the Mexicans] need is a lesson, a severe lesson, to knock
a little reason and justice into their heads. Furthermore, it is so easy to give it
to them!—Deffaudis to Molé, 18 June 1837

Blundering into War

If the renewed irritability between the two countries is readily ex-
plainable, the burgeoning of French *mauvaise humeur* within two years
into the bombardment and blockade of Veracruz by a sizable naval
squadron is more difficult to account for. The explanation given by
the Mexicans and that has found its way into the history books is that
France unleashed her might to collect money claimed by her subjects
for alleged damages in civil disorder. Because one of the claimants
was said to have been a pastry cook whose small shop had been
pilfered, the Mexicans, skilled in sarcasm, dubbed the attack the
"Pastry War." France was made out bully and fool in pursuit of a
risible aim.[1]

This interpretation has in it a modicum of truth. France did demand of Mexico an indemnity to compensate her subjects. Yet it is
inadequate to explain why the cautious government of Louis Philippe, after years of penny pinching and indifference to its Mexican
interests, suddenly embarked on a transatlantic expedition with costs
far disproportionate to the sums demanded.

Part of the answer must be sought in the French colony in Mexico
wherein arose the grievances for which the French sought redress.
According to contemporaries the colony had grown substantially
during the 1830s. By the time of the French attack its population was
usually reckoned at some four thousand, with occasional estimates as

high as six thousand.[2] These figures are not much better than guess-work and inspire little confidence. Given the absence of a reliable census for the period, no one could know with any accuracy who was living in the republic. Yet these estimates may not have been too wide of the mark. A poll of French subjects taken ten years later demonstrated the probable presence of between four and six thousand French subjects.[3] In the meantime hundreds of French had left the country as a result of the hostilities of 1838–39. Although most apparently returned, the colony at mid-century may not have been appreciably larger than it was in the late 1830s. Whatever their precise numbers, by 1838 the French were undeniably by far the largest group of foreign subjects in Mexico (except the Spanish, a special case). The size of the French colony in itself goes far to explain the frequency of their claims; the French complained more because there were more of them to complain.[4] Moreover, unlike the small British colony composed largely of wealthy wholesalers with means to protect themselves from Mexican officialdom, many of the French were poor artisans and small tradesmen. Deffaudis estimated that in 1837 there were seven to eight hundred of this class in the capital alone.[5] They were especially vulnerable during outbreaks of civil disorder.

The grievances of the colony escalated at a rapid rate during this decade. At the end of 1833 Deffaudis had made only a handful of claims in behalf of his countrymen. By 1837 his correspondence had become a continuous catalog of "outrages" and "atrocities."[6] His objectivity and accuracy are, of course, open to question. The very frequency of these occurrences in his reports may have been at least in part a reflection of his new policy of seizing upon each and every incident as an issue to take up with the Mexican government. Yet there can be no doubt that the colony met with increased hardship in the last half of the decade. The volume of French exports to Mexico, already disappointingly low, sank precipitously in those years. In 1835 exports had amounted to 13 million francs. The next year they fell to 7.5 million, not to rise again even to 10 million until 1840.[7] The tabulation of exports provided an infallible guide to the relative prosperity of French wholesalers and retailers within Mexico, who did two-thirds to four-fifths of their trade in merchandise from the mother country. The slump in exports translated inevitably into a proportionate decrease in their commercial activity.

The revolt of Texas against Mexico in 1835 and the military campaigns that followed had a troublesome fallout on the French colony.

At Tampico, for example, local military authorities tried to seize a French merchant ship for use as a transport vessel to carry men and munitions to Texas.[8] In November 1835 two French subjects were so misguided as to join a band of Texan and Mexican insurgents led by the Mexican general José Antonio Mexía. They were shot out of hand when they landed at Tampico. Deffaudis and the French government strongly protested the absence of judicial proceeding.[9]

The Texas war also brought with it imposition of forced loans of unprecedented magnitude. These exactions were no longer the minor irritants of earlier years. The Mexican government needed to raise some three million dollars to pay for its unsuccessful campaigns of 1836 and 1837 and large additional sums for the future if its pledge to subdue the rebellious province were to be taken seriously. Ever since independence the government had relied on taxes on imports and exports collected at the ports as its principal source of income. These had been insufficient at the best of times. Now faced with the slump in foreign trade and the exigencies of the Texas campaign, it resorted to extraordinary levies on capital wherever it could be found.[10] Commerce was an obvious target. In November 1835 the government shortened the interval of payment of customs duties from six months to forty to eighty days. Two months later it refused to accept customs bonds as partial payment of duties. In addition it suddenly required all merchants except simple artisans to purchase a *derecho de patente* at a cost of between one hundred and four hundred dollars.[11] The Mexican Congress followed in June 1836 with a decree levying a forced loan on foreign and native commercial houses to the amount of two million dollars. The maximum and minimum contributions were at first fixed at one thousand and one hundred dollars, respectively, but later changed to allow exactions as high as six thousand dollars per establishment.[12]

During these troubled years the French government utterly failed to come to grips with its Mexican problems. Political instability and a rapid turnover in the French Foreign Ministry were partly to blame. France had three foreign ministers in the year 1836: Broglie, who fell from office in February; Adolphe Thiers, who survived until the following September; and Molé, his successor, returning to the department for the first time since his brief term of office in 1830. But the fluctuations in French "policy" toward Mexico were even more frequent than the change of ministers. None of them seems to have had the time or inclination to think through a course of action.

Broglie, after taking a tough line on the Gallix affair, had allowed the negotiation of a treaty to sleep undisturbed throughout 1835 without so much as a comment on the "Alternative" or on Deffaudis's Provisional Convention. Suddenly either he or a subordinate awoke in February 1836 and ordered Deffaudis to resume negotiation straightaway and on terms that amounted to another giveaway. Deffaudis was not only to grant the Alternative, but also to use the unfortunate treaty of 1832 as his model. And if Mexico should refuse any concession whatsoever, continued the order from Paris, Deffaudis was to sign some treaty, any treaty, and send it immediately to the foreign minister for approval.[13]

Before these instructions could arrive at their destination Thiers entered office and temporarily halted the policy of appeasement. He instructed Deffaudis to hold the Mexican government strictly responsible for arbitrary action against French subjects and ordered the reactivation of the Gulf station at Havana.[14] Yet Thiers was far from a definition of Mexican policy. A month later he changed his tack, chided Deffaudis for his inflexibility, and counseled "prudence and moderation." The following July he reverted to a tough, even menacing line, in the affair of the French filibusters shot out of hand at Tampico.[15]

What was Deffaudis to make of these contradictions? Their harmful effects were magnified by their erratic delivery, often delayed over a period of months because of storms or interruptions of travel within Mexico. Deffaudis thus had too much time to work far out on a limb that would be sawed off behind him. Broglie's soft instructions of February 1836 had seriously embarrassed him. They had arrived while he was still acting on the energetic line set him in the Gallix affair. He had been obliged to climb far down in offering to resume treaty negotiation on what amounted to Mexican terms.[16] The Mexican foreign minister, preferring the status quo, sensed the lack of French resolve. He crowned Deffaudis's humiliation by rejecting his olive branch and refusing to open negotiations on any terms.[17] The French were thus left without the protection of a treaty, although by this time the United States, Holland, Prussia, Saxony, and Denmark had all successfully crossed this hurdle.

Soon after this rebuff Deffaudis faced the problem of the forced loan of June 1836. With Pakenham he believed that the levies discriminated unfairly against foreign houses. Levies on French merchants, reported Deffaudis, averaged between thirteen and fifteen hundred dollars, higher than the sums demanded of Mexican merchants of comparable resources.[18] Because the profits of the average French retailer even in a prosperous year amounted to only some twenty-seven hundred dollars,[19] the decree, if enforced rigidly, would spell hardship or even ruin for many of them in the adverse conditions of 1836. French merchants in the capital, in Tampico, and in Zacatecas petitioned Deffaudis to save them from what they regarded as spoliation.[20]

The uproar over the loan was at its height when Thiers's aggressive instructions of the previous March arrived at the legation. The about-face in Paris caused Deffaudis to mount his high horse and claim total exemption of his compatriots on the grounds that the distribution of the loan discriminated against foreign subjects. Stimulated by the prospect of naval support from a revived Gulf station, he decided to use the question either to bring Mexico to submit to French demands or to force a rupture in their diplomatic relations.[21]

He was still in this defiant mood when the misfortunes of a French warship, the *Inconstant*, came to his attention. She had been cruising in the Gulf, far from her base in Martinique, when her need of repairs became acute. Limping in to Veracruz in mid-July 1836, she was denied permission to anchor in the sheltered roadstead of the city instead of farther away at Sacrificios, the usual anchorage for foreign warships. Pleading inability to do otherwise given the condition of the ship and direction of the wind, she came in anyway. While the crew dismantled her rudder and repaired her sails her captain exchanged angry notes with the military commander of Veracruz. The argument resolved itself in a compromise that permitted the ship two days' grace in which to complete repairs. She left on schedule without more ado. The incident should have ended there had not Deffaudis taken offense at the language used by the Mexican commander in his correspondence. Deciding to demonstrate French resolution, he demanded satisfaction for the alleged insults and referred the matter to Paris for instructions.[22]

Deffaudis's reports on his summer of grievances were beginning to arrive in Paris just at the time Molé returned to the Foreign Ministry. Molé had never forgotten that he had presided over French foreign policy when France, against his better judgment, had made a gift to Mexico of diplomatic recognition without first negotiating a commercial treaty. At that time he had predicted trouble. Now he reacted angrily to Deffaudis's recital. The affair of the *Inconstant* caused him to order the minister of the navy to deploy immediately a frigate and two brigs to Veracruz to insist upon satisfaction.[23] The subsequent news of the forced loan aroused him to the point of fury. Mexico should be given a proper lesson, he decided. Believing that the small squadron that he had just summoned would not inspire "sufficient salutary fear" in the Mexicans, he countermanded it and decided instead to go to the king and council of ministers to obtain permission to send out a "greater deployment of force" to cow the Mexicans into submission.[24] In the meantime, on 7 November, he dictated instructions to Deffaudis advising him of the department's new resolution.

These instructions[25] were all but an ultimatum to Mexico and couched in language wounding to a weak, emerging nation. French subjects, began Molé, must be exempted from forced loans of any kind and at all times. The Declarations of 1827 must be honored in every particular. France could permit no exceptions, because Mexico, "a constant prey to civil war and devoid of financial order," would avail herself of them to treat foreigners like serfs, "taillable et corvéable à merci." The Mexican government should discover the error of its ways. Mexico needed Europe, whose commerce supplied her principal source of revenue and whose peoples carried with them the benefits of their "civilizing industry." "It is an example unprecedented in the history of international relations," he lectured, "for a country wherein everyone and everything—people, government, courts— yielding to the most base prejudices, seeks to outdo itself in displays of hatred and hostility against foreigners and appears to go out of its way to insult . . . the governments from which they come. Such nevertheless is the example of Mexico." Europeans were hounded, ransomed, pillaged, and assassinated "like Jews in the Middle Ages," even though they set an example of civilized industry "in the midst of an ignorant and barbaric society." But Mexico would be "dangerously misled," he concluded, if it continued "to fleece [French subjects] at its pleasure." The time would come when France would take no more, would call a halt to her policy of indulgence, and would "take justice into her own hands." Lest this moment arrive in the near future, Deffaudis should take up French grievances of every kind, one by one, and pursue them until complete satisfaction was obtained. And, to impress the Mexican government with the seriousness of French purpose, Molé authorized Deffaudis to communicate the dispatch in person and in its entirety to the Mexican foreign minister.

This harangue reached Deffaudis late in February 1837. He may certainly be excused if he inferred from it that his government had at last defined its Mexican policy and expected him to execute it to the letter. He was delighted to oblige. Tired of the repeated frustrations of his mission, he had come himself to believe that France needed to "teach Mexico a lesson." His dispatches leave no doubt of the satisfaction with which he delivered Molé's lecture and observed the apparent meekness with which it was received.[26] For some weeks thereafter Deffaudis seemed to make real progress. The Mexican government agreed to resume negotiation of a treaty and proposed appointment of special commissioners to examine dossiers of the claims. It also promulgated a new tariff in March more favorable to French commerce than that of 1827.[27]

Deffaudis was still riding high when, late in March, he received a letter from a French rear admiral in command of a frigate and two brigs. The admiral wrote from Havana, whither he had come on orders of the minister of the navy to follow up the affair of the *Inconstant*. Had France obtained proper satisfaction, he inquired, or should he appear with his squadron off Veracruz to obtain it?[28]

This communication plunged Deffaudis into uncertainty.[29] Why did the admiral ask only of the *Inconstant* when his own orders bade him threaten the deployment of force unless *all* French grievances were redressed? Almost a month had now passed since he had received Molé's thunderbolt of 7 November. Since then his government had relapsed into a silence with which he was only too familiar. Had the department once again changed its mind?

The answer to the enigma lay in the nonchalance amounting to recklessness with which the French government handled its Mexican affairs. Molé had dictated and sent off his demands of 7 November before he had obtained permission to order the large naval squadron that was to accompany them. He subsequently discussed French grievances in Mexico with the king and apparently failed to convince him of the necessity of force. He had then pushed the matter from his mind, turning to European affairs of more consequence. Negotiation of the marriage of the king's oldest son and a minor ministerial crisis absorbed his attention until April. Meanwhile, the minister of the navy had acted on Molé's earlier order for a small squadron to avenge the misfortunes of the *Inconstant*. By the time he received the order to countermand it in expectation of a larger one, he had already dispatched Rear-Admiral Bretonnière from Brest on a limited mission. Molé made no effort to explain the muddle to Deffaudis and seemingly made a quick recovery from his bellicosity. When he next wrote in April he had little to say. "Unable at this point to give you precise directions," he concluded aimlessly, "I can only rely with confidence on your zeal as well as your skill." [30]

This contretemps put the finishing touches on the destruction of the credibility of the legation. When Bretonnière, at the request of Deffaudis, visited Mexico in April he could treat only of the affair of the *Inconstant*, which had been all but forgotten. The Mexican government obligingly published an innocuous explanation of her reception in the port. When the admiral remained silent on the necessity of a general redress of grievances, the Mexicans concluded that Deffaudis's recent threats had been all bark and no bite. Soon after Bretonnière's departure the Mexican foreign minister refused outright to recognize the validity of the Declarations and withheld concessions on forced loans and practice of retail trade. [31]

Even Deffaudis's compatriots were losing their faith in him. Their elation at the arrival of Bretonnière's squadron turned to rage when they learned it had come solely to save the pride of the navy and not to redress their grievances. They could not understand why Deffaudis was unable to avail himself of the naval presence to press home his demands. [32]

His eroded position brought Deffaudis to take the step that in the past he had always sought to avoid: presentation to the Mexican government of a formal "memorandum-ultimatum" recapitulating French claims and demands. These included recognition of the Declarations of 1827, prompt negotiation and ratification of a treaty, compensation for acts of violence against French subjects and damages to their property (each case listed separately), compensation for miscarriages of justice, punishment of the assassins of the French at Atencingo in 1833, punishment of the "judicial assassins" of the two Frenchmen at Tampico, and redress of other lesser but "equally just" grievances. [33] This act pushed France across the Rubicon. A rupture between the two countries could now be avoided only by a retreat by France or by surrender by Mexico. Neither the one nor the other appeared likely.

In the ensuing months Deffaudis lived in a kind of limbo that must have seemed to him not far from hell. He heard not a word from Paris. The promised support of the Gulf station had not yet materialized. He became a virtual laughingstock in the capital. The Mexican newspapers were ridiculing his claims, making out that he had demanded thirty thousand dollars to indemnify a cook for pastries lost in the civil war of 1828.[34] Deffaudis's protests against fresh grievances—among them an attack on French textile workers at Orizaba and the seizure of a French merchant ship on charges of smuggling—were shrugged off with indifference. Bustamante, now president, and Luis Cuevas, foreign minister, appeared confident that France lacked the resolve to follow through on Deffaudis's demands. Cuevas definitively and totally rejected Deffaudis's "memorandum-ultimatum" and ordered the Mexican legation in Paris to lodge a formal complaint against his character and demeanor.[35] At the end of his tether, Deffaudis asked to be relieved of his post. Molé, receiving the request in August, promptly approved it, an act of apparent confirmation of French irresolution.[36]

Yet France was nothing if not unpredictable in her Mexican "policy." Molé was putting the finishing touches on another set of bland instructions to Deffaudis in September when he received the minister's account of the Mexican rejection of his "memorandum-ultimatum." Molé's anger of the previous year returned. He added to the foot of the ineffectual dispatch: "P.S., I have just received [your dispatches] through no. 151 [reporting the rejection]. I am going to take the orders of the king and I shall answer you later."[37]

This time Molé followed through. He submitted a long report to Louis Philippe on 1 October reviewing French difficulties with Mexico and recommending the dispatch of naval forces sufficient to seize the fortress of San Juan de Ulúa and to blockade Mexico's Gulf ports.[38] Meanwhile he ordered Deffaudis to remain at his post pending new orders. By 2 November the king had approved the report. The government resolved to issue a new ultimatum to Mexico via Deffaudis and to demand the immediate payment of an indemnity.[39] It would muster seven naval vessels (two frigates and five brigs) to compel Mexico to accept French terms. In December Louis Philippe announced this course of action to the Chambers, in order, he declared, "to assure to those French engaged in commerce in the interior [of the country] the justice and security that is their due."[40]

The Reasons Why

What had brought the Orleanist government, passive to the point of pusillanimity according to its enemies, to send out its fleet to Mexico? The answer is nowhere clearly spelled out. Certainly it is not to be found in the pressure of an aroused public in France. True, there had been scattered expressions of protest against Mexico and demands for French satisfaction. The Bordeaux Chamber of Commerce, for example, had petitioned the government for protection of French commerce.[41] Moreover, certain commercial houses in Mexico were sufficiently well connected in Paris to bring their claims to the attention of the government. The Adoue brothers, one of the four large French importing houses in Veracruz, were one. The "Sieurs Oxeda," former wholesalers in the Mexican capital who had suffered damages in the sack of the Parian, were another. The Oxedas obtained the support of the spokesman of the commission in the Chamber of Deputies responsible for investigation of Mexican claims and through him brought their grievances to the attention of the Chamber as a whole.[42] Another plaintiff, a M. Duport, described by Deffaudis as "one of our richest wholesalers," had a brother-in-law, Dr. Gabriel Prunelle, in the Chamber.[43] When the subject of Mexican claims came up for discussion on 11 March 1837, Prunelle, a former mayor of Lyon where the silk industry was strong, spoke out in favor of naval protection of French commerce. Other examples could be cited. But these cases were isolated and aroused no general public outcry. One may search the Paris press of 1836 and 1837 in vain for news of Mexico.

Moreover, French investments and interests in Mexico were insufficiently large for their preservation to constitute an economic necessity for France. The recent slump in exports could easily have been ignored. Nor did French grievances pose a serious political problem to the administration. Mexico seemed to generate as little interest in the politicians as in the public at large. It was discussed only once in the Chamber during the years 1836 and 1837 and on that occasion (as seen) prompted by the initiative of men who might be supposed to have had a personal interest in it.[44] The speeches went unreported in the French press and failed to trigger ministerial action.[45] When the king announced the dispatch of a squadron he made anything but a sensation. The peers, in preparing their answer to the king's speech, adopted without debate a short sentence expressing confidence in the ability of French naval forces to secure the welfare of the French in Mexico. The Chamber made no mention of Mexico whatsoever in its corresponding address.[46] The king's announcement seems to have made an impact only in the Mexican legation where, naturally, it was greatly resented.[47]

Nor were Molé and the king impelled to action by ideology. Unlike the Bourbons before them or Louis Napoleon after them, neither entertained visions of a monarchical solution to the Mexican problem. They totally ignored Deffaudis's broad and frequent hints of the need for a European intervention in behalf of a European prince to reorganize Mexican society and preserve it from disintegration.[48] The Mexican horizon of Louis Philippe and Molé encompassed no more than the coastline and customshouses and never extended into the interior of the country.[49]

If the French government had acted neither out of conviction nor out of economic or political necessity, what then? The explanation appears to lie in the very failure of France to define her objectives and policies in Mexico. A succession of French foreign ministers had improvised according to their mood and the seeming need of the moment, too often without reflection for the consequences. Their contradictions and vacillations propelled the government almost willy-nilly into confrontations they had neither planned nor sought. Through a series of blunders it had opened itself wide to humiliation. To avoid it the government thought itself obliged to send out its fleet.

Undoubtedly the factor of race intruded upon Franco-Mexican conflicts and exacerbated them. One of the reasons for the offhandedness with which France treated Mexican affairs was its contempt for the Mexican people. They were considered as undeserving of the time and thought of a European. Molé said it all in his celebrated lecture of November 1836. According to him, when France did deign to turn her attention to Mexico, when her subjects were willing to labor for the development of a barbaric country, the Mexicans should be grateful for French instruction and submissive to French demands. When instead Mexico declined to truckle and replied with impertinence, the resulting blow to French amour propre was much heavier than would have been the case if dealt by a European power.

Believing in the inferiority of the Mexicans, the French never doubted the ease with which the country could be subdued. Deffaudis had often declared that a single warship would need less than an hour to demolish the fortress of San Juan de Ulúa and bring Mexico to heel.[50] Molé apparently believed him. The minister of the navy was not quite so naive. But no one in the French government anticipated the quality of Mexican resistance. So confident were they of their own superiority and of Mexican cowardice, they conceived it as probable that Mexico would yield at the very sight of the French fleet and spare it the need to go into action.[51] For that reason the government had decided to send as many as seven ships at once, even though it assumed that fewer were needed to get the job done. The French could delude themselves the more easily as they had little idea of what they were getting into. Nothing in their recent naval experience had prepared them for the expedition on which they were embarking. Little did they comprehend the difficulties of mounting an attack on the other side of the globe on one of the most treacherous coastlines known.

Finally, the years 1837–38 were more propitious than previous ones for French involvement in the New World. By the autumn of 1837 the Orleanist government was entering on the period of its greatest internal and external stability. Molé and the king were then for some eighteen months securely on top of political dissension. In foreign affairs, although the Belgian question was still not completely liquidated, the European horizon was unusually unclouded. In the previous spring Molé had assured the future of the dynasty by arranging the marriage of the Duke of Orleans to Helen of Mecklenburg-Schwerin. The princess was charming and popular. The wedding ceremony and the ensuing reopening of the restored palace of Versailles by the king and his sons took place amid great public acclaim. The dynasty seemed at last to have attached itself to the minds and hearts of the French people.[52] With its hands nearly free, the government could attend to its neglected interests in the New World. Within the following two years France took punitive action against Haiti, imposed a long and extensive blockade on Buenos Aires, and after conducting a mission of exploration, granted diplomatic recognition to the infant Republic of Texas.[53]

Who was most responsible for the decision to act? Again the question is difficult to answer with precision. Certainly neither the public nor the Chambers played a major role. The contribution of Deffaudis is, of course, undeniable. His provocative reports whetted the appetite of the government for revenge. It is possible, although not demonstrable, that he meant to enrich himself from the appearance of a

French fleet. If he followed the practice of some of his successors he could have arranged privately with French claimants to take a percentage of any indemnities collected as a commission in reward for prompting the government to act. But probably he did no such thing. The unpopular minister had a host of enemies who would have been only too ready to raise the hue and cry at the slightest indication of venality. That none did is strong evidence of his integrity. His bellicosity can be adequately explained by the frustrations peculiar to his mission.

It was the king, of course, who made the formal decision and ordered out the fleet. It could not have been otherwise, as in the July Monarchy the conduct of foreign affairs was the constitutional prerogative of the sovereign. But the king relied very heavily on Molé for advice. In foreign affairs the work of the one was often almost indistinguishable from that of the other.[54] In this case what evidence that exists casts Molé in an active role and the king in a passive one. In 1836 Molé had penned his bellicose instructions on the assumption that a naval squadron would follow. He had then gone to the king, in whom he apparently failed to strike a spark. In 1837 again it was Molé who took the initiative when he learned of the rejection of Deffaudis's "memorandum-ultimatum." This interpretation of their roles is corroborated by so knowledgeable an observer as Lord Palmerston, British foreign secretary, who later told the Mexican representative, Máximo Garro, "All the past [the blockade and bombardment of Veracruz] was the fault of Molé. No other minister would have done what he did."[55] As for the king, he came to regret his own part in the affair, whatever precisely it may have been. "I don't like interventions," he was later heard to remark on more than one occasion.[56] Too bad for France and Mexico that he had to learn his lesson the hard way. As the French began their preparations, neither Louis Philippe nor Molé had any idea of the pitfalls ahead.

The Failure of Post Captain Bazoche

While the war councils were taking place in Paris, Deffaudis, all unaware, was thinking only of leaving his post as quickly as possible. A measure of serenity returned to him as he bade farewell to Mexican officialdom and presented his legation secretary, Edouard DeLisle, as the French chargé d'affaires. Confident that his next assignment would place him in Europe, he was pleased to remove himself from a country that seemed to him to make no progress except toward its own destruction. He left the capital on New Year's Day and boarded the French brig *Lapérouse* at Veracruz on 15 January. The following day he set sail for Europe and for civilization.[57]

Deffaudis was already several miles at sea when he saw a small ship on the horizon signaling energetically. It was the ten-gun *Laurier*, coming posthaste from the recently reactivated Gulf station at Havana with Molé's orders of the previous November. A rendezvous effected, Deffaudis scanned the dispatches. With a reluctance that must have been difficult to conceal, he ordered the *Lapérouse* to put over her helm toward Veracruz and signaled the *Laurier* to fall in as escort.[58]

By these instructions and additional ones brought soon after by special messenger, Deffaudis learned that he was to demand an indemnity of up to eight hundred thousand dollars of the Mexican government. He was also to insist upon total exemption of French subjects from forced loans, the guarantee of their right to engage in retail trade, and punishment and dismissal of certain Mexican officials for alleged abuse of French subjects. If Mexico accepted these terms France would declare herself satisfied. If not, France would place prosecution of her demands in the hands of Post Captain Bazoche, commander of the Gulf station, who was to arrive with two sixty-gun frigates and five brigs to take appropriate punitive action. Bazoche also carried secret orders authorizing him to strike immediately at the fortress of San Juan de Ulúa if, contrary to expectations, Mexico did not capitulate immediately at the appearance of his squadron. The overall direction of the mission was accorded to Deffaudis.[59]

Although these orders were all and more than Deffaudis had desired for the past eighteen months, he was less than enthusiastic as he began to act on them. While passing through Veracruz early in January he had visited the fortress on the invitation of the Mexicans. He had been sobered, if not by its substantiality, by the firm belief of the Mexicans in its impregnability. Contrary to his earlier blithe predictions, he now feared some genuine resistance from Bustamante and the "clerical-Spanish party"—either out of a misguided idea of their strength or because of a secret desire to provoke a serious intervention by France in favor of a monarchy.[60] He thus decided to defer drawing up his ultimatum until he had about him the reassuring presence of the reinforced squadron and could confer with its commander.

The little fleet was slow in coming. Unfortunately, the haphazardness of French policy toward Mexico had carried over into the direction of their naval operations. To have produced the desired results, Deffaudis's return to Veracruz in January should have been in the company of Bazoche and his ships. Instead, the squadron did not appear until March and even then not at full strength. Of the two promised frigates, only Bazoche's command ship, *Herminie*, materialized. The second, *Iphigénie*, detached from the station at Martinique, did not limp in until late in May, victim of storms and breakdowns for which the planners in Paris had made no allowance.

Meanwhile Deffaudis, on board the *Lapérouse*, fretted at the resulting incoherent appearance of the French initiative. Without the second frigate neither he nor Bazoche dared attack the fortress, which reportedly had been strongly reinforced during the weeks of French dalliance. But sitting in the midst of six war vessels, Deffaudis believed he could remain silent no longer without appearing ridiculous. He signed an ultimatum demanding an indemnity of six hundred thousand dollars on 21 March and dispatched it to the Mexican capital.[61]

This step merely widened the breach between the two countries. The Mexicans, sensing the French weakness, knew that the approaching summer and its concomitant, *vomito negro*, would work in their favor. Their reaction to the ultimatum was not only negative but insulting. Rushing an abbreviated translation of it to the Chambers, the ministers announced amidst loud applause their decision to treat with France while her warships remained on the coast. Their published reply urged the Mexican people to unite to repel an invasion. Bustamante followed with a manifesto accusing France of "unjust aggression" and of harboring designs on the republican form of the Mexican government.[62]

This accusation arose not from a misreading of the French purpose but from the exigencies of the internal political situation. Deffaudis's ultimatum had stated explicitly that France had no quarrel with the Mexican people nor any intention of interference in the internal affairs of the republic. Bustamante and the Centralists knew well that France was not planning an invasion of the interior. But they also knew that their political enemies, the Federalists, were ready to raise the cry of treason if the government indicated a willingness to treat with the foreign enemy. By falsifying the French purpose they could hope to unite the public behind them in defense of the republic and at the same time to disarm the Federalists. Cuevas tried the same tactic abroad in order to discredit the French government. Garro was ordered to spread rumors among Molé's opposition in Paris and in the British press of the alleged monarchical designs of the king.[63]

This stratagem had slight success in Europe but was very effective in Mexico. Protest their innocence though they did—shrilly and often—the French were always suspect while their fleet lay off the Mexican coast. The military disparity between the two countries was too great, the Mexican hatred of foreigners too strong, and the memory of the Bourbon alliance with Spain too fresh for the government of Louis Philippe ever to exonerate itself.[64]

When Bazoche and Deffaudis learned of the Mexican defiance, they came to the reluctant decision that their only alternative was the imposition of a blockade, which they announced on 16 April. They knew that the closing of the ports would inflict financial hardship on Mexico, but only by degrees over a period of many months. During this time the lives and property of the French colony would be vulnerable to reprisals from a Mexican public aroused by an inflammatory press. France would be deprived of the Mexican outlet for her exports, and French wholesalers and retailers within Mexico of the bulk of their merchandise. As summer approached, the *vomito* could be expected to decimate the crews of the blockading vessels. Finally, the blockade might evoke protests from other countries whose trade was interrupted, notably England, and embrangle French foreign policy in general. "Execrable mission," moaned Deffaudis in reviewing his position. "For my part, I shall fulfill it out of a sense of duty. But I would not take it on otherwise for any amount of money."[65]

Even the appearance of the elusive *Iphigénie* did not improve the French position. Bazoche still felt unable to attack the fortress or even to continue a semblance of a blockade much longer. In order to patrol the long coast from Matamoros to Veracruz and at the same time to bring in all supplies, including food and drinking water, from Havana or New Orleans, he had been obliged to disperse his squadron. Only the *Herminie* remained at Veracruz, and now she was in need of major repairs and almost unseaworthy. The inevitable attrition arising from sickness and accidents would soon render his position untenable.[66]

The end of their efforts was not long in coming. Deffaudis, physically and mentally weakened by the effects of the coastal climate and the realization of French impotence, had begun to experience violent headaches and hallucinations.[67] On 12 June he threw up the game, abandoned his post, and set sail for Brest on one of the brigs. Behind him lay the remnants of the forlorn squadron going through the motions of a blockade. By August over one-third of the crew lay ill or dying of the *vomito* or other pernicious fevers bred on the deadly coast. Bazoche, one of the sufferers, had to admit defeat and requested permission to return to France.[68]

The "Victory" of Rear Admiral Baudin

Apprised of the ill success of Bazoche, the French government decided that it had gone too far to retreat. Recalling the *Herminie*, it ordered the assembly of a much larger squadron to be composed of three frigates, nine brigs, two mortar ships, two steamers, and two supply ships. It reinforced their crews with the addition of three hundred marines for garrison duty and shore parties. Command of these forces and the plenipotentiary powers formerly vested in Deffaudis was awarded to Rear Admiral Charles Baudin, an older officer with a reputation for valor, who had lost an arm fighting the British under Napoleon.[69]

Baudin was ordered to repeat the French demand for immediate and total payment of an indemnity of six hundred thousand dollars and to insist on the exemption of French subjects from forced loans and on their right to engage in retail trade. These points were held essential to the welfare of the French colony and of French commercial interests in Mexico. He was also authorized to demand an additional two hundred thousand dollars to help defray the costs of the expedition if he believed by so doing he could improve his bargaining position.[70]

Despite this bold front, the government was beginning to regret its involvement in Mexico. Soon after the admiral's departure, Molé received Gutiérrez de Estrada in Paris and gave him the distinct impression that the French, at last realizing the difficulties in attacking Mexico, were "looking for some way out of their embarrassment with the least possible dishonor."[71] They were hoping that the mere sight of their great armada arising on the horizon would cause the Mexican government to yield. In this expectation, Molé instructed Baudin to settle the affair by negotiation if possible and to resort to arms only if Mexico remained intransigent. He also tempered the language of the French demands and permitted the Mexicans some latitude in the manner of the punishment to be imposed upon offending Mexican officials.

The French hope of a negotiated settlement was not without some justification. When Baudin arrived off Veracruz on 26 October he sent to the capital an emissary, who had little difficulty in arranging a conference between the admiral and Cuevas at Jalapa.[72] Mexico too was in a mood to parley. By July its government had suffered losses of revenue estimated at nearly three million dollars because of the blockade.[73] It had been required to impose heavy exactions on its citizens to meet the payroll of the army and to prepare its defense. At the same time the growing strength of the Federalists was evidenced by the outbreak of *pronunciamientos* in every direction: Michoacan, the mountains of Puebla, and Sonora. In Tampico the Federalist General José Urréa had placed himself at the head of the garrison and had seized the customshouses. And in Veracruz Santa Anna was threatening to pronounce against the government.[74]

During the conferences at Jalapa from 17 to 21 November both Baudin and Cuevas made concessions. The Mexican accepted an indemnity of six hundred thousand dollars and agreed to eschew future impositions of forced loans on foreigners (although without conceding the right of the government to impose them). Baudin, in violation of his instructions, accepted payment of the indemnity in deferred installments and omitted the demand of an extra two hundred thousand dollars. He also granted Mexico much leeway in the manner with which they were to punish their offending officials (virtually insuring their immunity). After several days the negotiators were able to agree on all points except that of retail trade.[75] Baudin was willing (again in violation of his instructions) to withdraw his demand of a guarantee of the French right to this practice if the Mexicans would agree to indemnification of any French subjects deprived of it. But Cuevas was totally inflexible on this subject. Not daring to concede more, the admiral departed for Veracruz. He informed the Mexicans that if by noon on 27 November they had not met his last terms on retail trade, he would commence hostilities.

The fact that the negotiations broke down over the question of retail trade rather than that of the indemnity is proof that the Orleanist government, in its blundering way, had finally grasped the fact that development of its commercial interests in Mexico was at least equally important as compensation of its subjects for past grievances.

That the government was going about the task irrationally, certainly counterproductively, is irrelevant. It had realized that the practice of retail trade was essential to its colony of urban little men and hence to the prosperity of its commerce in general. Britain and other countries with smaller colonies in Mexico and many fewer subjects working as retailers could afford to make concessions.[76] France could be nothing less than insistent on this right if the appearance of its fleet off Veracruz were to make any sense at all.

Mexico, on the other hand, had always held tenaciously to its right to withdraw this privilege. Cuevas had spoken the exact truth when he told Baudin that he could not yield on this point without the consent of Congress. None of Mexico's existing treaties granted this right freely and explicitly to foreign residents. The British, after years of haggling, had accepted an arrangement by which only those of their subjects "domiciliated" with their families had a clear right to this practice.[77] No other nation had done better.

The ability to threaten foreigners with deprivation of retail trade was an asset too precious to give up. It was a "sword of Damocles" that the Mexicans could hold indefinitely over their heads and as such was one of Mexico's few means of retaliation against a great maritime power like France. It could also be useful in discouraging immigration into Mexico of adventurers and speculators and, far more important, in inducing foreigners within the country to adopt Mexican nationality to rid themselves of this threat. Foreigners who took such action lost the protection of their legation and the right to make claims through it on the Mexican government for compensation for grievances. Any means of diminishing the chronic and heavy pressure of foreign claims on the Mexican treasury could not be lightly discarded.[78]

Because neither nation would yield on this point, the French resorted to arms. The last offer of the Mexican government, which reached Baudin on the morning of 27 November, refused to grant the French more than treatment of the most favored nation, a status in no way guaranteeing them the practice of retail trade. Rejecting the terms as unsatisfactory, Baudin immediately informed the commandante general of Veracruz, Manuel Rincon, that he would bombard.[79]

Baudin moved swiftly and competently to the attack. Under cover of night he had already sounded the waters around the fortress and had readied his plans to the last detail. He had also taken the precaution to send a neutral ship into the port of Veracruz to take away some 250 French subjects whose existence might be endangered during the hostilities.[80]

The admiral's battle plan relied on the concentrated fire of the three frigates as the center of his attack. He deployed them at anchorages that were relatively protected from the main batteries of the Mexicans but that afforded searoom for maneuver in the event of rising wind or broken anchor lines. The two artillery ships, towed into a small, protected cut, were ordered to bombard the other side of the fortress. The remaining vessels were to serve as observers directing the fire or as reserves. An exception was the tiny corvette, *Créole*, commanded by the king's third son, twenty-year-old Prince of Joinville. Possessing only two guns that could be brought to bear in the attack, she was ordered to tack offshore outside the range of fire.[81]

The bombardment began early in the afternoon and continued until evening, when Baudin withdrew his ships to safe anchorages for the night. By that time the fortress was a shambles. "Never was fire more rapid or better directed," reported Baudin later to the government.[82] Shells and bombs tore great gaps in the soft coral walls and silenced one battery after another. Some lucky shots blew up most of the ammunition. The French superiority was so quickly manifest that Baudin permitted young Joinville, burning to "uphold the honor of the race," to bring his *Créole* alongside the frigates and share in the action.[83] That night a Mexican council of war presided over by Santa Anna, who had hurried from his estate to offer his services, voted to capitulate. The following day, 28 November, a French garrison took formal possession of the fortress after permitting the defenders to retire with honors of war.[84]

Baudin had now redeemed the honor of the French navy, but he knew that he had done little more. He was master of the fortress but not of the city. Even were he to bombard Veracruz until it surrendered, he lacked the manpower to occupy it and hold it in subjection. While the city remained hostile it posed a threat to his forces. It possessed a garrison of soldiers that could prevent his crews from replenishing their stores on shore. Moreover, its gun batteries on the eastern and western extremities were reported to be receiving strong reinforcements that might enable them to bear on his squadron.

Realizing that he was in no position to dictate either to the commandante general of Veracruz or to the government in Mexico, he

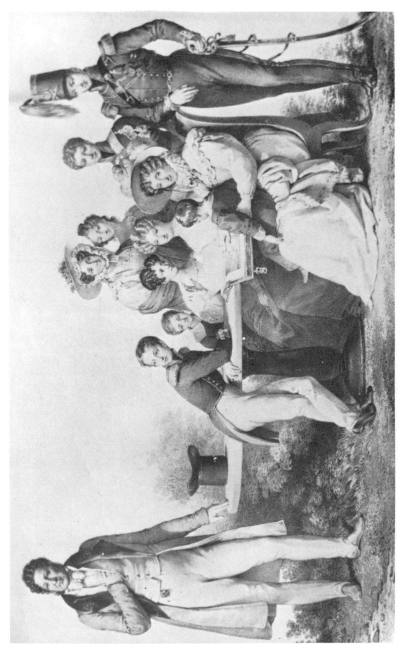

Louis Philippe, King of the French, 1830–1848, with his wife, sister, five sons, and three daughters (courtesy of The Bettmann Archives, Inc.)

Admiral Charles Baudin,
commander of the French fleet
off Veracruz, 1838-1839

signed a convention with Rincon and offered to negotiate with the Mexican foreign minister on the same terms as before the attack. The convention permitted the Mexicans to retain a garrison of one thousand soldiers in the city and the French to provision themselves on shore without hindrance. Baudin agreed to lift the blockade immediately and to return the fortress to Mexico when a peace settlement was signed. If these terms constituted but a meager reward for the conqueror of the "Gibraltar of the West," they would at least have the merit, thought the admiral, of bringing an early end to the conflict and of proving once and for all that France had no designs on the sovereignty of the republic.[85]

But Baudin had not yet come even close to a true comprehension of the difficulties of bringing Mexico to terms. The Mexican government not only rejected his offer to negotiate but repudiated the convention with Rincon and ordered his court-martial for having signed it. The government then proceeded to declare war against France and issued a decree of extreme severity expelling all French subjects from the country. By its terms they were ordered to leave their residences within three days and to be out of the country by the end of two weeks, conditions that were for the most part impossible of fulfillment.[86]

These measures had been dictated in part by political necessity, in part by the need of a safety valve for public effervescence to spare the French a worse fate. The capitulation of the fortress of San Juan de Ulúa had produced intense excitement in the capital. If the administration had showed itself even slightly less defiant it could not have withstood the fury of the opposition. At the same time newspapers and broadsides began to circulate the most sanguinary charges against the French. Cries of "Death to the Foreigners" were heard on the streets. The edict of expulsion was designed to satisfy the public desire for revenge. Its immediate purpose achieved, the government mitigated its terms by extending the time limits of departure to allow the French to put their affairs in order.

When he learned of the Mexican declaration of war, Baudin's first reaction was the immediate reimposition of the blockade. Next he organized three shore parties, two of which were to spike the guns of the city's batteries. The third was to advance into the city to seize generals Santa Anna and Mariano Arista as hostages. By this plan of action he could disarm the city so that it could do him no harm and avoid a general bombardment that would entail heavy civilian casualties to no purpose.[87]

These operations commenced early on 5 December and proceeded faultlessly except for the proposed capture of Santa Anna. Learning of his danger in the nick of time, the Mexican fled half-clad over the rooftops while the French column, led by Joinville, forced its way into the house below. Arista, less fortunate, was caught in his room and carried off. Joinville, frustrated by his failure, advanced rashly to the Mexican barracks of La Merced and trained a howitzer on the central gate. The result was a lively and costly exchange of fire. Baudin, appearing on the scene, ordered the prince to desist and to proceed to the quay to reembark with the other shore parties that had in the meantime accomplished their missions. Because Baudin was unable to occupy the city, he had no reason to fire on the garrison.

Unfortunately, the time spent by Joinville before the barracks delayed the French reembarkation and gave Santa Anna time to gather about him a column of men. Baudin and a small number of sailors were still on the mole when the Mexicans, Santa Anna at their head, dashed through the main gate of the city and opened fire. The five French longboats that were covering the reembarkation replied immediately with their cannonades. During the exchange Baudin and his men made good their departure, although with losses of one killed and two wounded. The Mexicans suffered higher casualties, one of whom was Santa Anna himself, wounded in the left leg and hand when his horse was shot out from under him.[88]

Baudin's foray on shore had assured him immunity from Mexican gunfire, but it still brought him no closer to a peace settlement. Hoping to induce the Mexican government to agree to negotiate, he entered on a thoroughly publicized correspondence with General Urréa, Federalist leader in Tampico. He was under no illusions that he could obtain better terms for the French should they arrive in power, and he steadfastly refused to offer them material assistance. Yet he was willing to lift the blockade in Tampico, permitting the Federalists to pocket the customs duties, and to profess his sympathy for their cause as a means of bringing the Centralists to the conference table.[89]

During this same time and to the same end, he greatly reduced the strength of the squadron, retaining only two frigates, the mortar ships, and such brigs as were needed to patrol the other Gulf ports. Among those who departed was Joinville, with his *Créole*; not, however, in time to extinguish the preposterous but inevitable rumors linking him to the throne of Montezuma. His presence had been an embarrassment from first to last and was another evidence of the insensitivity and shortsightedness with which the Orleanist government handled Mexican affairs. [90]

These measures taken, Baudin had about exhausted his options. As he reported to Molé, France had now inflicted all the harm it could on Mexico without launching on a "ruinous war" requiring an expeditionary force of some thirty thousand men. He would continue the blockade, of course, which would gradually diminish Mexico's financial resources, but the procedure would be long and slow. "Mexico is adapting itself to its poverty," he wrote, "and, ruined though it may be, it can long sustain the struggle against us relying simply on the force of inertia." [91] It might well mean another gruesome summer cruising off the fever-ridden coast. This state of affairs was deplorable for all nations that traded with Mexico, France not the least. All things considered, he came to the conclusion that mediation by a third party was perhaps the best and only means of bringing the two parties together.

The stalemate was broken by the return of Pakenham from a leave of absence late in December and the nearly simultaneous appearance off Veracruz of a sizable British naval squadron. Pakenham bore instructions from Palmerston to offer his services as mediator. The British, whose commercial interests had suffered from the blockade and other attendant disorders, had long desired to intervene as arbitrator, but in vain. The Mexican government had rebuffed them, suspecting that Palmerston intended to force French terms on Mexico. [92] It had preferred instead to rely on the climatic and geographical advantages of its position and the consequent lack of French resolution that had served Mexico well in the past. Molé, on the other hand, had seen French grievances as too demonstrable to justify the mediation of a third party and had taken offense at Palmerstonian criticisms of French methods and monetary demands. French pride would admit of no interference until its naval forces had taken punitive action. [93]

On his arrival Pakenham found that these objections were now passé. Baudin, he reported, was eager, even impatient to extricate himself from his "embarrassing position." The admiral was aware that Molé had rejected mediation in the past, but now that the honor of the French navy had been saved, he believed he could take on himself the responsibility of accepting the British offer. He demurred only at the prospect of negotiating while under the guns of a British fleet that outnumbered his own reduced squadron. Great Britain must not appear to be dictating to France. When Pakenham offered to order the retirement of the two British ships of the line, vessels that could outgun the French frigates, Baudin readily agreed to resume negotiations with Mexico with Pakenham as mediator.[94]

When he arrived in the capital Pakenham encountered some, but not much more, difficulty with the Mexicans. Gorostiza, who had returned as foreign minister in mid-December, at first raised a number of minor objections and declared that he could not treat with an enemy that lent encouragement to the cause of the Federalists. Yet by early February Pakenham persuaded him to accept a face-saving note of "explanation" from Baudin and to agree to travel to Veracruz to negotiate a settlement with the admiral.[95]

The acquiescence of the Mexican government stemmed in part from its knowledge of the vulnerability of the French and the expectation of lenient terms. Gorostiza had just received the report of Gutiérrez de Estrada from Paris of his interview with Molé, which had described the eagerness of the French to get out of the affair.[96] He had also received from Pakenham assurances that the treaty would be consistent with Mexican national honor. Moreover, he could scarcely have been unaware of Baudin's desire to remove his forces from the coast before summer. The time to drive a favorable bargain seemed to have arrived.

The internal political situation also necessitated an end to the debilitating struggle. Early in December the Federalists had all but succeeded in overthrowing the government. Bustamante had been reduced to the extremity of appealing for assistance to Santa Anna, with the price of that assistance being to place the authority of the government unconditionally at his disposal.[97] Recovering from the amputation of his wounded leg, Santa Anna was skillfully rehabilitating himself in the public mind by publicizing his skirmish on the mole at Veracruz. According to his version of events, he had performed an act of heroic martyrdom that had repelled the French from Mexican soil and had driven them into the sea. The Centralist government was in peril of total eclipse by the general's fast-rising star. Under these circumstances, and with the Texas war still upon them, they could but resign themselves to a negotiated settlement.

Negotiations opened in Veracruz early in March between Baudin and the Mexican plenipotentiaries, Gorostiza and General Guadalupe Victoria, and resulted in a treaty of peace and a convention signed on 9 March. The treaty was a brief instrument that proclaimed "constant peace and perpetual friendship" between France and Mexico (Mexico named first in the Spanish text). By it each party consented to submit to the arbitration of a third country the questions of restitution to Mexico of the war vessels captured by France after the surrender of the fortress of Ulúa and claims of indemnities by French and Mexican subjects for damages suffered as a result of the hostilities. Pending the conclusion of a treaty of commerce and navigation between the two countries, citizens, ships, and merchandise of each would be accorded treatment of the most favored nation. Finally, France promised to return the fortress of San Juan de Ulúa to Mexico as soon as Mexico ratified the treaty and convention (stipulated to take place within twelve days at most).

The convention was even briefer. Its only provision of any significance was the first, which required Mexico to pay France a sum of six hundred thousand dollars in cash in three installments over a period of six months beginning after the date of ratification by the Mexican government. When rendered in full, Mexico would be free of any further monetary claim by French subjects before 26 November 1838.[98]

The signing of these instruments did not assure the restoration of peace between combatants as contentious as these. The Mexican Congress immediately balked at payment of the indemnity and threatened to reject the settlement. The ratification by the two houses on 18 and 20 March was obtained only after Gorostiza explained that the word *pagar* ("to pay") in the text of the treaty was the equivalent of *entregar* ("to deliver or hand over") and hence did not imply Mexican recognition of the legitimacy of French claims or a moral obligation to pay them.[99]

This solution in turn angered Baudin.[100] Pakenham had to exert all his skills as a diplomat to persuade the admiral to accept the ratifications and to return the fortress to the Mexicans.[101] Privately, Baudin was only too glad to do so. The damp old walls seemed a perfect breeding place for disease. Despite precautionary hygenic measures, one-twentieth of the French garrison had died of yellow fever during the three and one-half months of occupation. And this was during the supposedly healthy months of the year.[102]

Even then the parties had not exhausted all their resources for troublemaking. Baudin refused to leave the coast until the government drafts on the customs duties for payment of the indemnity had arrived in Veracruz. The Mexicans, for reasons that are not clear but that seem to have arisen out of carelessness rather than bad faith, failed to deliver the drafts on the day they had promised, or at least on the day Baudin thought they had promised. As April wore on Baudin convinced himself that he was being gulled. He had actually dispatched an ultimatum threatening to open fire on the fortress when, mercifully for both nations, the papers arrived.[103]

Baudin no longer had reason to defer his departure. On 27 April he ordered four of his ships, including one frigate, to sail for Havana to attach themselves to the Gulf station. He dispatched most of the remainder to their home port in Brest. The following day the admiral and the *Néréide* disappeared over the horizon. Great was the relief on shore. "I sincerely hope [he will] not . . . return," wrote Pakenham wearily to his government. "For, from what I have observed of his irritable and violent disposition, I am convinced that he could not have remained long in command on the Coast of Mexico without bringing about a fresh rupture between the two countries."[104]

The restoration of peace was not official until France, too, had ratified the treaty and convention. Would Louis Philippe refuse to accept a settlement arrived at through the mediation of Great Britain? The king now had as foreign minister Marshal Soult, Duke of Dalmatia—Molé having been forced out of office in a ministerial crisis in March. Would Dalmatia advise the king to repudiate instruments signed by Baudin, the plenipotentiary of his predecessor? Garro, watching the scene from London, feared a French rejection was a real possibility. Palmerston, however, had a better understanding of the situation. "*Say what they will*," he reassured Garro, "it [the treaty] rescues them from the labyrinth in which they were lost . . . so at heart they are very pleased."[105]

As Palmerston had prophesied, both the king and his foreign minister were eager to accept the peace. As soon as he had entered office Dalmatia had ordered Baudin to return to France with his entire command excepting only those vessels needed for the Gulf station. In June he invited Garro to return to Paris in anticipation of resumption of diplomatic relations. When the official texts of the treaty and convention arrived in Paris, the king ratified them without hesitation on 6 July in his palace at Neuilly.[106]

Balance Sheet

What did the French have to show for their efforts of two years on the other side of the globe? Had they accomplished their purpose of protecting their subjects and promoting their commercial interests in Mexico?

The answers afforded by the peace settlement were not encouraging. The terms of the treaty and convention were less favorable to France than those demanded by Deffaudis before the beginning of the blockade or by Baudin before the capture of San Juan de Ulúa and the attack on Veracruz. As the French ran up against the unexpected difficulties of doing battle with an apparently weak foe they had, one by one, abandoned their objectives. Baudin not only had failed to bring Mexico to negotiate a treaty of commerce, but also had relinquished the privileges granted France by the Declarations of 1827. In the end he signed instruments that made no mention whatsoever of the two safeguards crucial to French interests: guarantee of the right of retail trade and exemption from forced loans. It was true that during the parleys he had elicited from Gorostiza a note declaring that Mexico would, of its own volition, henceforth eschew imposition of loans on foreign residents.[107] Yet such a unilateral declaration would have no weight in international law. Nor was it much of a guarantee for the future. What could prevent a subsequent Mexican government from repudiating it if it chose? In any case little ingenuity would be required to find other means of tapping the wealth of foreign commerce should the government so decide. Even that paltry satisfaction was denied him on retail trade. Finding that the Mexicans remained inflexible he had, as Gorostiza later explained to Congress, simply "ceased to insist" on that right.[108] And he had done this despite the fact that in the course of the negotiation and in violation of his instructions he had yielded on the question of punishment of offending Mexican officials and had given the Mexicans six months in which to pay the indemnity, while promising to restore the fortress within twelve days. Worst of all from the point of view of the French government, he had also accepted the arbitration of a third country to settle the questions of captured Mexican war vessels and claims for damages incurred during the hostilities.

The only tangible reward that France could show was in the long run the least important to the future of French commerce: payment of an indemnity. Even this satisfaction was not an unqualified success. The arbitrary manner in which Deffaudis had arrived at the figure of six hundred thousand dollars, for which he supplied no corroborating documentation, lent opprobrium to French claims and undermined their credibility. The French government was, in fact, later embarrassed when it tried in all honesty to identify subjects with bona fide claims worthy of indemnification.[109] Ten years later it still had not distributed all of the indemnity. Moreover, although the Mexicans delivered the six hundred thousand dollars, they had not recognized the *right* of foreign subjects to indemnification for demonstrable grievances. France had done nothing to insure the acceptance of their claims in the future. Even before Baudin's ships had reached Brest, DeLisle was complaining of the Mexican refusal even to listen to his list of recent grievances.

What else had France achieved? She had crippled Mexico financially by the imposition of a blockade over a period of nearly a year. But the blockade was a two-edged sword. If it had deprived Mexico of its customs duties it had also denied France her market for her exports. In 1838 French exports declined to a mere 6.5 million francs, a figure lower than any previous year for which records were available. Contemporary observers noted the irony of the situation by which the French were more injured than helped by the measures taken in their behalf.[110]

The peace settlement itself soon became a breeding ground of friction. In France its deficiencies were deemed so egregious that the government at first tried to cover them up and next to pretend that Baudin had in fact gained more than the terms of the treaty and convention allowed. When the opposition in the Chamber of Deputies requested copies of Molé's instructions to Baudin in order to compare them with the settlement, Dalmatia withheld the documents and defended the admiral on the grounds that he had achieved a peace "with which France could be satisfied."[111] Even before he returned to France Baudin had announced via a newspaper in New Orleans that he had definitively resolved the questions of forced loans, retail trade, and the punishment of Mexican officials in favor of France. Back in Brest he reported to Dalmatia that in negotiating the treaty he had simply made "a few concessions of pure form to satisfy the puerile vanity of the Mexicans."[112] This delusion soon became the official line. The government refused to admit that its fleet had retired with less than total victory. If the treaty and convention were less than explicit on certain points, ran this interpretation, it was because France, magnanimous in victory, had eschewed humiliation of a defeated foe.[113] Hence the foreign minister instructed Deffaudis's successor in Mexico to insist on the exemption of the French from all forced loans, on their right to practice retail trade, and on the punishment of the offending Mexican officials.[114] Thus did the French dress the stage for future confrontations.

While the French government was deluding itself, the Mexicans, too, were claiming an imaginary victory. In order to compensate for the humiliation of the indemnity, they transformed Santa Anna's skirmish on the mole at Veracruz into "a glorious action" that put to flight "the descendants of the warriors of Jena, Marengo, and Austerlitz." Amidst salvos of artillery Santa Anna received a diamond cross decreed on him by Congress for his heroism in repelling the "invasion."[115] In this mood the Mexican government was more brazen than ever in dismissing the grievances of foreign ministers. It was the opinion of both DeLisle and Pakenham that the French "lesson" had not been hard enough and that the Mexicans would be more, not less, intractable because of it.[116]

If the credit side of the French ledger was bare or nearly so, the debit side was crowded with expenditures of human and material resources. The number of casualties was smaller than would have resulted from a battle on land, but they could not have been fewer than four hundred.[117] Most of the dead were victims of fever. The ships of the squadron emerged almost unscathed with the exception of the crippled *Herminie*, which cracked up on the reefs of Bermuda on the passage home (her crew made shore in safety). But the costs of assembling and maintaining the fleet had far exceeded the naval budget for 1838–39. The government did not make public its expenditures on the expedition, but it was obliged to request a special allocation of nearly eight hundred thousand dollars and a special credit of almost one million dollars from the Chamber of Deputies to meet the operation expenses for its "exercises" in Mexico and Argentina and for protection of its commerce in the Americas.[118]

For French residents in Mexico the expedition was more curse than blessing. The bloody reprisals feared by Mexican and French officials alike did not, fortunately, materialize, and no civilian French subject seems to have died as a result of the hostilities. But all of the French suffered to one degree or another from the *mauvais temps économique* brought on by the blockade and shortages of French merchandise. Those who were hit hardest were those expelled from the country. As a rule they were residents of the capital, Veracruz, or points in between. Elsewhere the edict of expulsion proved virtually unenforceable. DeLisle estimated at seven hundred the number who left the country, which was probably not more than one-fifth of the colony as whole.[119]

The wealthier French were able to weather expulsion with less hardship than the poor. Rich merchants left their affairs in the hands of associates or proxies and upon the restoration of peace returned to business as usual. With financial cushions against adversity, the sum of their suffering amounted to income lost during their absence and hardships endured by themselves and their families on their travels. For the urban little men—craftsmen and retailers—expulsion could mean disaster. For them the journey alone spelled enormous financial and physical hardship. Moreover, because the first decree of expulsion had allowed them only three days in which to leave their homes, many had sold their tools and furniture, their only assets, at a great loss. The second, amended, decree gave them sixty days' grace, but by then, for many of them, the damage had been done. Although by the autumn of 1839 many of these men had returned, they were resuming their trades only with much difficulty.[120]

What had France done except to cripple her commerce, imperil her subjects, and embitter the Mexicans? She had also increased the pressures on a destitute Mexican treasury and pushed the country to the verge of anarchy. More than ever before, Mexico would need to turn to foreign capital to stave off bankruptcy and to fight for survival. More than ever before, the French colony would suffer in the deepening civil disorder. The expedition had not only failed to improve the position of French subjects in Mexico but had exacerbated the conditions on which their prosperity depended.

The French had not even obtained the mean satisfaction of humbling their foe. Protected by its rugged mountain ranges, Mexico was like a turtle in its shell. The French could hammer on its exterior as long as they liked without delivering the mortal blow. In a moment of realism Dalmatia later wrote, "Our experience in the use of force against Mexico, it must be admitted, is one that we would not wish to repeat."[121] If asset there were for the French in the miserable affair, it was only the hard-won discovery of the utter futility of gunboat diplomacy.

4

Franco-Mexican Doldrums: A Dangerous Drift

Men of reason are few in Mexico, where the people are as impressionable as children, where tinsel is more valued than solid worth, and where people are more concerned with pleasure and trifles than with serious and useful affairs.—Alleye de Cyprey to Guizot, 15 October 1843

The Mexican Sick Man

Mexico after the French war was a country cracking from outside pressure, disintegrating from internal strains. Its financial position appeared hopeless. The credit of the government was so weak that it had been obliged to contract indebtedness of three million dollars to raise the six hundred thousand dollars for the French indemnity. An international commission early in 1841 declared it liable for over two million dollars to satisfy claims of American subjects. The demands of the British were constant and heavy, not only for the sums owed the bondholders but for claims of its subjects in Mexico, many of them owners or operators of mining companies. More than once Pakenham felt obliged to threaten "something very disagreeable" to extract payments as they fell due.[1] The annual deficit of the Mexican government was rarely less than twelve million dollars and usually much more. The raising of the blockade did little to alleviate the country's plight. At least two-thirds of the revenues from customs had already been earmarked for outstanding debt. The remainder was not nearly adequate to meet the government payroll or to satisfy foreign claims.

In desperation, the Mexican government resorted to taxes on real estate and forced loans on its subjects. When these did not suffice it turned again, inevitably and predictably, to tap the wealth of foreign commerce. The promise to eschew forced loans on foreigners proved but slight impediment, easily circumvented. Instead of taxing the foreigners themselves, the government taxed their merchandise. Late in 1839 Congress decreed a surcharge on imports that had the effect of raising existing duties by nearly one-third and without allowing a six months' delay before implementation required by Mexican tariff law. Known as the "consumo," this duty triggered the united wrath of all foreign legations and prompted demands of some six hundred thousand dollars for reparations.[2] There appeared no way for Mexico to break out of the vicious circle in which it was trapped.

The very existence of the state as a geographical unit was in peril. The separation of Texas was a fait accompli, although the Mexican government refused to admit it. The Federalist movement, although defeated at Tampico, throve elsewhere, especially in the north where warlike chieftains talked of secession. Savage Indian tribes in Sonora and Chihuahua roamed unchecked, plundering Creole settlements. In the south Yucatán had all but achieved its independence and was reaching out to Texas for the aid of the Texan navy. The central government, lacking the funds to pay the salaries of its civil servants, stood by helplessly, unable to reassert its authority. Gómez Fárias, watching events from New Orleans, returned in the summer of 1840 to lead a revolt in the capital. After eleven days of street fighting Bustamante was able to persuade him to capitulate and depart. But the arrangement was little more than a reprieve. The need for a firm government was becoming ever more apparent. The dissolution of the country was so far advanced that Pakenham, never one to cry wolf, saw it on the point of "merging into a state of absolute anarchy."[3]

As Mexico put on the mantle of the sick man of the New World, the French government worried over the distribution of his worldly goods in the event of his demise. France assumed that the United States would not only help itself to the lion's share of Mexico but would attempt to hustle the patient into a premature grave. Texas was apparently destined to be the next addition to the Union. Even though the Washington cabinet had declined to annex Texas in 1838, few doubted the determination of the North Americans to dominate the entire continent. "We must face it," wrote the French chargé d'affaires to the Republic of Texas in a report typical of the day. "The Mexican republic is doomed. In my opinion the day is less far distant than generally supposed . . . when the Spanish race will be dispossessed by the Anglo-American race." [4]

The French saw other predators as well hovering over the expiring victim. The Russians, expanding their colonies in the northwest, might eventually push into California. Great Britain, France's oldest and principal maritime rival, gave the most serious cause for alarm. Always the French attributed to her designs on Yucatán, the Californias, and the silver mines of Mexico. They lived in fear of a bargain by which Mexico would hypothecate large parts of its territory to Great Britain as security for the debt owed to the bondholders. [5]

As Mexico's troubles deepened, many began to speak again of a monarchy under a European prince as its only means of salvation. The Plan of Iguala still had its adherents, chiefly among the wealthy classes who longed for a government strong enough to restore order and to release the productive energies of the country. Prominent among them was Gutiérrez de Estrada, who had returned from France to despair at the plight of his native land. In October 1840 he published a brochure in which he contrasted the present chaos with "the good old days" of Spanish rule and recommended convocation of a national convention to consider establishment of a constitutional monarchy. Although this publication was endorsed by many men of intelligence and experience (including all the European members of the diplomatic corps), it was condemned by the government. Gutiérrez de Estrada went into hiding and escaped to Europe at the first opportunity. [6]

But if the government had rid itself of the author of the brochure, it had not eradicated talk of a monarchy. With no end to the disorder in sight, the quotient of rumors of possible princely candidates and European governments who might support them increased. Much of this speculation inevitably revolved about France. She was Latin, Roman Catholic, and monarchical; her subjects were said to be free of the onus of hatred borne by the Spaniards in Mexico. The king of the French had five sons, all of them reputedly intelligent and vigorous. Surely he could spare one of them for Mexico. The recent French expedition, complete with the presence of Joinville, seemed proof of his interest. Perhaps next time the king would follow through with the reorganization of the country. In the opinion of DeLisle, who made it his business to plumb the thought of the *bien pensants* (men of "correct" views) in Mexico, France in 1838–39 "had ad-

vanced by ten years the foreign intervention necessary . . . [to sur-
mount] the destructive forces preying on the country and above all
to save it from the clutches of the United States." [7]

Those who desired or expected salvation from France totally mis-
read the mind of Louis Philippe. The old king now much regretted
his costly and unproductive forays into the New World. If he still
refused to recognize the totality of the failure of his Mexican expedition, he had no desire to repeat it. Farthest from his thought was a
plan to reassert the French presence on the American continent. In
the last years of his reign he desired merely to live and let live. In
1840 when a short-lived ministry of Thiers brought France to the
brink of war with England and Russia in a flare-up of the "Eastern
Question," the king took alarm. He dismissed Thiers in October and
with him the last possibility of adventurism during his reign. Under
the guidance of historian-turned-politician François Guizot, who
succeeded Thiers, the government entered a period of stability (some
would say paralysis) in which its policies rarely changed.

Instructions emanating from the Foreign Ministry after the Mexican war were moderate in tone, as befitted the unambitious goals of
the sovereign. "It is now to our interest to live on good terms with
Mexico," wrote the foreign minister to the minister plenipotentiary
in Mexico in October 1839. In Mexico the minister should protect
the rights of French subjects and promote their commerce and industry, but he should shun controversy, remain aloof from politics, and
above all refrain from "carrying matters to extremes." France stands
to lose too much, he continued, "by a rupture with a country whose
ports call our navigation and that offers the most promising outlets
for the products of our soil and industry." [8]

A Side Show in Texas

Yet these instructions and the king's pacific frame of mind were not
to usher in a more harmonious era in Franco-Mexican relations. For
if the king were sincere in his desire to live at peace with Mexico, he
gave the Mexicans undeniable reason to doubt it. At the same time
that he was welcoming the returning Garro in Paris, he extended
diplomatic recognition to the Republic of Texas in a treaty of friendship, navigation, and commerce signed 25 September 1839. Such an
act, coming on the heels of the French attack on Mexico and at a time
when Mexico had not relinquished its claims to its rebellious prov-

ınce, was seen inevitably as unfriendly, if not openly hostile. Garro immediately submitted a formal protest in which he expressed reserves on the rights of his country to the territory of Texas and to the option of exercising them to reconquer it in due time. In Paris, he reported, the public was favorable to the "Texians" (to use the spelling of the day), and he heard frequent mention of a French alliance with Texas against Mexico.[9] When the news reached Mexico it made a sensation. In Congress the Mexican foreign minister deplored the haste with which France had acted and compared it with her earlier long delay in recognizing the independence of the Mexican republic. Many Mexicans believed that France intended to support the pretensions of Texas and would even help it to extend its boundaries across the continent to the Pacific.[10]

In reply to the Mexican protest the French government disclaimed all hostility to Mexico. It had, it insisted, recognized Texas only after a thorough investigation of its situation and out of the conviction that its independence was an irreversible fact. Hence the government had merely followed its own interests in the area, which were purely commercial. The treaty with Texas was designed for the sole purpose of furnishing new outlets for the products of French soil and industry. As for Mexican claims to its former province, they were the affair of Mexico, in which France would not intrude.[11]

These disclaimers were true enough so far as they went. But they did not tell the whole story, which, as the Mexicans sensed, was less palatable to them. By stepping forth as the first European power to enter into diplomatic relations with Texas, France had made ostentatious profession of her sympathy for the Texas cause. The very act of recognition lent substantiality to the nationality of Texas and encouragement to the "Texians" to consolidate their political organization. It was also designed as an example for other powers. Sooner or later the mounting recognition would oblige Mexico to face reality and to "come to terms" with its lost province.[12]

On the other hand, France had no intention of taking up arms in behalf of Texas. Beyond expression of friendship and extension of her "good offices" to Texas she would not go. The instructions furnished the chargé d'affaires of the king in Texas reiterated the commercial purpose of his mission and emphasized both French neutrality between Texas and Mexico and the French desire to remain at peace with its former foe.

There was thus present in Orleanist policy toward Mexico the familiar ambivalence and absence of tact. While extending the olive branch with one hand, the French government inflicted a blow with the other. The Mexicans could well ask themselves which France valued more: friendship with Mexico or with Texas.

If the answer to the question were Mexico, the French choice of their agent in Texas was small indication of it. There the new chargé d'affaires was Alphonse Dubois de Saligny, an ambitious young man at the outset of a portentous career.[13] Service as legation secretary in Washington, D.C., and conduct of the mission of investigation in Texas in 1838 had already made of him a believer in the decadence of the Mexican and the vigor of the Anglo-American.

The youngster was a self-made man. Son of a provincial tax collector under the First Empire, he could call neither family nor fortune to his aid. But chance had made him the schoolmate of the Duke of Orleans, oldest son of the king. He battened on this friendship to obtain his entrance into the aristocratic diplomatic corps and to obtain his first assignment (secretary to the legation in Washington, D.C.) in the New World, in which the duke was keenly interested. When the opportunity arose to represent France in the wilderness of Texas, Dubois de Saligny grasped at it eagerly, even though the post promised to be arduous with no perceptible award for the incumbent. But the young man thought otherwise. He had well-laid plans for his mission, in which adjustment of tariff rates with rustic frontiersmen played but small part.

Taking up his duties in Texas in 1840, he soon disclosed the audacious scheme by which he intended to tap the *riqueza leyendaria* ("legendary treasure") of the American West. His proposal had three components. The first was a "Franco-Texian" trading company to divert the Santa Fe trade through Texas and to forestall the American traders from Missouri. French merchants, whom he had recruited before coming out to his post, were to supply the credit. The Texas Congress, he planned, was to grant him a monopoly of the trade and other commercial favors.

The second component was a colonization project remarkable mainly for its scale, which would bring eight thousand adult settlers to three million acres in western Texas and New Mexico. Like the first scheme, it required the cooperation of both France and Texas. The colonists would be mainly French; the land would be a grant from the Republic of Texas. Dubois de Saligny brought these two projects together in a legislative bill to create a "Franco-Texian Commercial and Colonization Company," which he arranged to have submitted to the Texas Congress in 1840. To assist its passage he entered on a lobbying campaign that included the staging of elaborate banquets designed to beguile and bedazzle the supposedly unsophisticated "Texians."

His third component encompassed the alleged mineral wealth of the area as well. The mines of Santa Fe, he wrote to his government, were "seemingly inexhaustible, and according to the most conservative estimates they could, if worked with more efficiency, supply the needs of all Europe for gold and silver." Why should France not help herself to this rich prize? To defend it the Mexicans would have to march an army across a desert affording no means of subsistence, a feat they could not be expected to perform. On the other hand, he argued, the "Texians" had only to ascend the Red River, which would bring them within some fifty miles of the Santa Fe settlements and the celebrated mines. They could be master of the area in a short time. France should strike a bargain with the young republic: Texas could supply the manpower to conquer the area. France could provide the money and the engineering expertise to exploit the mines. Together they would share the spoils.[14]

To say that this scheme was wildly speculative is to understate the case. In the first place, it was based upon a geography that was wholly imaginary. At that time the land between central Texas and Santa Fe was still largely unexplored, and neither the nature nor the extent of the terrain over which the traders and raiders would pass was known. Dubois de Saligny had simply composed a map most advantageous to his undertaking. On it, by assuming (erroneously) that the Red River was navigable throughout its passage along Texas and that its headwaters were located in the vicinity of Santa Fe, he had presented to the "Texians" the water route to Eldorado sought in vain over the centuries.

His proposal was also devoid of moral sense and a flagrant violation of the spirit and letter of his instructions, which bade him adopt a posture of neutrality between Texas and Mexico. Dubois de Saligny himself admitted to the French foreign minister that his scheme was a "delicate" affair. But for him the restraints of diplomacy could fall away before the glittering prize in sight. Were there not, he pleaded, "circumstances in which the strictures of the laws of neutrality . . . [might] be relaxed?"[15]

Fortunately for all concerned, his schemes had not the slightest

Alphonse Dubois de Saligny
as the young chargé d'affaires
to the Republic of Texas, 1840–1846
(courtesy of Barker Texas History Library)

Antonio López de Santa Anna,
Mexican general and statesman

chance of realization. In Paris the government immediately rejected
the mining proposal on the grounds that it involved conquest of
Mexican territory and hence a violation of French neutrality toward
Mexico.[16] In Texas the Franco-Texian Commercial and Colonization
Company had no more success. After becoming a political football
in a heated presidential election, it failed in the Texas Senate early in
1841. Foiled on both counts and having no further interest in remaining at his uncomfortable post, Dubois de Saligny looked about for an
excuse to quarrel with the government. Within weeks he found it in

the wild pigs that roamed the streets of the frontier capital (Austin) and invaded his rooms to devour his linen and papers. Escalating the "Pig War" to the level of international diplomacy, he ruptured relations with the republic in May 1841 and stamped off to Louisiana to remain for the better part of a year. [17]

This comic sideshow in a remote part of the American West had no direct repercussions on French relations with Mexico. The Mexicans were unaware of Dubois de Saligny's scheme to invade their territory, and they were pleased rather than otherwise at the risible performance of the French agent. On the other hand, the manner in which the French government treated its bellicose agent reveals the low value that it set upon maintenance of good relations with Mexico. Although the French foreign minister rejected the plan of invasion, he neither reprimanded nor recalled its author. He found the subsequent "Pig War" harder to swallow because, as Guizot later remarked of the incident, "France could on occasion afford to be wrong, but she could not afford to be ridiculous." [18] Even so, the government retained him as chargé d'affaires in Texas and ordered him back to his post in 1842.

The forbearance of the government may have been at least in part a reflection of the potency of the patronage of Orleans. However, it also was a clear indication that if the Orleanist monarchy in its last years had sufficient prudence to avoid adventurism, it lacked the desire to inaugurate an era of goodwill in its relations with Mexico.

The Mission of Alleye de Cyprey

The disdain, if not outright contempt, in which the Orleanist monarchy held Mexico was nowhere more clearly displayed than in its choice of a successor for Deffaudis. Given the bad feeling between the two countries, the Foreign Ministry might have taken great pains to seek out a minister plenipotentiary with experience in the New World and of proven tact. Instead, it filled the vacancy by a shuffle of ministers in which the legation in Mexico became a dumping ground for a diplomat who, if not in actual disgrace, was clearly undesirable. In need of a post to award the returning Deffaudis, the Foreign Ministry removed its minister plenipotentiary from Frankfurt, who was giving less than satisfactory service. It assigned Deffaudis to the German mission and packed the displaced minister off to Mexico. [19]

Although both posts held the rank of legations, that in the New World was much the less prestigious of the two and was a step down for its new occupant.

The new minister to Mexico was Baron Isidore Elizabeth Jean-Baptiste Alleye de Cyprey, a career diplomat of modest means then in his mid-fifties. His record in the diplomatic corps revealed not only an absence of skills and experience befitting him for the post but also certain blemishes that should have disqualified him for it. Although born on the island of Guadeloupe, he had had no adult experience in the New World. What Spanish he could muster was halting and heavily accented. He had come to France as a youth of twenty and done most of his diplomatic service in Germany. He had held the Frankfurt post since 1830. The reasons for his demotion are not entirely clear but are strongly suggested by certain letters and notations in his personal file. According to these, Alleye de Cyprey had ostracized himself from polite society in Frankfurt by living openly with a mistress and had thereby cut himself off from important channels of information. He had also acquired a reputation for bad temper. "[He] is easily maneuvered into flying into a rage," wrote one informant. "Everyone knows what he thinks, he does not know what anyone else thinks." [20] What a type to send out to represent France in a country with which she had just been at war! Although Alleye de Cyprey could, and did, correct his social position by marrying his lady before leaving Europe, he could not so easily change those traits of personality that had impaired his mission in Frankfurt.

When Alleye de Cyprey arrived at his post in February 1840 the situation would have taxed the skills of the most accomplished diplomat. Resentment at French recognition of Texas was at its height. Bustamante, who had resumed the presidency, and Foreign Minister Juan de Dios Cañedo were in heated altercation with DeLisle over a long list of French grievances postdating the recent war. The French legation was demanding monetary compensation for, among other things, the imposition of the "consumo" duty on exports, several assassinations and cases of assault and battery, profanation of the French cemetery at Veracruz where lay the French casualties of the war, and enormous material losses suffered in a fire in the government customshouse the preceding March just as the blockade was lifted and the warehouse was piled to the rafters with merchandise.

Having strained to pay the French indemnity in full and on time, the Mexican government was indignant at these fresh demands on its depleted treasury.[21]

Alleye de Cyprey was not the man to pour oil on these troubled waters. Apparently he had been much embittered by his "exile" from Europe and assignment to the distasteful post. He arrived with a chip on his shoulder and from the start was determined to impress the Mexicans with his superiority as a European. His was not to be a mission of propitiation. He managed to give offense even before setting foot on shore by ordering the French warship on which he was a passenger to advance immediately into the harbor of Veracruz without putting in first at Sacrificios to ask permission, as required by port regulations. He then disembarked as ostentatiously as possible, in full uniform, with an honor guard of fifty men, and followed by a cortege of attachés, marines, and sailors. Still in a truculent mood, he took the road to the capital, quarreling acrimoniously over prices of meals and accommodations along the way. By the time he had arrived at his post his reputation for irascibility seemed as firmly established as it had been in Frankfurt.[22]

Immediately after presentation of his credentials he began a vigorous pursuit of French claims for compensation for grievances new and old. He was prepared to see an insult to France in the slightest incident: a newspaper editorial casting doubt on the legitimacy of his claims, a random remark critical of his predecssor, even the nonchalance with which Bustamante referred to the recent hostilities (as if Mexico, not France, had won the war!). Always he went about armed with a cane, which he brought into play at slight provocation.[23] It seemed as if scarcely a day went by without its fracas and high words. The French minister was making a sensation in the capital.

He was also generating much alarm. What could lie behind this pugnacity? It appeared out of all proportion to its causes and most unnatural in a diplomat of his age and experience. The professionals in the diplomatic corps began to fear that Alleye de Cyprey must be acting on orders from his government to provoke Mexico and to seek an excuse to finish the job left undone in 1838–39.[24]

If Alleye de Cyprey's colleagues could have had access to his correspondence they would have learned that if their fears were indeed justified they were totally misdirected. It was not the French government that was seeking a quarrel with Mexico but rather its minister plenipotentiary. He had come to bring not peace but a sword. Instead of avoiding "unnecessary unpleasantness" as his instructions bade him, he was actively in search of an issue or incident on which he could fasten to bring about a rupture.

Alleye de Cyprey was not long in finding what he wanted. On 31 May 1840 Archbishop of Mexico Manuel Posada y Garduño, was to be consecrated in the cathedral in a solemn ceremony to which all the members of the Mexican government and diplomatic corps were invited. Alleye de Cyprey was almost certain that in so grand an affair involving many levels of functionaries and dignitaries a breach of etiquette offensive to the diplomatic corps was bound to take place. Perhaps to make sure it did, he and his entourage arrived at the cathedral a half hour late, after the ceremony had begun and when all the other dignitaries had been seated. As the French advanced toward their reserved places, the baron's alert eye saw that the Mexican ministers had been seated above the diplomatic corps on armchairs of red velvet. The diplomats, on the other hand, had been placed in the second rank and on chairs upholstered in black horsehair like those of lesser functionaries.

Alleye de Cyprey immediately turned to Pakenham, dean of the diplomatic corps, and to the newly arrived minister from Spain, Angel Calderón de la Barca, to ask them to leave with him. But neither of these diplomats wished to make a scene and remained serenely in their places. Unmollified, the baron crossed over to Cañedo to protest the violation of etiquette. Receiving no satisfaction, he stationed himself ostentatiously several paces in front of the Mexican. Five minutes later he swept out of the cathedral trailed by his chancellor, consul general, and legation secretaries.[25]

The aftermath of this incident was as unpleasant as Alleye de Cyprey could make it. From Pakenham and Calderón de la Barca he wrung the admission that the seating arrangements in the cathedral had in fact constituted a departure from international usage, although neither believed that an insult had been intended. Reluctantly, Pakenham agreed to write a note of protest against the innovation. Alleye de Cyprey followed with a hotter one of his own. From there, while the other diplomats dropped out of the affair, he escalated his verbal attacks in a series of notes in which he all but accused Cañedo of physical cowardice.

If Alleye de Cyprey did not succeed in rupturing relations, he came very close. Cañedo, who happened to be short, slight, and nearsighted, took offense, as the baron had intended. Early in July the Mexican sent copies of the cathedral correspondence to Garro and instructed him to ask for the recall of Alleye de Cyprey and his replacement by one "more well mannered and moderate," who would know how to reconcile "the interests of France with the consideration due the government and citizens of the republic." [26]

Alleye de Cyprey was exultant at his handiwork. "I confess," he wrote his government, "I am experiencing a good deal of satisfaction at having induced this quarrel over etiquette, I have fought it with pride, and I believe my country will profit from it." [27]

He continued to provoke trouble the rest of the summer. After Gómez Farías staged his unsuccessful rebellion in July, Alleye de Cyprey offended the government by giving him shelter in the legation. In September he went so far as to incite his compatriots to armed attack on a group of offending Mexicans. The occasion was a coffeehouse brawl in which his young legation secretary, the Count of Breteuil, had been roughed up. Learning of the melee, Alleye de Cyprey ordered Breteuil to gather up a party of French and return to the scene of action to take revenge. Obeying, the French found the Mexicans armed and waiting for them. A bloody encounter would doubtless have taken place had not a Mexican officer and guard made an opportune appearance to separate the combatants. [28]

Alleye de Cyprey was thoroughly frank in explaining to his government the motive governing his behavior. The moment had arrived, he declared, for France to establish a monarchy in Mexico. "If this beautiful country succumbs to its internal dissensions, its ruin will be complete." he wrote. "European commerce will no longer find in it . . . a treasured market." Partition of Mexico between the United States and England was inevitable unless a stable government were imposed on it. It was France who must take upon herself the duty of organizing the Mexican monarchy and regenerating its people.

But if duty it were, it was no heavy one, he continued. The Mexican people, "like spoiled and obstinate children," were easily governed by firmness. [29] The difficulties of conquering the country had been greatly exaggerated. Even Baudin, he wrote, had fallen into this error. In the past the Spaniards had failed only because their expeditions were badly commanded and executed and because they were hated by Creoles and Indians alike. But a French army of fifteen to twenty thousand men could easily conquer the country. And it would find on arrival a monarchical party ready and willing to flock to its support in establishing a stable government.[30]

The French government, of course, rejected Alleye de Cyprey's advice and declined to take up the gauntlet he had thrown down. First Thiers and then Guizot reprimanded him for having needlessly provoked a sterile quarrel over etiquette. They adjured him to guard his tongue, bridle his temper, and (a reference to the baron's needling of Cañedo) avoid remarks of a personal nature in his official correspondence.[31]

So far so good. But why did not the government recall him? He had obviously now lost all value in Mexico except as an agent provocateur. He could be only an embarrassment to a policy of peace. Alleye de Cyprey seems not to have possessed the protection of a powerful personage such as enjoyed by Dubois de Saligny in the son of the king. And yet Guizot accepted as satisfactory the baron's explanation of his conduct, even though it amounted to a defense of his methods and even a declaration of his determination to continue them.[32] The obvious inference is that the government preferred to run the risk of future confrontations with the Mexicans rather than to give them the satisfaction of recalling an agent objectionable to them.

Diplomatic Crosscurrents

Franco-Mexican relations in the early 1840s would have been stormy enough even without Alleye de Cyprey on the scene. A revolution in 1841 evicted Bustamante from office and brought Santa Anna to the capital, where he remained for the better part of three years either as dictator, president, or manipulator behind the scene. Bearing a decided grudge against the French for the loss of his leg, he displayed his animus from the moment of his arrival, which he marked by a public ceremony recalling his "victory" at Veracruz in the French war. The severed limb became an object of veneration. Disinterred from Santa Anna's estate in Manga de Clavo and transported to the capital, it was given Christian burial under an imposing monument. The better to drive home his anti-French message, Santa Anna gave ostentatious promotion to one of his officials, Gregorio Gómez, whose dismissal had been demanded by the French in 1838, and lodged an additional complaint against Alleye de Cyprey without, this time, clear provocation.[33]

The dictator's hostility toward France soon burgeoned into an assault on foreign capital in general—partly by reason of economic necessity, partly as a matter of political expedience. In February 1842 the government decreed the cancellation or at least the suspension of payment of foreign debt except that owed to the British bondholders. The following year in April it placed new and heavy surcharges on all imports. Three months later Congress passed a bill prohibiting entirely the importation of a long list of useful articles (carriages, saddlery, pianos, cutlery, fishhooks, for example), which Mexico had no possibility of producing in the foreseeable future.[34]

The climax in the campaign against foreign commerce came in a decree of 23 September 1843 prohibiting foreigners from the practice of retail trade. The only exceptions permitted were those foreigners holding certificates proving that they were married to Mexican citizens, had themselves adopted Mexican nationality, or were residing in the republic with their families. Retailers were given six months either to obtain the necessary papers or to sell off their inventory and shut up shop. At the end of the period, on 23 March 1844, merchandise of foreign retailers not in compliance with the law would be confiscated.[35]

To Alleye de Cyprey, who had never despaired of provoking a war with Mexico, this prohibition came as a godsend. France had been willing to fight for the practice of retail trade in 1838. Surely he could use the decree to bring on a crisis now. He immediately accused the Mexican government of violating its treaties with England, United States, and Spain and, by implication, of violating Mexico's treaty of 1839 with France that granted French subjects the right of the most favored nation. Mexico alone, he declared, would have to bear the responsibility for the consequences if it persisted in its illegal intentions.[36]

Confident that spring would bring a rupture of relations, the baron set about preparation of a memorandum elaborating his monarchist thesis and refining its military solution. This document he dispatched to Paris on a French warship in the safekeeping of a legation secretary.[37] In writing it he wore the hats of both sociologist and military specialist. "Mexicans like distinctions, they like titles, decorations, frivolous pleasures," he began; "they detest austerity, constraint, [and] that severity of habit that must accompany republicanism." They do not know how to govern themselves, but they are docile and easy to govern. Without the institution of monarchy the country was doomed to destruction; with it Mexico could quickly be rescued from its anarchical state. A prince of any branch of the Bourbon family (except the Spanish branch), he continued, would be the most suitable for this great mission. And he should come at the head of an army. France should beware of the half measures of the past and strike at the heart of the country. Twenty-five thousand infantrymen and two thousand cavalry would be needed to overthrow Santa Anna. For, he concluded, "he who desires the end must supply the means." [38]

When Guizot received these proposals he rejected them out of hand. [39] But he found it impossible just at that moment to take no notice whatsoever of the denial of retail trade to the French in Mexico. The opposition in the Chamber had not forgotten the assurances of Baudin and the government in 1839 that the attack on Veracruz had guaranteed the French that right, and they had seized on the issue as a stick to browbeat the ministry. Guizot had been compelled to admit, after reviewing the appropriate documents, that France had no treaty explicitly assuring its subjects the right of retail trade; but to counter the attack he had affirmed in the official *Moniteur* of the preceding January that France still claimed it by virtue of past usage. [40]

This explanation served Guizot for the time being in France, but it did nothing to help French subjects in Mexico. How was he to compel Mexico to respect his claims if he did not back them up with force, which he was unwilling to do?

The solution to this problem that came most easily to Guizot was the enlistment of British support. Ever since he had entered the Foreign Ministry the *entente cordiale* had been the keystone of his foreign policy. When the Tory, Lord Aberdeen, had become British foreign secretary late in 1841, the two had largely repaired the damage to Franco-British relations done by the Near Eastern crisis of 1840. They had developed a habit of cooperation and had picked their way successfully around a number of diplomatic potholes in Europe. In the New World the two powers appeared to be following similar, if not identical, courses. Both had extended diplomatic recognition to the Republic of Texas—France in 1839, Great Britain in 1842—and both were on record as desiring the containment of the United States and the preservation of Texan independence. In Mexico the British like the French had resented the attacks on foreign commerce although they had but scant interest in the practice of retail trade. But, thought Guizot, perhaps for the sake of the entente Britain would lend its support to France in this question. If the two great maritime powers spoke loudly and as one, probably Mexico would heed their voices even if they did not threaten coercive action.

Unfortunately for the success of this plan, the solidity of the entente on which it was based was more apparent than real. Its fragility was exposed almost at the very moment Guizot was about to invoke British aid by the intrusion of another New World crisis on the diplomatic scene: the question of annexation of Texas by the United States. The Texas question had entered the acute stage the preceding January 1844 when President John Tyler signed a treaty arranging for the incorporation of the Republic of Texas into the Union. Although the treaty had still to pass the Senate, its existence obliged England and France to decide what, if anything, they were prepared to do to block it.

The British were single-minded in their determination to "stop America." Viewing the growing colossus across the Atlantic as their principal rival for control of the seas, they were prepared to resist annexation even at the risk of war if they could obtain the help of France. The response of Aberdeen to Tyler's treaty was, therefore, to propose to France to sign a pact by which the two countries would guarantee not only the independence of Texas but its boundaries as well. Known in its fullest form as the "Diplomatic Act," the agreement called on Mexico to recognize the independence of Texas and placed both countries under the military shield of England and France, who had the right of intervention to deter violations of its provisions. Stated in simplest terms it meant, among other things, that if the United States went ahead with the annexation of Texas it would face a war with England and France.

This proposal seriously embarrassed the French government, whose attitude toward the United States was inherently ambivalent. She too desired to halt its expansion across the American continent, but she also saw in the young giant a valuable ally against her traditional maritime enemy, which was England. Ever since the time of Lafayette and the Franco-American alliance of the eighteenth century there had been much talk of the celebrated friendship between France and the United States. And as Louis Philippe and Guizot knew full well, the liberal opposition in France still drew its inspiration from the "American example," and was solidly in favor of a Franco-American entente. Even if the Orleanist government were willing to embark upon an adventurous foreign policy, which it was not, it could not possibly entertain the prospect of a war with the United States.[41]

The French answer to the British proposal was not, therefore, long in coming. France attached a genuine importance to the preservation of Texas as an independent state, Guizot informed Aberdeen in June 1844, and she would join with Great Britain in urging Mexico to accept the loss of its former province. But beyond moral suasion France could not go. A pledge to defend the boundaries of either Texas or Mexico for an indefinite period, he concluded firmly, presented "insurmountable drawbacks."[42]

While Guizot was outlining his policy of peace to Aberdeen, Alleye de Cyprey was hot in pursuit of war. Far from regarding the annexation question as an embarrassment, he welcomed it as a timely means of broadening the theater of military operations. He shared neither the ambivalence of his government toward the United States nor its hesitation in risking a war with the Americans. In his book they must be stopped at all costs. The thought of France's taking on Mexico and the United States simultaneously daunted him not at all. To the contrary, he saw the prospect of annexation as an additional incentive for France to hasten its army into the Mexican interior. Then if the United States moved into Texas the French would be in a position to combat them. With but one army France could kill the Republic of Mexico and at least clip the wings of the giant republic in the north.[43]

The baron devoted his days to the search for fresh outrages with which to fuel French indignation. All summer long he regaled his government with umbrageous reports of grievances, among which were an additional promotion for the celebrated Gómez, the incarceration and beating of a French sailor in Mazatlán, and subjection of French subjects to a forced loan to finance the reconquest of Texas. He was in constant altercation with José María Bocanegra, Mexican foreign minister, on the degree of hardship imposed on the French by the prohibition of retail trade. The Mexican argued that the many exemptions allowed permitted most French subjects to continue business as usual. Alleye de Cyprey replied, accurately enough, for that matter, that the decree was enforced with great inconsistency and that especially in the interior many French houses had been forced to close. For those individuals he made demands for reparations.[44]

The Mexicans played into his hands by a shocking display of

brutality in punishment of an inept band of filibusters of mixed nationality that blundered onto the shore of Yucatán in June 1844. The forces of General Pedro de Ampudia easily rounded them up, declared them pirates, and shot almost forty of them out of hand (eleven of whom were French). Then, the better to discourage imitators, Ampudia cut off the head of the leader, Francisco Sentmanat, had it boiled in oil, and displayed it to the public in a cage.[45]

Loud was the indignation of Alleye de Cyprey. Holding Santa Anna responsible for ordering the atrocity, he planned to exploit it to generate a revulsion of feeling in the public in which monarchists would dare to call openly for the overthrow of the republic and the rule of a European prince. By August he was claiming the success of his operation, which included inspiration of articles in the opposition press and excited conversation with all who would listen. The majority of the Mexican Chambers, the clergy, the landowners, and even an element of the army, he declared, were now in favor of a French intervention. "The revolution is prepared," he wrote Guizot. "On the day [that a French army appears] it will break out in force."[46]

The baron's huffing and puffing may have generated a breeze in Mexico, but it failed to carry across the ocean. In Paris Guizot was unwilling to do more than to add the Sentmanat affair to the list of grievances for which France desired British support in protesting. In London Aberdeen was smarting at the French refusal to help England in Texas. He dismissed the French complaints with an indifference amounting to coldness. Through a subordinate he expressed to the French ambassador in London his opinion that pirates who were seized, arms in hand, could scarcely expect forbearance from their captors. On the subject of retail trade he was equally obdurate. The crown lawyers having decided that British subjects had no legal guarantee of the right of this practice, the British government would decline to insist upon it.[47]

By the late autumn of 1844 Guizot had been forced to recognize that the breakdown of the entente had condemned France to a policy of immobility in Mexico. Wiser, or at least more prudent, than Molé, he knew better than to make threats he had no intention of carrying out. Without British support he dared not raise his voice to Mexico. Establishment of a blockade, he wrote Alleye de Cyprey, would create more problems than it would solve. A monarchical intervention was out of the question. "This enterprise would entail so many difficulties arising from the present political situation in general and in . . . [Mexico] itself, that we could not dream of undertaking it."[48] To save face, France would refuse either to recall or to reprimand Alleye de Cyprey, would even promote him to the rank of grand officer in the Legion of Honor. But, concluded Guizot, Alleye de Cyprey should recognize the limits of the possible, should lower his voice, and cease his manufacture of diplomatic correspondence on occasions of trifling importance.[49]

Meanwhile, the Texas question, which lay at the root of the Anglo-French estrangement, was moving toward its denouement. The Tyler treaty of 1844 had failed to pass the United States Senate, but this failure had provided no more than a brief reprieve. The election of proannexationist James K. Polk as president in November 1844 was a clear indication of which way the wind was blowing. Even before the new president took office, Congress adopted and Tyler signed (1 March 1845) an annexation resolution.

Again Aberdeen proposed active resistance to annexation and again Guizot refused.[50] At cross-purposes, the most the two powers could agree upon was the exertion of their good offices to induce Mexico to grant diplomatic recognition to Texas and to induce Texas to resist annexation. Guizot, however, was reluctant to take any action, no matter how innocuous, that might be regarded by the United States as less than friendly. Consequently, when he instructed Dubois de Saligny in Texas and Alleye de Cyprey in Mexico to foster the preservation of Texan independence by moral suasion, he warned them to avoid any statement that could possibly give offense to the United States and to confine their demarches to informal, unofficial conversations.[51]

Thus watered down and delivered by agents as unpopular as Dubois de Saligny and Alleye de Cyprey, the French message had little or no effect. In Texas Dubois de Saligny cut a poor figure next to the respected British chargé d'affaires, Charles Elliot, who took the lead in inducing President Anson Jones to hold off the United States and to give Mexico a last chance to recognize the republic. After a single conversation with Jones, the French chargé d'affaires retired to Louisiana, by now his habitual residence, while Elliot carried the negotiation on to Mexico.[52] There he obtained but perfunctory help from Alleye de Cyprey, who had lost all interest in the question, now that he knew it was not to lead to a war and a French intervention.[53] It was Elliot and Charles Bankhead, British minister in Mexico, working feverishly against time, who overcame the reluctance of the Mexican Congress and obtained the consent of the government to recognize the independence of its former province.

Twentieth-century readers may well believe that Elliot and Bankhead were fighting a hopeless battle. Most historians who have studied the Texas question have concluded that annexation would have taken place no matter what the British did.[54] By the time the two negotiators had obtained the consent of the Mexican government to recognize the republic, Jones was calling a convention in Texas to decide the question. In July 1845 the delegates voted nearly unanimously in favor of annexation.

Yet to contemporaries annexation by no means appeared a foregone conclusion. It must have been bitter gall for Guizot to know that by his own hand he had helped hasten an event that he had wished to prevent. True, he had no alternative unless he had been willing to expose France to a war with the United States. And if he had cast in his lot with Britain in defiance of the United States, he might well have been forced from office by the anglophobes in the liberal opposition.[55] Britain, in turn, was unwilling to risk war without France as an ally. Under these circumstances the Texans were isolated, and inevitably they opted for annexation.

The unfortunate coincidence of crises in both Texas and Mexico rendered French policy impotent in both countries. Guizot's denial of French support to Great Britain in Texas proved to be the perfect foil to his simultaneous efforts to enlist British aid in Mexico. And by maintaining in Texas and Mexico two agents far out in their own Cloud Cuckoo land, the Orleanist government spoke with a voice that was not only ineffectual but despised.

The Battle of the Baño

No one was more disappointed with these results than Alleye de Cyprey. Even he, by no means a faint heart, was beginning to despair of ever teaching his government its civilizing mission in Mexico, its duty to step forth as the champion of *les races latines* and to administer the *leçon complète* ("thorough lesson") that would both chastise and regenerate the moribund country. If only the king, he wrote to his daughter, could be made to follow in Mexico the example of the old empire ("that lifted up my soul!")[56] set in Europe. But, far gone in solipsism, he was willing to give his government one last chance. The war he saw shaping up between Mexico and the United States promised too good an opportunity for France to pass up. France could step in to prevent the dismemberment of Mexico; in the course of the hostilities her navy could seize the two Californias "without firing a shot," [57] while a French army landing at Veracruz was marching by the conventional route to the capital. But if his government could not be made to see the grandeur of the plan he, Alleye de Cyprey, would return to Europe. He could no longer bring himself, he wrote, to stay on as the spokesman of a "timid and shameful policy." [58]

Even before the Texas question was settled, the baron was on the alert for an opportunity to put his government again to the test. Only one of his singular mental outlook could have found it, as he did, in a dustup in a livery stable with the unlikely name of the Baño de las Delicias.

The trouble began on 25 May 1845 when the baron's servants, grooming their master's horses in the establishment as usual, quarreled with the Mexican stable boys and fled. One of the baron's horses remained in the Baño as hostage to fortune. Learning of the fracas, Alleye de Cyprey thrust two pistols in his saddle, called two aides to his side and sallied forth to claim his property. Arrived at the Baño, the trio found gathered the assistant *alcalde* of the city and a swarm of *léperos* ("derelicts of Mexican society") armed with stones and shouting "Death to the French." Alleye de Cyprey was later to claim that he had been ambushed. However it may have been, the French were sore pressed to make their escape through a hail of stones. One grazed the baron's leg; another wounded an aide in the head. A shot rang out from the crowd—intended, reported the baron, for himself. Forcing his way to the exit, Alleye de Cyprey himself fired into the people, with what result it is not recorded.

Emerging into the street, the French were still not out of trouble. They were retiring at a gallop when an officer of the Mexican army and his squad, appearing on the scene, forced them to halt, ordered them to dismount, and, amidst the jeers of the crowd, marched them off to the Citadel. There their torment ended when the commander of the post, realizing the perils of treating foreign ministers like ordinary mortals, immediately placed them at liberty.[59]

Seeing that he could use the incident to rupture relations with Mexico, Alleye de Cyprey immediately wrote out terms of a dramatic reparation that he knew would insure rejection. He demanded of the Mexican government (1) exemplary punishment of the assistant *alcalde*, (2) dismissal and exemplary punishment of the officer who arrested him, (3) the death penalty for the individual who had fired at him (whom he claimed could be identified), and (4) punishment of the *léperos* and owner of the Baño. When the government returned the anticipated refusal, the minister reported the affair to Paris. So that Guizot could not possibly mistake the method behind this madness, he attached to the dispatch another memorandum dilating on the need for the *leçon complète* and describing the most feasible route of invasion.[60]

When the news of the Battle of the Baño reached Paris, the government began at last to regret having retained Alleye de Cyprey at his post. Like Dubois de Saligny and his "Pig War," the baron had made France ridiculous. Yet it could not recall him now without suffering a humiliating loss of face in Mexico. And in Paris the liberal opposition, incessant in its attacks on the "pusillanimity" of French foreign policy, would be sure to see in the baron's return another example of truckling to a foreign country.[61]

The best Guizot could manage was a compromise that would preserve French dignity and rein in its unruly minister. He sent the baron two dispatches. The first, designed to be shown to the Mexican government, approved his conduct and bade him obtain reparation for a "crime almost unprecedented among civilized peoples." The second, in cypher, was for the baron's eyes alone. It reprimanded him for having gone in person and with arms to the Baño and instructed him to mitigate his demands for reparation. It was the desire of the government that he negotiate his way out of the contretemps. Of the *leçon complète* Guizot said not one word.[62]

Alleye de Cyprey was now prepared to admit defeat. By the time Guizot's dispatches arrived in September he had already broken relations with Mexico and received his passports. The prospect of crawling back to the Mexican foreign minister was unbearable. He preferred instead to leave the country, even without authorization. Setting the date of his departure for early November he began, head high, to put his affairs in order. The obligation of protection of the rights and security of French subjects he turned over to the Spanish minister, who was now Salvador Bermúdez de Castro.[63]

Even though the baron had ceased his official functions, he had not exhausted his resources for mischief making. Given the notoriety that he had acquired and the atmosphere of opprobrium in which he lived, another outbreak of temper was, as his colleagues in the diplo-

matic corps sensed, perhaps inevitable. The minister's pell-mell retreat from the Baño had delighted the public and the gentlemen of
the press, who had commented on it with insatiable vivacity. One
newspaper in particular, the liberal *El Siglo XIX*, had outdone itself
in impugning the minister's honor, intelligence, and integrity. These
gibes were more than the baron could take. Coming across *El Siglo*'s
editor in the crowded lobby of the opera one evening in September,
he strode toward him and, while the elite of Mexican society looked
on, he spat in his face and smote him with his cane.[64]

This time even Alleye de Cyprey realized that he had overstepped
the limits of the permissible. Instead of fighting the duel he had
hoped to provoke, he accepted the advice of his colleagues and the
pleas of Mexican officials, who feared for the baron's life in the
envenomed atmosphere, and advanced the date of his departure.
Leaving the capital for Veracruz on 9 October, he sailed for Havana
early in November, there to await the reaction of his government.

With this incident Alleye de Cyprey terminated not only his so-
journ in Mexico but his career in the diplomatic corps. Although
Guizot would not admit it to Garro, he was as thoroughly disgusted
with the baron as were his colleagues in Mexico and the Mexicans
themselves. Guizot authorized Alleye de Cyprey's return to Europe
and, once he was in Paris, gave him the reception demanded by
protocol for diplomats who had already retired from service. Never
again did Alleye de Cyprey represent France abroad.

By a bizarre twist of fate the baron departed the scene just at the
moment the Mexican monarchists were beginning to stir. In December 1845 the conservatives under the leadership of General Mariano
Paredes y Arrillaga rose in revolt and issued a proclamation unmis-
takably monarchist in tone. Once in power, Paredes called for the
convocation of a constituent congress to discuss and decide on the
form of government. Although he did not call openly for the establishment of a monarchy, his action carried the implication that the
present, republican constitution would be changed. Many believed
that he was working toward the enthronement of a European prince.
For several months he permitted the publication of *El Tiempo*, a
newspaper that freely expressed its faith in national unity under a
hereditary monarchy. Its major contributors, among them Lucas
Alamán, were thought to be planning to carry out Iturbide's Plan of
Iguala in the forthcoming congress.[65]

Under the circumstances it was natural that many Mexicans should turn to Europe and to monarchy. The imminence of war with the United States gave rise to the fear that Mexico would disappear entirely from the map unless it were saved by a European army. Paredes confessed to Bankhead (who agreed with him) that in his opinion Mexico's "sole hope" lay in a European intervention.[66]

The Spanish government was thinking along the same lines and had chosen this time to promote the cause of the infante, Enrique de Borbón. It had instructed its ambassador in Paris to inform Louis Philippe of its intention and to enlist his cooperation.[67] The Spanish minister in Mexico, Bermúdez de Castro, seems to have borne very explicit (albeit confidential) instructions to prepare the way for the infante. According to Paredes himself, who told the story later to monarchists in Paris, it was the Spanish initiative, together with the rupture of Franco-Mexican relations over the affair of the Baño that had foiled his plan. He, Paredes, had been on the point of sending Alamán to Europe to negotiate a monarchical intervention with the cabinets of France, England, and Spain, he related, when Alleye de Cyprey departed and left Bermúdez in charge of French subjects. The young Spaniard's "exaggerated zeal" and indiscretions in distributing the largesse supplied him by his government for the purpose gave the game away. The opposition raised the cry of treason and obliged Paredes to avow his republicanism. When Paredes left the capital late in June to assume command of the troops in the war against the United States, the plan fell to the ground.[68]

Paredes's scheme had faint chance of success in any case. Neither Aberdeen nor Louis Philippe would have underwritten an intervention; nor would they have been likely to support an ultra-royalist Carlist candidate like the infante. Moreover, it is difficult to suppose that the continued presence of a man like Alleye de Cyprey could have exerted a calming influence on Bermúdez. Yet undeniably, Alleye de Cyprey, by his unpopularity and rash rupture of Franco-Mexican relations, had helped foil the work of those very Mexicans he would have wished to support.

Revolution Prevails

With Alleye de Cyprey out of harm's way the break in Franco-Mexican relations appeared at first glance easy of repair. Paredes, on the brink of war with the United States, was anxious to keep on good terms with the European powers. In a show of goodwill he ceased to enforce the prohibition on retail trade (although he refused to repeal it) and hinted at other concessions to French commerce to be made as circumstances permitted. He was careful not to sever his line to Paris. When Garro died of cancer in February 1846 the Mexican government accredited Fernando Mangino as chargé d'affaires and dispatched a special agent to Paris to undertake the negotiation of the resumption of diplomatic relations.[69]

The French government at first appeared willing to meet Mexico at least part way. Guizot informed Bermúdez de Castro that although France would insist on satisfaction for the affair of the Baño, she would be "less demanding" than before. And Goury du Roslan, secretary of the French legation in Mexico, was authorized to remain in Havana and to correspond with Bermúdez on the terms of reconciliation.[70]

As the two countries appeared on the point of rapprochement, other events intervened to hold them apart. In Mexico the American war brought not only Mexican defeats at Matamoros and Monterey but renewed revolution. In 1847 Gómez Farías and the *puros* returned to power only to give way to Santa Anna, who had managed to trick the Americans into permitting him to slip through the blockade at Veracruz. Santa Anna, who still harbored deep resentment toward the French, recalled the special agent in Paris and declined outright the offer of satisfaction. Guizot, offended in turn at this attitude, fell back on a "policy of reserve" that metamorphosed into a prolonged silence.[71]

During the year 1847 the question of resumption of Franco-Mexican relations paled into insignificance as the Mexican government hurtled headlong down the slopes of destruction. As the American army of General Winfield Scott invested the capital, the chaos in Mexico was indescribable. Santa Anna fell back on guerrilla warfare to continue the struggle. Diplomats on the scene reported that the dissolution of the country was at hand. Mexico appeared to be lapsing into anarchy when Manuel de la Peña y Peña, chief justice of the supreme court, established a Mexican government at Querétaro and opened peace negotiations with the Americans.

In Paris Louis Philippe and Guizot spared few thoughts for the plight of French subjects in Mexico, terrible though it was. Perhaps through indifference, or perhaps owing to preoccupation with domestic problems, Guizot left Bermúdez de Castro and Goury du Roslan for eight months without guidance. Goury made one last attempt at reconciliation on his own initiative, but in vain. When he at last tracked down the Mexican government at Querétaro, he found it unwilling to treat with him.[72] Relations between the two countries were still broken when the February revolution in Paris of 1848 suddenly wrote an end to the Orleanist chapter of history.

The Orleanist government simply had no Mexican policy in the decade of the 1840s. The government had just sense enough not to repeat the naval action of 1838–39 but found nothing to take its place. Conscious of its ineffectiveness, it sulked and snapped, and, while professing officially its desire to live on good terms with Mexico, maintained representatives in the field with manifestly hostile intentions. Objects of ridicule and scorn, these agents hindered, instead of helping, the interests they were there to serve. French subjects in Mexico were left to their own devices to cope with the civil wars and Francophobe administrations. French commerce never recovered from the blows dealt it by the French war of the previous decade and by 1847, when Mexico was under the American blockade, it all but ceased entirely.

It was of course true that many of the elements necessary for the prosperity of the French in Mexico were beyond the control of the French government. Nevertheless, the policy of laissez-faire, at least as practiced by the so-called bourgeois monarchy, proved more curse than blessing to its subjects and trade in Mexico. Its deplorable record might well serve to demonstrate to a more energetic and visionary French ruler the perils of aimless drift and the need for a bolder course.

5

Intervention Foreshadowed:
The Turkey of the New World

As is well known, nothing equals the ambitious designs of the [American] except his persistence in pursuing them.—Hippolyte Du Pasquier de Dommartin, *Les Etats-Unis et le Mexique*, 1852

Today Mexico resembles a Being who is going to die without heirs and whose remains will become the prey of whoever gets there first.—Goury du Roslan to Guizot, 9 April 1846

The Two Republics

For the men in the Mexican government the outlook after the war with the United States was dismal enough. The Treaty of Guadalupe Hidalgo of February 1848 required Mexico to relinquish claim not only to Texas but also to California and the vast expanse of territory between them and left its people exhausted and spiritless. There would have been few who would have denied the ability of the United States to help itself to the remainder whenever it chose.

Republicans, however, could take some comfort in the overthrow of the government of Louis Philippe. The Orleanist monarchy had made itself so thoroughly detested in Mexico that its downfall was deeply satisfying. Its replacement by the Second Republic effected an ideological rapprochement between France and Mexico that had its practical benefits as well. No longer would the Mexicans need to alarm themselves over alleged plots by a French king to create a throne for a French prince. And France, weakened internally by revolution, might be expected to be less forceful in her monetary demands.[1]

117

Diplomatic relations were quickly restored. Luis de la Rosa, Mexican foreign minister, agreed to receive the persistent Goury du Roslan as chargé d'affaires late in April 1848, even though the Frenchman now represented a defunct regime. The minister also sent instructions to Mangino in Paris to call on the French foreign minister to congratulate him on the "republican government, gloriously established in France." [2] At that time the French government had its hands full quelling the terrible uprising of the "June Days," but it too was no less willing than Mexico to forget the affair of the Baño. As soon as order was restored, the foreign minister, Jules Bastide, received Mangino and accepted his credentials as chargé d'affaires. [3]

To direct its legation in Mexico the new republic chose a minister plenipotentiary of appropriately egalitarian views. This was André Nicolas Levasseur, son of a sergeant major under Napoleon, a man of the people whose entire career was a reflection of his hatred of legitimate monarchy. The men of the First Republic and the First Empire were his heroes. Appointed a scholarship cadet at the École militaire, he had been still in his teens when he followed the emperor in the campaigns of 1812 and 1814–15. Unable to accept the Bourbon restoration, he had been arrested and cashiered from the army for having joined a conspiracy against Louis XVIII at Belfort in 1822. The Revolution of 1830 brought him out to fight in the July Days and to serve under Lafayette in the National Guard. It also began his service in the diplomatic corps, first as consul in Trieste (where he aroused the distrust of the conservative Austrian government) and, after 1838, as consul general in Haiti. At that post in the New World he had had the satisfaction of arranging for the abolition of the slave trade. But he had never been a fervent admirer of Louis Philippe. When the February revolution broke out in France, "Citoyen A. N. Levasseur" addressed a memorandum to the French Foreign Ministry expatiating on his republican credentials and requesting promotion to the rank of minister plenipotentiary and assignment to Mexico. [4]

This background qualified Levasseur for his new post in many ways. His republican views prepared him in advance to admire the men and institutions he expected to meet. His military experience enabled him to play the bluff old soldier and to ingratiate himself with the Mexican generals-turned-politicians, whose martial skills he took care to flatter. [5] His extensive service as consul had given him a thorough knowledge of commerce and of the intricacies of reparation claims. And last but not least, because he had himself sought the post, he brought to it a spirit of goodwill.

Levasseur's mission began in an atmosphere of cordiality. On his arrival at the Mexican capital in December 1848 he saw everything through rose-colored glasses. His journey inland from Veracruz, he reported, was a triumphal procession in which natives and foreigners had hailed him in a joyous display of fraternity. He was delighted with the reception given him by José Joaquin Herrera, Mexican president since the preceding June, whom he characterized as intelligent, honest, and loyal. Herrera and his foreign minister, Luis Cuevas, were apparently equally pleased and not a little astonished at the French minister's conciliatory words and ready smile. He was a most welcome contrast to his unfortunate predecessor.[6]

In France the election of Louis Napoleon Bonaparte as president of the Second Republic in December 1848 also augured well for the future of Franco-Mexican relations.[7] Like his uncle, Napoleon I, Louis Napoleon was a man of global vision. He had given much thought to the New World, to which he was strongly attracted. Already in his mind was the germ of the *grande pensée du règne* ("the great idea of the reign") by which he intended some day to regenerate Central America and to halt the encroachments of the United States. As early as 1847 while a prisoner in the fortress of Ham (for having conspired against Louis Philippe), he expressed this thought in a pamphlet entitled *Le Canal de Nicaragua, ou projet de jonction des Océans Atlantique et Pacifique au moyen d'un canal*. The thesis of the prince was that the completion of an interoceanic canal would not only benefit commerce but produce political change as well. The joining of the oceans would trigger the rise of a new state that, astride the main artery of global commerce, would become rich and powerful, the hub of a great empire. Would not this new power be able to release the productive energies of its people and resources and even to hold its own against the United States?[8] European powers, especially those that had possessions in the Caribbean Islands, he believed, should themselves take the initiative in digging the canal; for they had a special interest to see that no one power, certainly not the United States, monopolized the trade route to Central America or obtained special privileges there.

But this was not all. As a student of Saint Simonian economic theory, Louis Napoleon saw the canal as a stimulant to the economies of France and Europe as a whole. The increase in world trade would foster production at home, create new employment, and bring lower prices for all. In the resulting takeoff of "enlightened capitalism," poverty would die out (he was also the author of a brochure entitled *L'Extinction du paupérisme*) and the standards of living would rise.

But captivating though these theories were, the prince-president had no possibility of realizing them in 1848. First he must put his own house in order. Public confidence must be restored and his own authority established. He must win the acceptance of the crowned heads of Europe and chart his diplomatic course. Europe as usual came first. During the early years of his rule Louis Napoleon could do little more in Mexico than to attempt to assure its government of his goodwill and to watch over the interests of French subjects there.

Evidence that the Franco-Mexican détente was a reality soon appeared when Herrera appealed to France to aid Mexico in reforming its armed forces and defense industries. The lamentable deficiencies of these had been exposed in the recent war against the Americans in which Mexico had shown itself totally unable to mount a defense against invasion. In the past Mexico had usually armed itself in Great Britain (from the Tower of London), buying, out of economic necessity, obsolete models and in small lots. This practice had resulted in a collection of firearms of a variety of calibers and of inferior quality. Now in 1849 Herrera turned to France, which was still the acknowledged leader in the arts of war and which possessed the best munitions factories and technological schools in the world. It was his desire to effect a complete rearmament of the Mexican army with French weapons and also, by tapping the skills of French artillerists, medics, engineers, strategists, and other specialists, to reorganize its entire system on the French model.[9]

Herrera found old soldier Levasseur very receptive to his proposals. They struck an initial bargain in May 1849 by which drafts to the amount of two hundred thousand dollars were sent to Mangino for purchase of arms. These were to be the latest models, identical to those then in use by the French army, and were to be purchased directly from government arsenals or from the munitions factories that supplied the French army.

The prince-president cooperated readily with Mexican plans. He gave Mexico the requisite permission to purchase current models and to remove them from the country. Only at the sale of the advanced carbines *à tige* did he draw the line. He was also willing to permit Mexican officers to inspect French military installations, salt-peter refineries, and the great fortresses in Lorraine, and to enroll Mexican students in French technological schools.[10] Perhaps no better proof of his benevolence toward Mexico exists than his readiness to share with it the weapons and expertise of his army and defense industry.

The agreement between Levasseur and Herrera was thus the small beginning of large-scale purchases of arms and equipment that continued into the 1850s under Mariano Arista, who succeeded Herrera as president, and under Santa Anna, who returned as dictator in 1853. The transactions were not without attendant complications.[11] Mangino, for example, saw in them a means to line his pocket. An indignant Herrera dismissed him when his chicanery became evident.[12] Even so, the quantities actually purchased were impressive. By the autumn of 1849 close to one million dollars had been advanced to Paris for the purpose. By 1851 over twenty thousand muskets had been received in Mexico. A report from the minister of war of January 1852 announced the arrival of approximately twenty-five thousand rifles and thousands of sabers, carbines, and other weapons.[13] The Mexican army adopted the French system of gymnastic evolution, purchased drill manuals and books of army regulations, and installed military hospitals on the French model where possible. Skilled French workmen, patent machinery, and models of cannon were introduced to serve Mexican gun factories to replace the heavy artillery destroyed in the recent war. The government also substantially increased the enrollment of Mexican students in the École Polytechnique, the School of Roads and Bridges, the School of Mines, and other French technological or medical institutions.[14] As a result of all this activity, when the troops of Louis Napoleon later battled their way inland in Mexico in 1862, they were, ironically enough, to encounter forces in large part trained and equipped by their ruler's hand.

While the Mexican government was arming itself in France, the French government was taking up the question of the reparation claims of its subjects in Mexico. By the time Levasseur arrived at his post these amounted to a total of some 1.6 million dollars, a reflection of the ineffectiveness of the unpopular Alleye de Cyprey in protecting French subjects and of the chaotic conditions during the war, when many French had been compelled to subscribe to loans or to perform services for the Mexican government for which they had not been paid. The very first instructions given Levasseur bade him assume responsibility for the dossiers of these claims and to pursue them with "firmness," and "perseverance." [15] The republic, in fact, proved itself more alert to its financial interests in Mexico than its sluggish predecessor.

Levasseur soon showed himself a skillful negotiator who knew how to alternate carrot and stick. His system was first to remind the Mexicans of French favors to Mexico and then to threaten their withdrawal if a quid pro quo in the form of monetary reparations were not forthcoming. As carrots he had available not only French aid to Mexico in its military reform but, for a time at least, another almost entirely of his own making—a French "national guard" of which he was the proud commander. It had originated as a vigilance committee for the protection of foreigners in the Mexican capital in the period of near anarchy after the departure of the American army. It was entirely French except for a small German infusion and had welcomed Levasseur enthusiastically. Under his direction the unruly band had developed into a disciplined corps that functioned as a security force for the Mexican government. Herrera and subsequently Arista treasured its presence, as it spared them the necessity of surrounding themselves with Mexican troops, whose loyalties could not be relied upon. [16]

Unfortunately for Levasseur's system of negotiation, the French foreign minister took what Levasseur felt was a perverse view of his beloved guard. Seeing the guard as incompatible with the position of political neutrality he desired the legation to maintain, he ordered Levasseur to dissolve it. This order embarrassed Levasseur. But he extracted what advantage he could from the directive by disobeying it for slightly over a year (until July 1850), meanwhile informing Herrera that he was "risking his career" for the sake of Mexico. In this way he began to make substantial progress on his claims. By June 1849 he had extracted nearly five hundred thousand dollars for his compatriots, many of them poor laborers and artisans whose payment for services performed for the government had been for years in arrears. [17]

During the next two years Levasseur pressed the Mexican government relentlessly, for he saw one bright spot in its otherwise bleak financial picture: the American promise to pay Mexico an indemnity of fifteen million dollars in return for Mexico's territorial losses in the war. To be paid in installments over a period of five years, the indemnity represented Mexico's most regular and certain source of revenue in the near future. The French government had tried unsuccessfully in 1848 to tap this source even before it left the United States and had asked (only to be refused) the Washington cabinet to withhold from Mexico a sum equal to the amount of the claims of French subjects in Mexico.[18] Now Levasseur was determined to obtain at least a part of the bonanza for his compatriots before it vanished forever in the quagmires of Mexican finances.

The effectiveness of his efforts can be seen by the claims convention that he signed with the Mexican government in the autumn of 1851 in behalf of the company of Serment and Fort, holder of the largest French claim. By it the Mexican government was obliged to recognize indebtedness to the amount of 1.1 million dollars and to retire it on terms astonishingly favorable to the claimant: amortization at a rate of 30 percent guaranteed by three hundred thousand dollars from the next installment of the American indemnity and allocation of one-half the duty on the export of specie from the country. Levasseur boasted that his British and Spanish colleagues were shocked and dismayed when they learned of the terms of the convention, which were far better than those they had been able to elicit in behalf of their nationals.[19]

Levasseur could be justifiably proud of his accomplishments. By 1851 he had brought the Mexican government to admit to an obligation of a total of over 1.7 million dollars to French subjects, an amount exceeding the total of claims outstanding at the time of his arrival. Part of this money had already been paid, and the balance was assured by sources of revenue sounder than any other credit against the Mexican government. No other French minister plenipotentiary before or after him could match his record as a collector of claims.

The French Colony at Mid-Century

The government of the French republic was interested not only in coming to the financial assistance of its subjects in Mexico but in defining who they were. In August 1848 the foreign minister sent instructions to his representative in Mexico to undertake a canvass of French nationals across the country and to submit his findings in a "Register" resembling an elementary census. This order seems to have been the first systematic attempt by a French government to ascertain how many and what kind of its subjects made up the French colony in Mexico.

Levasseur had found these instructions waiting for him on his arrival. Although aware of the difficulties of accounting for a population scattered across an enormous state with primitive means of communication, he and his consuls and vice-consuls set obediently to work. By the end of April 1849 he had located and listed by name 1,810 French heads of families and for a large majority of them gave their occupations, places of birth, places of residence, and marital status.[20] Apologetically, in the submission of these findings, he warned his government of the imperfections of his study and concluded pessimistically that he might not have located even half of the French in the country.[21] Yet even making full allowance for its shortcomings, Levasseur's *Registre de la Population Française au Mexique* is a gold mine of information. Given the absence of a Mexican census and the paucity of French demographic documentation for the period, the *Registre* is the single existing source of quantitative data on the French population in Mexico at mid-century.

After subtracting the number of those who had left the country or who had died while the survey was being drawn up, Levasseur arrived at the figure of 1,737 French heads of families resident in Mexico as of April 1849. All of these were adult males, with the exception of eight widows and two spinsters. Consequently, they signify the presence of a much larger colony of French nationals, although precisely how much larger is difficult to say. Levasseur noted the reluctance of some, whose families were in France, to disclose their marital status. Frequently these men were living with *femmes du pays* ("local women") whom they represented as legitimate wives in their community.[22] Children of these unions would have been French according to French law. Servants who had left France with their masters were not listed separately, even if male, as they were considered part of the family with which they traveled. There must have been many of them, but how many is impossible to know. Reporting on the British population in Mexico at close to the same time, Sir Percy Doyle, British minister, listed a total of 755 British subjects, of whom 61 percent (458) were men, 14 percent (110) were women, and 25 percent (187) were children.[23] If this ratio were applied to the French list it would yield slightly over 3,000 French men, women, and children. If Levasseur were correct in his fear that he had located less than half of his compatriots, the total community might have been as large as 6,000 or more. This figure is in part corroborated by a subseqeunt French minister, Viscount Jean Alexis Gabriac, who in 1860 estimated the French population at between 5,000 and 6,000, although without

having taken a methodical survey.[24] The British representative believed the French numbered as many as 6,000 or 7,000 in 1856.[25] On
the other hand, an educated Frenchman who had lived in Mexico for
twenty-five years, Mathieu de Fossey, held that between 4,000 and
5,000 in the mid-1850s was a more accurate estimate. Given the
present state of Mexican demographic history, greater precision is
probably impossible. In any case, the exact figure is less important
than Levasseur's demonstrable evidence of a visible and significant
French presence on the Mexican scene. At mid-century it was by far
the largest group of European nationals in Mexico except the Spanish, a special case.[26]

On the other hand, these estimates are not markedly larger than
those of the thirties during the "Pastry War" and indicate that if the
French colony in Mexico was sizable, it probably was not, at mid-
century, experiencing rapid growth. And yet in France herself the
usually low rate of emigration jumped sharply in the years 1846 to
1851, reflecting the depressed economy and political instability.[27] No
doubt the explanation for the seeming paradox may be found in the
chaotic conditions in Mexico during and after its defeat at the hands
of the Americans, and the interruptions of trade and commerce, all of
which would have deterred would-be settlers. The United States
offered many more attractions to French emigrants, especially after
the discovery of gold in California in 1848.[28]

How were the French in Mexico earning their living at mid-century? The occupations professed by those on Levasseur's register
indicate that the colony had continued to develop along the lines dis-
cerned earlier. Craftsmen of nearly every conceivable skill made up
42 percent of the whole, with carpenters, cooks, tailors, bakers, lock-
smiths, and jewelers, in that order, the most numerous. Almost equal
was the percentage of merchants of one kind or another (40 percent).
The largest single category of the traders was wholesalers (*négociants*),
with retailers (*commerçants* and *marchands*) forming the next largest
group, and their many clerks (*commis*), the third. Only 9 percent were
members of professions, which were, in descending order, doctors,
teachers, pharmacists, and dentists. Agricultural workers made up
only 6 percent, none of whom was a landowner. Unskilled workers,
such as porters, woodcutters, or day laborers, were even scarcer,
comprising less than 1 percent of the whole. Fourteen artists and
others defying classification, such as three travelers, four jugglers,
and one professional strongman (*hercule*) made up the rest. Only

Occupations of the French in Mexico in 1849

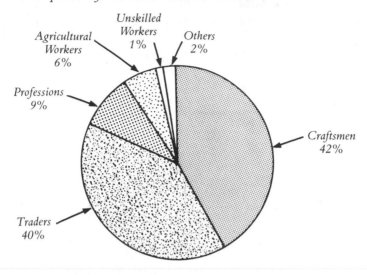

From Registre de la Population Française au Mexique au 30. Avril 1849, by André Levasserur, AMAE.

sixteen of the entire list declared themselves without occupation, and only one described himself as a *rentier*.

There is little in the configuration of the colony that is not either self-explanatory or fairly easy to account for. The virtual absence of lawyers (only one) is not surprising. Why would a French lawyer go out to an alien society to practice his profession in a foreign tongue? The scarcity of landowners (only eight) is explained by Mexican law by which few foreigners were eligible to own real estate. The virtual nonpresence of the French in mining (only six) might at first glance seem astonishing in a land celebrated for its mineral wealth. It was not that the French were disinterested in gold and silver. French agents and travelers in Mexico unfailingly dilated upon the alleged riches of Mexican mines. Dubois de Saligny had been willing to make war to obtain them. But in the 1820s the French had been forestalled in the mines by the British, who at mid-century still owned those mining companies that had survived.[29] Although France imported specie from Mexico (the official figures are meaningless owing to the ease with which it was smuggled), and although the mines of Sonora were soon to attract French interest, Levasseur's

register is incontrovertible proof that few French were directly involved in active exploitation of mines.

The heavy concentration of the French in crafts and commerce
(over 80 percent of the colony) was no doubt in part owing to their
exclusion from mining but even more to the opportunities presented
them by the earlier departure of many Spaniards, whom they replaced as retailers. It must also have reflected the manner in which
they had emigrated to Mexico, i.e., as individuals or as families, not
as members of organized bands. As a rule the Frenchman went to
Mexico on the invitation or recommendation of a friend or relative
already established there, who had prepared a place for him.[30] The
famous "Barcelonnettes" that dominated retail trade in the capital
typified this pattern of emigration that, like French emigration in
general, represented a sum total of individual initiatives.[31]

The register also demonstrates that the French were mainly urban
dwellers, a fact in keeping with their occupations. Levasseur listed
places of residence for only some four-fifths of his respondents and
must have overlooked many country dwellers. Even so, the urban
pattern is clear enough. Mexico City, Veracruz, and the towns and
cities between them received the largest numbers. Important colonies
of French were also present in the ports of Tampico and Mazatlán.
On the Gulf coast the concentration of merchants was high; in the
capital, craftsmen made up by far the largest group (48 percent of the
French there).

The only exception of any size to this pattern of emigration and
urban living in Mexico at mid-century was an agricultural colony
founded in 1834 in Jicaltepec near Veracruz. There the French had
been the clients, or perhaps one should say the victims, of *empresarios*
with land grants from the Mexican government, who had lured
them from their farms in Burgundy (in the Department of Haute
Saône) with promises of rich land and quick wealth.[32] Once in
Mexico they faced a grimmer reality. But, unlike their unfortunate
predecessors at Tehuantepec, they had managed to hang on and eke
out a poor living.

How prosperous were the French and what was the socioeconomic
configuration of their society at mid-century? Answers to these questions must of necessity be tentative. Levasseur's survey affords little
means of evaluating the degrees of wealth or poverty, since occupation is but a poor guide to economic status. Other contemporary
sources, however, permit a rough sketch of its contours. They sug-

gest the presence of a small number of big fish who were *négociants* and bankers, and a host of smaller fry, urban little men who were retailers and craftsmen, often both at the same time.

The wholesalers (*négociants*) were the consignees of merchandise, most of it of French origin. As early as 1838 the major French importing houses in the capital possessed inventories showing assets in excess of ten million dollars. At mid-century the French consul in Veracruz reported that four great importing houses dominated trade with France. They had connections in Le Havre and Bordeaux and possessed individual assets amounting to six hundred thousand dollars in two cases. One of them, Garruste and Company, was also a bank that had ties with Parisian financiers. Mexico City was the great commercial center of the state and most of the French houses on the coast were branches or were otherwise linked to a parent firm inland. According to Levasseur's register, there were eighty French wholesalers in the capital alone. Veracruz, on the other hand, showed only fifteen. The capital also boasted three French banking houses: Garruste and Company; Jecker, Torre, and Company; and C. A. Formachon. These large merchants and bankers were often well connected and could make their voice heard in Paris. Before the "Pastry War" they had brought their grievances to the floor of the Chamber of Deputies. The claims of the house of Adoue Frères for years enjoyed the solicitous attention of the French Foreign Ministry.[33] Banker and merchant Jean-Baptiste Jecker enjoyed the protection of Levasseur. (Jecker had in fact been born in Switzerland, but he claimed French citizenship on the ground that his natal village of Porentruy had been part of the French empire [Department of Haut-Rhin] at the time of his birth in 1812.)[34] Later he was able to interest the Duke of Morny, half brother of Louis Napoleon, in an enormous claim he held against the Mexican government. After the French intervention of the 1860s Mexico honored this claim by regular installments until the duke's death in 1865. In the 1850s more and more claimants began to work through the French ministers or through liaison men with the French court to bring their cases before Louis Napoleon himself.[35]

Information on the retailers and other urban little men is more difficult to obtain. If skilled craftsmen and clerks are included in the category of retailers, this group outnumbered the wholesalers by a ratio of nearly 3 to 2. Some idea of the disparity of wealth between wholesalers and retailers may be perceived from a report of the French minister in the mid-1830s, who estimated the total assets of 21 whole-sale houses at 8,830,000 francs and the total worth of 138 retailers at 20,310,000 francs.[36] According to these figures the assets of the "average" retailer would have been slightly in excess of one-third the assets of the "average" wholesaler. Aristocratic French ministers in Mexico such as Alleye de Cyprey or Viscount Jean Gabriac, Levasseur's successor, often drew a sharp distinction between "the decent class" of French, by which they meant wholesalers and bankers, and "the turbulent and undisciplined class of workers," who had radical ideas, drank to excess, and demonstrated noisily in the streets.[37]

These little men were not as successful as the *négociants* in drawing to themselves the solicitous attention of French officialdom. But even if they could exert no special influence, they could and did appeal to the French legation in Mexico for redress of their alleged grievances. Before the interventions of 1838 and 1861 claims emanating from retailers and craftsmen greatly outnumbered those of the major commercial houses.[38] While most of the French ministers had but small sympathy for these men of the lower social echelons, they still found their claims useful in swelling the volume of alleged injustices to totals sufficiently impressive to justify their pleas for intervention. In this way even the little man in the French community might make his mark on Franco-Mexican relations.

The undeniable clannishness of the French must have contributed to their difficulties in Mexico. French merchants hired their compatriots as employees and dealt in French goods. The preferential treatment they gave each other elicited Mexican complaints against their monopolization of retail trade.[39] Their exuberance in celebration of French national fetes and other political events (at least among the lower classes) at times elicited protest from Mexican authorities. The advent of the Second Republic, for example, was observed in Veracruz by a public banquet attended by nearly two hundred Frenchmen. After an elaborate collation and many toasts they escorted the republican-minded French consul through the streets amid loud renditions of the "Marseillaise" and "the Yankee Doodle."[40] In the capital the French national guard was another and conspicuous example of *fraternité*. While it existed it not only guarded the safety of French subjects and property but also, with the consent of the Mexican government, maintained a jail for French subjects who ran afoul of the law, sparing them the ordeal of incarceration in Mexican prisons.[41]

The French had become something like a small state within a state. They seem to have mixed very little in Mexican society except at the official level. The French minister formed social ties with prominent Mexicans, attended the opera, and received Mexican guests at the legation. But he was an exception. Those who could afford it, careful to preserve their national identity, sent their children to French-speaking schools and subscribed to French newspapers. The working classes kept much to themselves, spending their days in their shops and their evenings or other free time at a café or in a game of *boules*.[42] Not even to attend mass did the French need to mix with Mexicans, at least in the capital. In 1849 Levasseur reported the consecration of a church especially for French use. Beneath vaulted arches hung with the *tricolore* the French curé presided over their spiritual life and the more dignified, sober displays of French patriotism.[43]

The French were also remarkably assiduous in caring for each other's welfare. Paupers, vagabonds, and other social derelicts were rarely to be seen in the French community. By mid-century in both Veracruz and the capital substantial French and Swiss Sociétés de Bienfaisance collected money for distribution to impoverished compatriots. In 1849 the savings account of the society in the capital showed a balance of over seventy-one thousand dollars divided among the three French banks.[44] French consuls and ministers also opened their purses to victims of misfortunes, often reimbursed for their largesse later by the French government. Since the recipients of such aid usually made their way back to France as soon as possible, they did not remain to encumber the Mexican scene.

French subjects needing medical attention could turn to their compatriots for care. Their doctors and pharmacists were considered the best in their field. A certain Mme Labourdette, best known of foreign midwives, was said to have brought nine out of ten French babies into the world in the capital at this time. For serious illnesses the French could go to their own hospital. In times of emergency, such as a cholera epidemic, the legation cooperated with the Société de Bienfaisance to insure the delivery of medicines and the care of physicians for those unable to afford them.[45]

Why did the urban Frenchman in Mexico cling so tenaciously to his *qualité de français* and resist assimilation into Mexican society? One reason no doubt was the relatively short time he had had to learn the Spanish language or to adopt a Mexican life-style. For almost without exception the French in Mexico at mid-century were first generation. Only 3 in Levasseur's survey gave Mexico as their place of birth, and none of these can be proved to have been in Mexico as early as 1820. Only 12 had been born elsewhere in the Americas. Indeed, only 47 out of the entire 1,810 on Levasseur's list had been born outside the French *métropole*.[46] The French were thus newcomers not only to Mexico but to the New World in general. The earlier French of the eighteenth century had departed, and a new generaton had replaced them.

How does one account for this lack of continuity? The decree of expulsion of 1838 seems to have had little permanent effect. Most of those who departed returned. Undoubtedly more important was the *esprit de retour* ("intention of returning") with which the average Frenchman arrived in Mexico. Levasseur noted in his survey that fifty French heads of families either were on the eve of returning home or had wives and children in France. A longing for the homeland was a leitmotiv in the many published descriptions of Mexico by Europeans who had traveled there.[47] With their disdain for the Mexican people and culture they portrayed the country as a place to exploit, a place in which a clever Frenchman might make his fortune, after which he would go back to his native land. The townspeople of Barcelonnette followed this pattern of emigration almost without exception. Having prospered as retail merchants in Mexico, they returned to comfortable retirement to the Basses-Alpes. "[The Frenchman] camps out in a foreign land; he does not put down roots," wrote one resident of Barcelonnette. "Our native land is too beautiful, and there is a desire to return to it."[48]

This type of *émigration viagère* ("emigration for one generation only") apparently typified the French community as a whole.[49] As early as 1830 the French commercial agent in Mexico observed, "Because of the way in which business is conducted [in Mexico], and because of the threat of revolution, pillage, etc. [the Frenchman] has but one idea, to get rich and to leave as soon as possible."[50] This feeling of transience made the Frenchman remain aloof from Mexican society. It must also have enormously increased his chances of clashing with Mexican authority.

Sonora, the New Eldorado

The state of Sonora in northwestern Mexico surged into worldwide prominence in the decade of the 1850s. Part of its new fame was a matter of geopolitics. The treaty of Guadalupe Hidalgo that awarded to the United States Upper California, Texas, and the land in between, made of Sonora a frontier state bordering on American Arizona. Ravaged by hostile Indians, sparsely settled, and all but beyond the control of the Mexican government, it lay exposed and helpless, the next probable target of the American expansionist drive. Soon after the war with the United States, the Mexican government, mindful of Sonora's peril, had sponsored various plans for military colonization of the state to defend it from the Indians and to establish a barrier against the United States. But in vain. As the decade of the fifties opened, the state was a sort of no-man's-land, a hunting ground for the lawless and adventurous.

Its reputation as a miner's paradise was another and no doubt more important reason for its celebrity. The famous Planchas de Plata, silver deposits on what is now the northern border of Mexico (after the Gadsden Purchase of 1853) discovered in the eighteenth century, had prompted an earlier rush to the locality. But the mines had been claimed by officials for the Spanish crown and seem never to have been worked profitably. Yet their fame endured and grew with the passing years. In the early 1840s a French traveler had exalted their potential in a widely circulated book published under the aegis of the July Monarchy. Then came the discovery of gold in California in 1848 and the gold rush of 1849. The old stories gained new credence. Was it too much to hope that the mountains of Sonora would give up similar treasure, especially if they, like those in California, could be wrested from the hands of the Mexicans and placed in more energetic (and/or rapacious) hands?[51]

Small wonder that in the fifteen years following the Mexican war with the United States, Sonora became the site of half a dozen major and many minor colonizing and/or filibustering expeditions seeking to exploit its mineral wealth and, more often than not, to wrest it from its lawful owner. In these enterprises the French played a major role, breaking their record of abstinence, or near abstinence, from mining enterprises.

The cast of actors for the forthcoming drama was already assembled and waiting in California. Victims of hard times at home, the French had flocked to the gold mines in hope of repairing their fortune. The French police, eager to rid themselves of the indigents, had sped their exodus by organizing lotteries whose fortunate winners received free passage to California.[52] By 1851 contemporary accounts estimated the number of French in and around the mines and cities as high as twenty thousand. This figure was no doubt much exaggerated, but it is at least evidence of a sizable and visible French presence. Once on the scene, few of them had prospered. The majority had had to abandon the placers and to fall back to the cities, primarily to San Francisco, where they lived as best they could by their wits. Frustrated but impetuous, possessing little incentive to return to France, they were a restive proletariat receptive to a call to the Promised Land.[53]

The first of the French impresarios, or would-be impresarios, in Sonora was Hippolyte Du Pasquier de Dommartin. He differed in important ways from those who followed. He was a man of independent financial means, and his interest in the American West, which antedated the discovery of gold in California, was never primarily metallurgical. After extensive travels in South America he had decided that the major drama of his day would take place on the northern continent where the Anglo-Americans intended to extend their sway to the Pacific. He believed that if not checked they would dominate commerce and industry across the continent and mold the civilization of the Western world. As a European he was profoundly depressed by this prospect, and like a nineteenth-century Don Quixote he decided single-handedly to do what he could to prevent it. He was remarkably perceptive of the geopolitics of the region. A journey across northern Mexico from Matamoros via Chihuahua and Sonora in 1849–50 convinced him that the land south of the Gila River in northern Sonora and Chihuahua (now southern Arizona and New Mexico) was the strategic location for forestalling of the Americans. There lay the mountain passes that the United States would need to possess to construct a transcontinental railway, vital to the transmission and diffusion of their commerce and industry.[54]

Beginning in Chihuahua, Dommartin at first made unbelievable progress toward his goal. In December 1849 he applied for and the following April received a concession of unoccupied land in that state between thirty degrees of latitude and the Gila River. This grant placed at his disposition territory equivalent in size to approximately half the land of France and encompassing the strategic Paso del Norte and the Paso de Guadalupa. By its terms he was obligated as concessioner general to introduce into the area between 140,000 and 150,000 colonists of the Roman Catholic faith within a period of twenty years. In return he could claim certain lands of his choice for himself and construct any railroads necessary for his commerce. The immigrants would receive from Dommartin plots of land in full owner-ship and from the state exemption from taxes for thirty years. The colonists would promise to obey the laws of Mexico and to defend its territory.[55]

Not content with this coup, Dommartin, learning that the state of Sonora likewise wished to foster European colonization, applied to its governor for the lands in the north contiguous to those granted him in Chihuahua. In May 1850 Governor José Aguilar sent Dom-martin a copy of the decree granting his request, with the same terms as those of the concession in Chihuahua. The enterprising French-man now had established rights to land encompassing but greatly exceeding that of the later Gadsden Purchase.[56]

In these initial successes Dommartin had had the approval of but not the active support of the French government. Through channels that are not known, he had been able to bring his enterprise to the favorable attention of the French foreign minister, who instructed his ministers in Washington, D.C., and Mexico to use their good offices to further his plans. Levasseur could thus vouch to the northern governors and to the men of the federal government for Dommartin's good faith. Dommartin seems not to have come in person to the Mexican capital but to have communicated with Levasseur by letter and by the intermediacy of Fernando Cubillas, a French-speaking deputy of the federal Congress from Sonora who had married the daughter of the French vice-consul in Guaymas. Through Cubillas and probably others, Levasseur obtained the passage of a bill by Congress designed to protect the lives and property of Dommartin's colonists.[57]

Levasseur had fallen in readily with Dommartin's plans, as he had by now come to believe that Mexico had need of Europe to save itself from destruction. Two years in the country had sufficed to replace his former optimism with a pessimism bordering on despair. The men he had once admired in Mexico he now despised. He was convinced that Mexico was "condemned to lose its nationhood in the near future, unless Providence stepped in soon to its aid."[58] By Providence, however, he did not mean a French army. As a soldier he could appreciate the difficulties of invading and holding in subjuga-tion so vast and underdeveloped a state. "Far from me that fatal thought," he wrote.[59] The solution to Mexico's ills lay, he believed, in the introduction of Europeans (preferaby French) for the triple purpose of regeneration of Mexico, development of French commerce, and the establishment of a barrier "against the encroaching power of the United States."[60]

Even with the aid of Levasseur, Dommartin's project soon foundered, for reasons that are by no means clear. In the spring of 1851 the Mexican Senate declared the concession of land in Sonora unconstitutional; the following year Congress failed to ratify the grant in Chihuahua. Dommartin, defeated, returned to France where in 1852 he published a brochure renewing his plea for European colonization. In it, by means of explanation of his defeat, he referred obliquely to the formation of a rival company of Anglo-Mexicans with which he could not compete.[61] Yet the rights of this company too were declared null and void by the Mexican Congress. Levasseur, even less explicit, blamed "plots hatched in the midst of Congress itself" for the ruin of Dommartin's prospects.[62]

When the Mexican Senate scratched Dommartin's enterprise early in 1851, Levasseur himself seized the initiative. Somehow he obtained access to the records of the famous Planchas de Plata (which seem to have been fraudulently purveyed from the Mexican treasury) and with Manuel María Giménez, a retired colonel in the Mexican army, and other associates, he applied for a claim to mines in the region of Arizona in the late spring and summer. The Sonora government replied in January 1852 with an act of concession of the stipulated lands, mines, and placers. What Levasseur had in mind was a colonizing enterprise similar to that of Dommartin but on a smaller scale (ten thousand colonists) and in which the search for mineral wealth would play a more prominent part.[63]

In order to avoid the pitfalls that had brought down Dommartin, he himself presided over the organization of the enterprise and drew into it the most important men in the Mexican government. To this end he "initiated and fostered" the formation of a joint stock company called the Compañia Restauradora de la Mina de la Arizona in which, in addition to himself, Arista, Aguilar, and other important personages held shares either honorary or profit bearing. At the same time he pledged his word of honor, offering to put it in writing, that the colonists would submit themselves to Mexican law and that France under no circumstances would seek to assert its sovereignty over any part of Mexican territory.[64]

To finance the enterprise he turned to Jecker, Torre, and Company. The bank became the sponsor of Restauradora, responsible for advancing on its account money for initial expenses to the amount of thirty thousand dollars. When the lands and mines had been located and taken possession of, there was to be a division of property by which half would go to the leader of the colonists, to be shared among them, and half to Restauradora and its sponsor.

Finding the manpower for the undertaking was the least of Levasseur's problems. He had only to write to the French consul in San Francisco, Patrice Dillon, who placed him in contact with one of the many disappointed French fortune hunters in the city. This was Count Gaston de Raousset-Boulbon, wayward son of an old French noble family in Avignon with a history of failure behind him. After running quickly through an inheritance, he had dabbled in politics and journalism in Paris and at one time tried his hand in vain at establishing an agricultural colony in Algeria. In California, where he arrived in August 1850, he had been no more successful and eked out an existence by hunting, fishing, or trading in cattle for the markets of northern California. As ambitious as he was restless, he jumped at the opportunity to lead an expedition to Sonora. Furnished by Dillon with passports and letter of recommendation, he departed for Mexico City in February 1852 to make his plans with the members of the Restauradora.[65]

In the Mexican capital all was quickly arranged. Impressed by Raousset's handsome appearance, energy, and determination, Levasseur and his associates signed a contract authorizing him to recruit a band of 150 Frenchmen in San Francisco and to bring them to the port of Guaymas, on the coast of Sonora, as quickly as possible. There he was to meet Giménez, the agent of Restauradora, and march inland to take possession of the mines. Spring was not far advanced when he returned to San Francisco to gather up his men.

The affair seemed well in hand when complications arose in the form of two additional colonizing bands of French that arrived at Guaymas before Raousset could bring in his company. The first of these was composed of some ninety men and was led by an unprincipled young Frenchman, Charles de Pindray (*Pindret* in French). It had been formed under the aegis of the Mexican vice-consul at San Francisco, who had obtained for them the promise of a favorable reception by Mexican authorities in Sonora. The second, about which less is known, was a poorly organized band of armed miners recruited apparently by one Lepine de Sigondis, an agent of a French company in Paris that speculated in gold mines. When Levasseur learned of these arrivals (in December 1851 and April 1852, respectively), he worried lest by their misconduct or claims they prejudice his own carefully laid plans. Pindray, especially, was undesirable as he was wanted for forgery, among other things, in France.[66]

Yet Levasseur need not have worried; neither expedition had any staying power. That led by Pindray dissolved during the summer of 1852 when its leader was killed in mysterious circumstances while reconnoitering near the northern border. The remnants of his men later joined forces with Raousset when he passed through the area. The second band, having settled in the Santa Cruz valley, soon dispersed when they failed to locate the anticipated treasures. Some of them too may have later rallied to Raousset.

More formidable was the competition that arose within Mexico in the shape of a rival company, this one organized by the British firm of Barron, Forbes, and Company, then the financial lords of Mexico's west coast with headquarters at Tepic. Displeased at the intrusion of Restauradora, they too sponsored a corporation, the Sociedad Esploradora de Metales de Sonora, also known as the Forbes-Oceguera Company, designed to claim and exploit the mineral wealth of Sonora. Levasseur, dismayed at the emergence of the competition he believed he had forestalled, denounced it as a mere speculation devoid of the beneficial colonizing aspects of his own company. In any case, this company, claiming rights prior to those of Restauradora, proceeded to stake out large claims and, probably through liberal distribution of money, obtained the protection of Calvo, of Cubillas, now provisional governor of Sonora, of General Miguel Blanco, military commander of the Occidente Frontier, and perhaps even of Arista. Levasseur asserted, and he may well have been correct, that Barron, Forbes had bribed all of the chief officials of the country. Certainly the affair smacked of chicanery. But Levasseur too was suspected of venality. He had withdrawn ostentatiously from Restauradora lest he be accused of a conflict of interest.[67] But who indeed can say what arrangements he may have made with Jecker, Torre, and Company, or, for that matter, with Arista and others to obtain their patronage in the first place?

However it may have been, Levasseur's enterprise was already derailed when Raousset and some two hundred men arrived in Guaymas on 30 May. They found difficulties of every description in their path. The route prescribed them by the Mexican government to reach the mines was a circuitous one designed to impede rather than speed their progress. They were even denied permission to remain in

Sonora unless they renounced their nationality or accepted imprac-
tical restrictions on their activities and organization. Blanco made
repeated efforts to separate Raousset from his men, perhaps hoping
that the unruly band would mutiny or quarrel among themselves, or
perhaps for a more sinister purpose.[68]

From almost the moment of his arrival Raousset understood that
he was being tricked and prepared himself for battle. Perhaps all
along he had had in mind setting himself up as an independent chief-
tain of a frontier state. He realized that his small band, even with the
reinforcements that he anticipated, could not by themselves long
withstand armed forces sent from the capital. As he later wrote to a
friend, "I could achieve success only on condition of revolutionizing
the country, or turning it against the government of Mexico. Therefore, I needed a party desiring independence and the proclamation of
a Republic of Sonora."[69] Consequently, while Blanco was attempting to lure Raousset to his headquarters at Arizpe, the Frenchman
was canvassing the villages, picking up the remnants of former French
bands and recruiting Mexican partisans for the coming revolution.

While Raousset and Blanco were heading toward a collision on the
frontier, Levasseur was caught up in a battle in the capital. He faced
an enemy on two fronts: the British legation headed by Sir Percy
Doyle, and the Mexican government. In May, just as Raousset and
his men were about to disembark at Guaymas, Levasseur had learned
that the Mexican government proposed to export specie in the
amount of 2.5 million dollars to London, supposedly in payment of
the bondholders, and on that ground without paying export duty.
Levasseur claimed this action was a violation of his convention of
December 1851, which had awarded to Serment and Fort Company
one-half the duty on exported specie to retire the debt owed the
house by the government. Doyle, Arista, and the Mexican foreign
minister expostulated that the money should not be taxed, as the
bondholders should not have their dividends reduced in such a fash-
ion. As well tax the money Mexico sent abroad to pay its diplomatic
personnel, they cried. Not so, countered Levasseur. The specie was
not in reality intended for the bondholders, who, he claimed, had
been paid earlier with drafts on the American indemnity that had
passed directly from Washington to London. Rather, the exported
specie was destined for British speculators and was part of a "scandal-
ous" intrigue hatched by Doyle in collusion with the venal Arista.[70]

By the beginning of summer Levasseur was so outraged by the

violation of the convention that he fell back, like his predecessors on a military solution. True, he avoided Alleye de Cyprey's advocacy of a *leçon complète*, invoking instead Deffaudis's prescription of the gunboats, whose appearance would, in a matter of hours, bring Mexico to its knees. "I am firmly convinced," he wrote the French foreign minister in June, "that with firm language and a serious [naval] demonstration, the government of the prince-president will enable me to settle up all our national interests in an honorable way." The same month he packed his legation secretary, Alphonse Dano, off to Paris to fill the government in on the details he dared not commit to paper in the hope of his early return with "a vigorously formulated ultimatum." If followed by several French men-of-war, he was confident they would suffice to "bring Mexico quickly to submit to our will." [71]

In his wrath he also began to act like his predecessors. A disgraceful squabble over a theater box, to which he claimed he was denied admittance after having paid its rent, and a hot exchange of words over the Serment and Fort convention brought him to the brink of a duel with the Mexican foreign minister. Only the timely intercession of the Spanish minister averted the building scandal. So violent was his behavior and so unrestrained his language that both the British and the Mexican representatives in Paris submitted formal complaints and requested his recall. [72]

What lay behind the minister's sudden bellicosity? Certainly his sense of outrage was genuine. He was sure of the accuracy of his charges of speculation, as he was acting on information received from Jecker, who, ironically enough, had been one of the bankers who had made up the boodle for the British and who knew its inside history. [73] Moreover, Levasseur may have reasoned that the authoritarian republic of Louis Napoleon would react more energetically than had earlier regimes to redress grievances. Also, his anger had in it a generous share of anglophobia, which was perhaps not unnatural in a veteran of the Napoleonic wars. His reports reverberated with charges not only against Doyle but also against perfidious Albion in general. Always he rejected the cooperation of the British legation and advised his government against concerted action of the two powers in Mexico. [74]

How much, if any, connection was there between Levasseur's Restauradora and the quarrel over the Serment and Fort convention? Levasseur's existing reports did not accuse Doyle of having been the demon behind the Forbes-Oceguera Company, although Doyle was free with his criticism of the French minister's role in Restauradora. Yet undeniably the two affairs interacted on each other. When Levasseur learned of the measures taken to paralyze the progress of Raousset he had all but ruptured relations with the Mexican government and could do nothing in the capital to help his protégé.[75] The supposition is reasonable that his call for a French fleet was at least in part the release of pent-up fury at the dirty trick played on Raousset.

Meanwhile on the frontier Raousset and his men, left to their own devices, were not long in meeting with adversity. Although the count possessed both courage and intelligence, he lacked the steadiness of purpose and devotion to principle necessary for greatness. By late September all negotiations between the French and Blanco had broken off, and each prepared for hostilities. Taking the initiative, the French had their day of glory on 13 October when they attacked Hermosillo, a city some seventy-five miles inland that was invested by Blanco. In less than two hours the 250 French defeated a Mexican force of 800 and mastered the city.[76] At that point their luck ran out. The populace failed to rally to the banner of revolution and Raousset, stricken violently with dysentery, stepped down from command. Disheartened, the French abandoned Hermosillo and returned to Guaymas where they meekly surrendered to Blanco and renounced their plans. Most of them soon returned to San Francisco. Raousset, after several months of convalescence in Mazatlán, followed them early in 1853.

The fallout from this summer of turbulence was remarkably small, principally because of the moderation and goodwill of the government of the prince-president. In the autumn of 1852 Louis Napoleon was about to convert the Second Republic into the Second Empire, an act that he knew would alarm the European powers.[77] He was particularly desirous of reviving the entente with England, the keystone of his foreign policy during the 1850s. "The Empire means peace," he announced in 1852 at Bordeaux. He would not begin his reign by dispatching a fleet to Veracruz or mounting a quarrel with the British cabinet.

Louis Napoleon's foreign minister, Édouard Drouyn de Lhuys, acted promptly to pour oil on the troubled waters in Mexico. He assured the Mexican representative in Paris that Raousset had no instructions whatsoever from the French government and that he had acted at his own peril. Drouyn de Lhuys even admitted regret over Levasseur's role in Restauradora. As for the question of the Serment and Fort convention, the minister defended Levasseur in principle but deplored his tactics and language and promised to bring him home in the near future. As an appropriate termination to the quarrel he proposed a token payment of forty or fifty thousand dollars to Serment and Fort as acknowledgment by Mexico of the validity of the convention of 1851.[78]

Not even Levasseur suffered unduly by these measures, although his mission was thereby brought to a close. Although reprimanded, he was not disgraced. In the spring of 1853 he was able to terminate the Serment affair along the lines laid down by Drouyn de Lhuys and save face. To effect his removal the government granted him an ostensible leave of absence with permission to delay his departure to avoid the appearance of a recall.[79] On his return to France Louis Napoleon rewarded him with the post of Prefect of the Department of Tarn and Garonne. Thanks to these arrangements the French government was able to make peace with both England and Mexico.

The Two Napoleons and the Lengthening Shadow of the United States

Not long after Louis Napoleon assumed the imperial crown as Napoleon III in December 1852 Mexico too seemed on the verge of adopting a monarchical form of government. Arista was overthrown in January 1853. After a period of confusion the conservatives assumed power and elected Santa Anna as dictator with a one-year term. The "Bonaparte of the West," as he called himself, arrived in the capital in April 1853. The new regime, whose guiding spirit was Alamán, took energetic measures to centralize the authority of the government and to censor the press.

Again there was an ideological rapprochement between France and Mexico that manifested itself in the cordiality of their relations. Even Santa Anna was willing to forget his grudge against the French now that they were governed by a Bonaparte. In moving against the federal system in Mexico the dictator and Alamán were consciously copying the strong centralized institutions of France. "We would even like to follow her example to the point of establishing a hereditary monarchy," Alamán told Levasseur; but failing that, he continued, "we would like him [Santa Anna] to have [an emperor's] . . . authority and strength."

Alamán desired more than a model from France. He also desired her protection. "Would not the extension of the power of the United States over all Mexico and perhaps to the Isthmus of Panama be dangerous to Europe from the point of view of maritime influence?" he asked Levasseur. "We are convinced that if the Emperor Napoleon desires to save us, he can do it, he can assure our independence and contribute to the development of our power that would become a counterweight to the United States."[80] Would not the emperor consider guaranteeing the territorial integrity of Mexico? That the emperor might see that the Mexican government was serious in its proposal, Alamán designated a conservative who shared his views, Ramón Pacheco, as minister plenipotentiary to France and charged him with its negotiation.

Pacheco found Napoleon III in a receptive mood. The emperor greeted the minister warmly and invited him to dine informally at the palace with his Spanish wife, Empress Eugénie,[81] herself a long-time champion of monarchy in Mexico, who had for years been urging the emperor "to do something" for that country. The emperor seemed very nearly as desirous as the Mexicans of halting American encroachment on Mexican territory. His government was carefully following the negotiations of right of passage across the Isthmus of Tehuantepec that had gone on for several years between Mexico, the United States, and American entrepreneurial companies. Tehuantepec had now replaced Nicaragua in the emperor's mind as the most favorable location for an interoceanic canal, and he was determined to prevent this area from passing under the sovereignty of the United States.

In a few weeks Pacheco made encouraging progress. The emperor appeared on the point of accepting at least a limited responsibility for the preservation of the Mexican state. Through Drouyn de Lhuys he informed Pacheco that France would be willing to enter into a guarantee of Mexican borders if he were joined by the other European maritime powers. He was also ready to sign an international convention guaranteeing the neutrality of passage across the Isthmus of Tehuantepec. Although not ready to break French ties of friendship with the United States, the emperor believed he could intervene "amicably" to prevent a seizure by the United States of all or a part of Mexican territory.[82]

This promising negotiation was interrupted by the sudden death of Lucas Alamán early in June 1853. Left to his own devices, Santa Anna lurched in the opposite direction. Faced with a treasury deficit

enormous even by Mexican standards, he broke his pledge not to part
with additional Mexican territory and sold the area south of the Gila
River for ten million dollars to the United States in December 1853.

Yet the very act of yielding more territory to the Americans made
Santa Anna more aware than ever of Mexico's need for European
protection. During the negotiation of the sale he had heard the American minister, James Gadsden, admit that the United States coveted
the entire northern half of what remained of Mexico and would be
willing to fight a war in the not-distant future to annex it. Other
proofs of the voracious appetite of the Americans were present in
abundance: a recent filibustering expedition by William Walker into
southern California thought to have been secretly sponsored by the
American government, attempts by a company of New Orleans
entrepreneurs to obtain right of passage across Tehuantepec, and the
growing clamor in the United States for acquisition of Cuba. The
"great American disease"—Manifest Destiny—seemed to have broken out in epidemic proportions.

Fearing that Mexico was in imminent danger of annihilation, Santa
Anna issued an urgent appeal to England and France. In Paris Pacheco described Mexico's plight in a long memorandum, which asked
the emperor to pledge his word to defend the territorial integrity of
Mexico.[83] Meanwhile in Mexico Santa Anna went so far as to invite
an Anglo-French military invasion of the country to reorganize the
country from within and to establish a European prince on a Mexican throne. Because he, Santa Anna, lacked a successor, he told Doyle,
he would be willing to prepare the way and step aside for a European
ruler, convinced as he was that Mexico could never survive another
war with the United States. In line with this proposal he ordered
Gutiérrez de Estrada, still in exile and still faithful to the idea of
monarchy, to make the round of the European courts in search of a
suitable prince.[84]

Whether Santa Anna was sincere in his offer to step aside is certainly
a question worth asking. But it required no answer at that time. In
Europe another irruption of the "Eastern Question" intervened to
cut off the negotiation. For months the governments of England and
France had been maneuvering slowly toward war with Russia in
defense of the Turkish empire. By the time Gutiérrez learned of his
mission it was already a lost cause. Late in February 1854 the two
powers presented Russia an ultimatum and in March declared war.
For the next two years they had neither time nor resources to spare

for the New World. Informed of their decision not to pledge to defend Mexico, Santa Anna could but resign himself, but he was nonetheless bitter at what he regarded as the desertion of England and France, who would fight for the Turks against the Russians but leave the Mexicans to be destroyed by the Americans.[85]

It is idle to speculate whether Mexico might have slipped into the status of a European protectorate had not the Crimean War broken out when it did. Yet obviously many of the elements that prompted the intervention of the 1860s were already present: a fear of the United States amounting to desperation; virtual bankruptcy of the Mexican treasury together with indebtedness to the maritime powers; a visionary half-genius on the throne of France with plans for regeneration of the Latin world. With the shadow of the United States falling across the entire nation, Mexico was apparently at the cross roads. Santa Anna's invocation of European protection was a sure sign that the years of crisis were at hand.

The Last French Filibuster

While the Crimean War was going on in Europe the concept of French colonization as a means of strengthening Mexico received a last test. When Santa Anna and Alamán had called for French protection in the spring of 1853 they had also returned to the project of a French colony as a means to settle and civilize the land south of Arizona. Levasseur promptly suggested Raousset-Boulbon as its leader and organizer, vouching unhesitatingly for the loyalty of his character. Having remained in contact with Raousset since his return to San Francisco, Levasseur was aware of his desire to try again in Mexico. When Alamán and the dictator agreed, Levasseur arranged for the count's passage to the capital. Santa Anna especially waxed enthusiastic in what he said was his desire to compensate Raousset for his bad experience with Arista the previous year. "I shall myself open Sonora to him," he told Levasseur. "He shall colonize at his pleasure and call in as many French as he pleases . . . he will aid me in destroying the barbarian Indians and defend the frontiers of the north against the adventurers from California."[86]

In response to Levasseur's call Raousset came immediately to Mexico to negotiate. Yet by the time of his arrival in July 1853 the enterprise was already in jeopardy. The two principal believers in colonization had already departed the scene: Alamán to his death,

Levasseur to France. Dano, accredited as chargé d'affaires, had no enthusiasm whatever for the project. He had taken a dislike to Raousset, believing him more freebooter than colonizer. Nor had he any confidence in Santa Anna. He was then not at all surprised when the dictator, after greeting Raousset warmly, objected to each and every one of the proposals he set forth. Those he offered in return (the rank of colonel in the Mexican army, for example) were calculated to invite rejection. It became clear to Dano that Santa Anna had never thought seriously of employing Raousset as an impresario and had instead lured him to Mexico to separate him from the San Francisco bayfront French with whom he was reportedly planning a filibustering expedition. Raousset-Boulbon left the capital empty-handed late in 1853.[87]

Dano was also correct in his assessment of Raousset. The Frenchman too was playing a double game. Despite his professions of loyalty to the Mexican government he was in reality its enemy. Before coming to Mexico the second time, he had offered his services to Gadsden as leader of an expedition to conquer Sonora. Rejected in that quarter,[88] he had decided to exploit the Federalist movement within Mexico to help him carve out an independent state composed of Chihuahua, Sonora, Durango, and Sinaloa. To this end he had entered into a conspiracy with Vega, ex-governor of Sinaloa, who was to serve as a front man to appeal to Mexican patriots while Raousset recruited a band of French in California. Their plans extended even to an invasion of the heartland and an attack on the capital itself if their revolution came off as planned in the north. Letters between the conspirators intercepted by the Mexican government and published in the Mexican newspaper *Universal* in January 1854 left no doubt of the existence of the conspiracy and of Raousset's role in it.[89]

The sequel to these proceedings may be quickly told, for once the colonizing principle had been lost from sight, the ensuing action became a meaningless if bloody sideshow on the frontier. In April 1854 some four hundred Frenchmen set sail for Guaymas from San Francisco on a charter ship, *Challenge*, ostensibly at least, as peaceful colonists enlisted by the Mexican vice-consul. Raousset followed a few weeks later with 250 rifles. Going ashore to join the others, he found the local population hostile. After brief negotiations with General José María Yañez, governor and military commander of Sonora, he impetuously attacked the Mexican forces. But he could not repeat his success at Hermosillo. Although the French outnumbered the

Mexicans by a ratio of two to one, they were badly defeated and forced to surrender. Their casualties were heavy: fifty dead and nearly eighty wounded . Among the three hundred prisoners was Raousset himself.

The repercussions from Raousset's exploit were slight. The victorious Yañez, known as a humane commander, was the first to decide to spare the prisoners. Santa Anna subsequently talked of decimation, but he too relented and eventually turned them over to Dano, who embarked them on French ships at Veracruz. Only Raousset was executed, but even he was given a court-martial.[90] Such proceeding provided marked contrast with the punishment meted out to Sentmanat and his men in 1844.

Historians who have studied Raousset's expeditions have asked themselves in vain to what degree, if any, the French government should be held responsible for them.[91] Was Raousset acting on orders from above? Was he in fact a little-noticed precursor of the better-known Maximilian? The answers can be found only in the diplomatic correspondence that passed between the French Foreign Ministry in Paris and its legation in Mexico, which those historians did not consult, and which is preserved in the archives of the ministry in Paris. Those records demonstrate conclusively that neither the emperor nor his foreign minister had inspired, ordered, or in any way guided Raousset's activities. The filibuster had acted on his own responsibility. The correspondence also shows that, far from encouraging Raousset to take up arms against the Mexicans, the French government had made no small effort to prevent Raousset from embarking on his second expedition when it learned, from Dano, of his hostile intent. The foreign minister immediately ordered the commander of the French naval station in the Pacific to patrol the San Francisco Bay area to try to cut off the passage of the would-be filibuster. And Dano wrote the French consul in San Francisco to warn him against recruitment of French subjects for Raousset's band.[92] After Raousset surrendered at Guaymas, the emperor made no attempt to save him. His minister of war was even heard to remark that Raousset was a rogue who deserved to be shot.[93] Dano, who worked hard to obtain the release of the other French prisoners, expressed no regret at Raousset's death.

The emperor could be held responsible for the expeditions only to the extent that (1) he expressed approval to Pacheco and through his Foreign Ministry to Levasseur of the principle of peaceful colonization as a means of regeneration of Mexico and (2) he kept in Mexico for a time a minister plenipotentiary who initiated and sponsored Raousset's colonizing activities. But even if Levasseur's role is viewed in the worst possible light, he can be accused of nothing worse than venality. Always he intended Raousset to work with the consent and cooperation of Mexican officials; never did he encourage his protégé to revolt against them.

To sum up, then, no one in the French government—not the emperor, not the foreign minister, not the French representatives in Mexico—made use of or intended to make use of Raousset either to plunder Mexico or to overthrow its government. The pronouncement of Dano on learning of the filibuster's death was an appropriate expression of the French official view of him: "M. de Raousset died as he had lived, a bit theatrically but with excessive courage. He dreamed of nothing less than the Empire of Mexico and attaining it with the aid of adventurers from California . . . he was a bad wretch."[94]

If lesson there were in this saga it would teach the folly of attempting the regeneration or the defense of Mexico with fortune hunters and adventurers. The California French were not the stuff of which new civilizations are made.[95] They carried with them the seeds of their own destruction. The French emperor evidently understood their futility. Raousset had no French successors. But if Sonora fell away from the emperor's mind as the site of French colonization, the memory of its alleged mineral wealth did not.

6

The Maturation of the Grand Design

Instead of desiring to weaken Mexico or to dismember it, as the United States has done in each of its wars, France has but one goal: to save this beautiful land from imminent ruin, to rescue its civilization from almost total decay, and to establish in Mexico, with the willing assistance of the Mexicans, a flourishing state that will govern itself in full independence.— Michel Chevalier, *Le Mexique ancien et moderne*, 1864

The Mission of Viscount Gabriac, Proponent of Intervention

The last years of the 1850s in Mexico were the scene of a social revolution known as the War of the Reform. A rebellion led by Juan Álvarez and Ignacio Comonfort toppled Santa Anna from power in August 1855. By the following December Comonfort assumed the presidency and entered on the insurmountable task of gaining the consent of the clericals and reactionaries to a program of anticlerical reform. Under a new constitution of February 1857 Benito Juárez, a liberal of Indian descent who was to become the leader and symbol of constitutional government, was elected Comonfort's vice-president and president of the Supreme Court. The reactionaries, rallying to the cry "Religión y Fueros" ("Religion and clerical privileges"), worked to use Comonfort's innate desire for a strong executive as a blind for a coup d'etat. But Comonfort was unable to assert his authority and went into exile in January 1858; Félix Zuloaga, leader of the reactionaries, declared himself president in the capital. Meanwhile Juárez, the lawful president according to the constitution, escaped to the provinces. After a long and circuitous route he established his government at Veracruz. The much-tried country plunged into the vortex of the most bitter and most destructive of its civil wars, a guerrilla struggle tinctured with religious fanaticism in which armies and local bands plundered the countryside and besieged towns and cities.

During much of this terrible period the French representative in Mexico was Viscount Jean Alexis Gabriac, a career diplomat who had served previously only in Europe and in ranks no higher than legation secretary or chargé d'affaires. He seems to have had nothing better to thank for his promotion to the rank of minister plenipotentiary than the patronage of Foreign Minister Drouyn de Lhuys, who was his close friend.[1] Why he should have been sent to Mexico is not easily explained; he had no discernible skills, linguistic or other, qualifying him for the post. Perhaps in their preoccupation with the Crimean War neither the emperor nor Drouyn de Lhuys gave much thought to the Mexican appointment.

They could scarcely have done worse. Gabriac's political and religious views were those of the extreme Right. Assigned to a country torn asunder by a war with strong ideological overtones, he was not the man to remain neutral. Under his direction the legation became a nexus of intrigue against the proponents of constitutional government. By the time he was brought back in 1860 he had succeeded in identifying the French legation with the cause of clerical reaction.

He also succeeded in linking the legation publicly with the advocates of monarchical intervention. For Gabriac the salvation of Mexico lay in the destruction of the federal republic and introduction of a European monarchy. His entire mission may be summed up as one prolonged call for French arms and a French prince.

To a certain degree Gabriac's ideas were a logical reflection of the chaos about him and were shared by many of his contemporaries. Few would have disputed his contention that internal peace must be restored if Mexico were to be saved from destruction. Nor would anyone gainsay his fear of the encroachments of the Americans. His dictum that the Mexicans were the Poles of the nineteenth century seemed an apt articulation of a truth that was self-evident, with the single difference that the Mexicans seemed destined to be swallowed whole by one power rather than divided among three. His monarchical solution was also well within the norm of contemporary thought in the circles in which he moved, and it was an idea that gained ground with every additional year of civil war.[2]

What placed him beyond the pale of all except a small clique of reactionaries was his rigid clericalism and his hatred, amounting to a phobia, of the Mexican masses. In him the usual European prejudice against Mexicans had hardened into a crabbed dogma governing his every thought. "Of all the people on earth," he pronounced, they were "the most despicable." Or they would be, he would amend, "if they were not the most ignorant and the most frivolous."[3] Left to themselves they would go quickly from *pronunciamiento* to *pronunciamiento* to total anarchy. If Gabriac could have had his way (and at times he had sense enough to know he could not), he would have imposed on Mexico a monarchy that was antidemocratic to the highest degree. His preference lay not in a liberal empire whose ruler owed his mandate to the people, at least in principle (as in France under the Bonapartes), but in a theocracy in which church and state kept their subjects in tutelage.

His aristocratic elitism also served to alienate him from the French colony in Mexico. Repelled by the boisterous behavior and radicalism of the urban little men in the capital, he was nearly as contemptuous of them as of the Mexicans. He announced at the outset of his mission that the French foreign minister should beware of the avalanche of claims filed by retailers and craftsmen. Many, he wrote, were corrupt in their business practices and made a business out of claims for which there was little or no justification. He refused to do battle with the Mexican government on their behalf, permitting their claims to pile up in the legation while he gave his attention to a privileged few (usually *négociants* or bankers).[4] Nor did he come to the assistance of poor French subjects who protested forced loans or other fiscal impositions. When the Comonfort government imposed a heavy forced loan on foreigners in 1857, Gabriac not only made no move to contest it but declined even to try to scale down its rates. "Those brigands of French," he was heard to remark on the occasion of another Mexican tax on foreign capital, "I shall make them pay to the last *tlaco*."[5]

Such attitudes naturally earned him an unpopularity in the French community that became notorious. There he was seen as not only a snob but a hypocrite who took money under the counter from the Mexican government in return for the docility with which he permitted it to tax the French workingman. Whether justified or not in these beliefs (his reputation for avarice was well established, according to contemporary accounts), the French public left him in no doubt of their opinion of him. Catcalls greeted him in the theater; hostile editorials calumniated him in *Le Trait d'Union*, newspaper of the French radicals. The French in the capital refused to subscribe to his fete to celebrate the French victory at Sebastopol and on one occasion, much to the amusement of the diplomatic corps, among whom he was no more popular, they staged a noisy charivari in front of the legation.[6]

But Gabriac refused to let his ill fame deter him from what he regarded as his real mission: the establishment of a European monarchy in Mexico. As soon as the Crimean War ended he set to work. By September 1856 he had gathered together a number of wealthy conservatives who decided to appeal directly to the courts of England and France for support of a monarchical intervention. Among them was no less a personage than Luis de la Rosa, foreign minister in Comonfort's government. Although formerly republican in political conviction, the Mexican was one of those who had come around to the belief that only a monarchy could save the country from anarchy and conquest by the United States.[7]

After some hesitation the group chose as its princely candidate the Duke of Aumale, fourth son of Louis Philippe. The selection was not entirely pleasing to Gabriac, because Aumale, as an Orleanist, was insufficiently clerical and authoritarian for his taste. But at least he was French. Gabriac did not want a Spaniard, and he knew that the French Bourbon line had all but died out (the pretender himself was the sole male survivor). Moreover, Aumale was reputed to possess both intelligence and strength of character. If his consent could be obtained, Gabriac was confident that they would need little material aid to establish him on his throne. A few thousand troops and a squadron of British and French warships would carry the day. If the scheme were carried out with proper secrecy, the new ruler could be presented to his subjects before the United States knew what was happening. By then it would be too late for the Anglo-Americans to go against the will of "Providence."[8]

As his emissary to carry the proposition to the European courts and to Aumale, Gabriac selected an aristocratic but impoverished compatriot who had come to Mexico to repair his fortunes. This was Aimé Louis Victor du Bosc, Marquis of Radepont, a former *capitaine d'état* in Algeria, who could claim kinship or friendship with the elites of French society. During the July Monarchy he had been one of the charmed circle around the Duke of Orleans where he had made the acquaintance of the Count (later Duke) of Morny. Under the empire he could boast of a brother-in-law, Aynard Clermont Tonnerre, in court serving the emperor as aide-de-camp, and a friend, Morny, who was the half brother of the emperor.[9]

Radepont had arrived in Mexico in 1847 ostensibly on a mission to

Napoleon III, Emperor of the French, 1852–1870

observe and report on the military operations of the American army. In fact the mission had been manufactured for him as a favor on the request of the widow of the deceased Orleans. By the time he had arrived in Veracruz the American army had already reached the capital; his long report based perforce on secondhand evidence, lay filed and forgotten in the archives of the French Foreign Ministry.[10] At the conclusion of peace he had stayed on but, possessed of an unlucky

Viscount Alexis Gabriac,
French minister plenipotentiary to Mexico,
1854–1860

hand, had gone from one failing enterprise to another. By the 1850s he had become almost a dependent of the legation where he had managed to place his nephew, Auguste de La Londe, as secretary by invoking the patronage of Morny. Yet despite this record of failure Radepont was not an inappropriate messenger for Gabriac. His name alone would open doors and suffice to insure him a hearing.

When Radepont arrived in Europe in the autumn of 1856 he found the two powers still too close to the Crimean War to consider a serious material commitment in the New World. Lord Clarendon, British foreign secretary, expressed a hope that the plan might succeed, but added that the British government would decline to interfere in the internal affairs of another country. In Paris Radepont found the atmosphere warmer. The emperor told him that the plan had his complete approval and that he regarded Aumale as a "very distinguished man" whose success would afford him great pleasure. As for military assistance, however, he could offer no more than a corps of volunteers. Consequently the affair fell to the ground. Despite Radepont's arguments Aumale, whose reputation for intelligence was not unjustified, refused to consider showing himself in Mexico without a French army behind him.[11]

With the failure of the Aumale schema Gabriac turned his energies on Comonfort, whom he intended to groom for the role of Monk in anticipation of a monarchy. Throughout 1857 during his many conversations with the vacillating president he hammered on the need to break with the liberals and anticlericals and instead to seek the only reliable bases of power in Mexico: the clergy, army, landholders, and merchants. He was, he told Comonfort, the confidant of many conservatives who would like nothing better than to rally to a clerical dictatorship.[12] Many were hoping and planning to organize their own *pronunciamientos*. They would all flock to Comonfort's support if he would seize the helm boldly and lead a coup d'etat. By December Gabriac believed his preachments had had their desired effect. The president confided to him that the very next day he would "pronounce" for a dictatorship. He appealed to the French minister to obtain the approval of France for his regime and to raise a war chest of one million dollars to put down the liberals.[13]

Yet there must have been some miscalculation somewhere. When the coup took place on the morning of 16 December, it was led not by Comonfort but by Zuloaga and surprised Gabriac as much as anyone else. But the French minister did not long remain at a loss. He quickly switched his allegiance to the new leader and helped propel Comonfort into exile.[14]

By the summer of 1858 Gabriac had so won the confidence of Zuloaga that the two had worked out a plan to defeat the constitutional regime with the hired military might of France. By it the

Mexican government would emit bonds to the value of ten or twelve million dollars, with the lands of the church as collateral. The sums borrowed would be used to put a French army of ten thousand men in the field, supported by four French warships. A French general would administer the country during its reorganization. The adherence of England and Spain would be requested. "If Napoleon III rejects this proposal," Zuloaga reportedly told Gabriac, "he will condemn us to die." [15]

These plans too fell to the ground. In Paris Count Walewski, foreign minister from 1855 to January 1860, was then strongly opposed to a major French involvement in Mexico. He stood little risk of being overruled by the emperor under the circumstances. [16] Napoleon knew that the British government was opposed to the dispatch of a French army to Mexico, and he dared not embark on such a venture without its cooperation or at least without its consent. In any case he was too deeply involved in Europe to expend his resources in the New World. He was already engaged with the Sardinians in secret negotiations that were to culminate in the Italian War with Austria in the spring of 1859. While making plans for a war that might involve the German states as well, he could spare no troops for monarchists in Mexico, no matter how attractive their cause.

Yet Gabriac was indefatigable. When the Italian War ended in July 1859 he and Radepont immediately tried again. The minister dispatched Radepont to Paris in the autumn, this time as the spokesman of those "unfortunate French" with claims against the Mexican government (they were a handful of wealthy *négociants* and bankers). Received by the emperor, Radepont waxed eloquent on the plight of French subjects in a country torn by civil war. Developing an early version of the domino theory, he predicted that unless France acted immediately, the Americans would soon control not only Tehuantepec—gateway to China and India—but Cuba, Santo Domingo, and the French Antilles as well. [17] They would seize the silver mines in Sonora and leave France helpless to compete with the dangerous giant. Radepont's prospects apparently reached their zenith when the emperor, after listening quietly, promised "not to forget" the claimants and to offer them "his all powerful protection." [18]

No doubt Radepont exaggerated the effectiveness of his mission, because the emperor had not yet decided on intervention. Nevertheless, the arguments of a man as highly connected as Radepont and with the force of thirteen years' residence in Mexico behind them must necessarily have commanded respect—the more so since he was on this mission the spokesman for the French legation in Mexico, which should have been the most objective and trustworthy source of information available to the French government.

The Ravages of War

In addition to Radepont's appeal the emperor received other petitions for his intercession. During the period from December 1858 to May 1859 a group of Mexican monarchists addressed themselves successively in three petitions to Napoleon and also to queens Victoria of England and Isabel of Spain. The petitioners did not spell out the form of government to be established by the intervening powers but by implication, since interventions by the powers in Europe in behalf of princes were cited as precedents, it would be a monarchy. Claiming to represent "the wishes of the enlightened men of the nation as a whole," the signers either were men of high rank in the army, church, or courts, or were prominent industrialists and landowners. There were forty-three signatures on the first petition and twenty-seven on the second. The third bore seventy names, many of which had figured in the first and second appeal.[19]

These petitions seemingly well expressed the feelings of desperation and hopelessness of many Mexicans and foreigners alike as they observed the continuation of the seemingly interminable War of the Reform. According to the British minister, Charles Otway, Mexicans of the best class were coming increasingly to desire a European protectorate, seeing no alternative except the "complete absorption of the Mexican Republic by the United States of the North." Otway himself shared this conviction. The Mexicans, "degenerate descendants" of the Spaniards, he pronounced, were incapable of ruling themselves. "*It is only from a Foreign Power* that we can expect to obtain an efficient Govt here."[20]

The deepening of the civil war apparently well justified this pessimism. At the end of 1858 there was still another coup d'etat in the capital. The troops there turned against Zuloaga and declared Miguel Miramón, youngest of the reactionary generals, president. The new Miramón government proposed to strike directly at Veracruz and led an army to the coast in the spring of 1859. The forces of the Juaristas planned to surround the capital in the hope of triggering a liberal rebellion within the city. The country was subjected to additional years of battles and guerrilla warfare.

Commerce during these years was at best precarious and often totally blocked. The roads in the interior were chronically unsafe. Whatever merchandise survived the trip from Veracruz to the capital was subjected to a second taxation by the reactionaries. Suspension of payment on the foreign debt became virtually the norm. The European maritime powers and the United States had recognized the government in the capital as the "legitimate" one; but that regime, cut off from customs duties and starved for funds, resorted to forced loans and other unpredictable impositions on foreign capital. Miramón could neither pay the London bondholders nor honor the conventions with England, France, and Spain. The Juaristas controlled the customshouses in Veracruz and most of the other ports as well. But they pocketed the revenues for their own uses and refused to hand them over to powers that declined to recognize their legitimacy. Both governments at length resorted to outright robbery of *conductas* that were largely the property of British mine owners. The Miramón government even broke into the British legation and made off with one million dollars earmarked for the bondholders. By 1858 Otway was predicting that if no improvement took place, "there will hardly be a solvent Merchant in Mexico within two years!!"[21]

The figures on the tables of French exports in the late 1850s were a sad reflection of the ravages of war. The value of exports to Mexico fell from 19.5 million francs in 1856 to 12.3 million in 1860, and this during years of exceptional growth of the French economy and overseas trade as a whole. Seen over a longer time span the contrast between the progression of French trade with Mexico and French commerce in general is even sharper.[22] In 1827 French exports to all countries had amounted to a mere 507 million francs while those to Mexico totaled 13.6 million. In that year Mexico ranked tenth in importance in the volume of general commerce of all countries with which France traded. By 1860 French exports overall had shot up to 2,277 million francs, an increase of over 250 percent. During these same decades French exports to Mexico fluctuated erratically but in general followed a downward trend, so that in 1860 they were valued at 9 percent *less* than exports to Mexico in 1827 and represented no more than .005 percent of the value of French exports to all countries.

While the large French colony of merchants and retail traders suffered more in the conduct of their business in the Mexican civil war than the British, it was the British who felt most keenly the chronic suspension of payment of foreign debt. In the years 1857 to 1859 the British representatives in Mexico clamored unceasingly for a naval squadron to force the constitutional regime to set apart a percentage of the customs duties for the amounts owed to the London bond-holders and on the British convention. These sums were indeed sizable. By mid-1859 they amounted to over fifty-six million dollars, nine-tenths of which was owed the bondholders.[23] The French debt was negligible in comparison. On the eve of his departure in 1853 Levasseur had negotiated a convention that allocated 25 percent of the Veracruz customs duties on merchandise imported on French ships for the payment of French claims.[24] Owed on that convention and on Levasseur's previous one in favor of Serment and Fort were a mere four million dollars in 1859.[25] Unlike the British, French subjects in Europe held no bonds of the Mexican government. But the governments of both France and England began to comprehend that in extending diplomatic recognition to the reactionaries they had, in a manner of speaking, bet on the wrong horse—i.e., the horse that could not bring in the money. It was with Juárez, who controlled the customshouses, that they must treat. Moreover, if Gabriac were to be believed, French lives and property in Veracruz were in dire peril and in desperate need of protection.[26]

The British and French were again in the familiar quandary: how to enforce their will on the anarchical country without outlays of resources and men disproportionate to the ends in view. The upshot was the dispatch of a small Anglo-French naval squadron to Veracruz in the autumn of 1858. Its objective was limited negotiation of a new scale of payments on the foreign debt with the Juárez regime.

From the French point of view, at least, a more futile display of the flag can scarcely be imagined. The French commander, Admiral Pénaud, seems not to have understood matters very clearly and agreed to terms less favorable than Levasseur had obtained in 1853.[27] The British fared slightly better, but not much. But in the end it mattered little. The Juárez government negotiated politely while the warships were offshore but disregarded the terms and again suspended payments on their departure. French merchants in Veracruz complained that they were worse off than before the naval demonstration. Juárez, in retaliation for the show of hostility, discontinued a discount on the tariff that he had earlier granted them.[28] The Pénaud expedition was further proof, if that were needed, of the uselessness of gunboat diplomacy in protecting either French subjects or French commerce.

The time appeared at hand when Mexico would have to make its choice between acceptance of the tutelage of one or more of the

European maritime powers or submission to and absorption by the United States. "This unfortunate country feels itself to be dying," wrote Gabriac in the spring of 1858. "It makes no attempt to conceal the fact that it is out of its power to restore order by its own efforts."[29]

In the years 1857 to 1859 the second alternative appeared more likely of realization than the first. During those years the government of the United States or its representative made several initiatives either to the Comonfort government or to the Juaristas that left no doubt of its intention to complete the job left half done in 1848. The first was the negotiation with Comonfort of a series of treaties in 1857 permitting American merchants to monopolize the Mexican market in return for a loan of fifteen million dollars; the treaties were described by their author, John Forsyth, United States minister in Mexico, as intended to "pave the way" for territorial acquisitions later.[30] Certain as his method appeared, as Mexico was unlikely to escape the burden of such indebtedness, it was too tedious for the impatient Washington cabinet. The secretary of state repudiated the treaties and ordered Forsyth to replace them with an instrument by which the United States would purchase outright Baja California and the greater parts of Sonora and Chihuahua.

The third and boldest initiative was made to the Juárez regime when Comonfort rejected the bid of the United States to purchase the northern provinces for cash. Rupturing relations with the reactionaries, the United States recognized the Juaristas in the spring of 1859. The American minister in Veracruz, Robert M. McLane, then negotiated with Melchior Ocampo, Juárez's foreign minister, a treaty granting the United States, among other things, perpetual right-of-way across the Isthmus of Tehuantepec, two railroad routes across northern Mexico, the right of conveying troops and military supplies across Mexico, and the right to extend a general power of protection of United States citizens over the entire country by force of arms. In return for these terms that reduced Mexico to the status of an American protectorate, Mexico would receive a loan of four million dollars.[31]

This treaty too failed to go into effect, defeated in the United States Senate by the antislavery forces of the North in the spring of 1860. Yet its impact in Europe in the months following its negotiation can scarcely be exaggerated. It was the flashing red signal that the maritime powers must either resign themselves to the disappear-

ance of Mexico, or at least of most of it, or themselves find a way to
end the enervating civil war.[32]

But the treaty found Napoleon still occupied with European affairs. He had brought the Italian War to a close before it could broaden
into a general war, but he had succeeded only partially in his wartime
goal of eviction of Austria from the north of the Italian peninsula.
During the autumn of 1859 and most of 1860 he was attempting to
achieve by diplomacy what he had failed to do by force of arms. The
difficult parleys involved him in a cold war that threatened to flare
into a resumption of hostilities.[33]

Consequently, it was Great Britain who took the initiative in
Mexico. Lord John Russell, British foreign secretary, proposed early
in 1860 an Anglo-French mediation between the two Mexican regimes. The plan called for a cease-fire of six to twelve months during
which time a provisional regime would be established and a national
assembly elected to decide on the form of the new government.[34]
Édouard Thouvenel, the emperor's new foreign minister, accepted
this proposal in February 1860 and instructed Gabriac to cooperate
with his British colleague in negotiating an armistice.

The proposed mediation had not the faintest prospect of success.
Miramón wanted to defeat the Juaristas, not to parley with them. He
refused to consider the proposal and instead embarked on a second
campaign to capture Veracruz, this time with the aid of two Spanish
vessels fitted out in Havana. Only after its failure in April 1860
(brought about by the help of a United States naval squadron that
captured the vessels) did he give his consent.[35] Even then he accompanied his acceptance with a note insisting on the resurrection of
the Plan of Iguala: the creation of a constitutional monarchy with
Catholicism as the only religion. Juárez was even less receptive to the
offer. He would have nothing to do with a negotiation in which
Gabriac, to him anathema, would play a part. Buoyed by the support
of the American navy and confident of ultimate victory, Juárez rejected the proposal out of hand.[36]

The Intrusion of Affairisme

The attempt at terminating the civil war by mediation had at least the
merit of exposing the need for the removal and replacement of the
French minister in Mexico. Thouvenel ordered Gabriac home on a
six months' leave of absence in March 1860.[37] This would certainly

have been a step in the right direction had he followed it with the appointment of a less partisan and more personable diplomat. Instead he chose as Gabriac's successor ad interim none other than Dubois de Saligny, veteran of the "Pig War," who had disgraced his country as the unprincipled chargé d'affaires in Texas. Truly France lived under a special curse in her choices of representatives in Mexico.

Why was such a person entrusted with so difficult a post at so delicate a moment? The answer was not to be found in the record of his post-Texas career, which was checkered, to say the least. On his return from the New World in 1846 he had been denied further assignment (his patron, Orleans, having died in 1842) and relegated to the inactive list of the diplomatic corps. After the revolution of 1848 he emerged briefly into public life as the protégé of General Nicolas Changarnier, commander of the troops in Paris, who procured his promotion to the rank of minister plenipotentiary and assignment to the legation at The Hague. There he soon brought disgrace on himself with intemperate criticism of Louis Napoleon, then prince-president. When Changarnier fell from favor in 1851, Dubois de Saligny was returned to Paris and the inactive list. Since that time he had obtained but one short and paltry assignment to a boundary-fixing commission after the Crimean War.[38]

Dubois de Saligny later boasted that, comprehending the emperor's desire for a monarchy in Mexico, he had gone to his post determined to *casser des vitres* ("smash windows"),[39] i.e., to provoke a quarrel and to offer the emperor the opportunity to intervene. Yet this explanation is borne out neither by the circumstances surrounding his appointment nor by his behavior during the early months of his mission. He was appointed for a period of six months only. During those months he negotiated willingly, even eagerly, with the Mexican government. He remained to preside over the rupture of relations in July 1861 only because Juárez triumphed over Miramón late in 1860 and rendered the return of the reactionary Gabriac out of the question.[40] Dubois de Saligny remained at his post to continue the negotiations in hand.

The only possible explanation for his appointment once again lies in the patronage of an influential person, this time that of Morny. The two had known each other since their school days in the circle of friends around Orleans, so many of whom seem to have shared and developed the prince's passion for the New World. Morny, a keen businessman, had a special interest in the financial opportunities in

Mexico and had built up an enormous portfolio of investments there, many of them highly speculative, among which were shares in the Jecker bank. Always Morny was able to keep abreast of the latest developments through his ties to the legation via Radepont and Radepont's nephew, La Londe. That he was the man behind the reopening of Dubois de Saligny's career is strongly evidenced by the assiduous care lavished by the new minister on Morny's interests in Mexico (especially the Jecker bank) and by their collaboration in other financial combinations.[41]

When Dubois de Saligny went out to his post he had in his mind ideas much less elevated than the creation of a monarchy. A man whose thought turned naturally to commissions, mergers, and shares, he was in the act of putting together a number of combinations that promised a handsome return for himself and his collaborators. Far from desiring to smash windows, he was intent on striking a bargain with whatever regime he found in the capital.

One of his projects was the formation of a French-sponsored company to construct a railroad across the Isthmus of Tehuantepec. The idea had arisen out of a private agreement he had made with an old friend, Judah P. Benjamin, United States senator from Louisiana, later secretary of state for the Confederacy, and a noted financial plunger. Dubois de Saligny had made his acquaintance while serving as chargé d'affaires in Texas and had been a frequent guest at Benjamin's plantation, Bellechasse, near New Orleans.[42] The American had come to grief in the 1850s in a bold attempt to build a road across Tehuantepec designed to bring to New Orleans the rich trade from the Orient.[43] He had hoped to operate under the aegis of the United States flag and had been a prime mover of the McLane-Ocampo Treaty. The rejection of the treaty by the Senate in the spring of 1860 had dealt him a heavy blow. He spent the winter and spring of 1859–60 in Paris attempting to raise capital for his nearly bankrupt company. There he had renewed acquaintance with Dubois de Saligny, so opportunely designated minister to Mexico, and with him schemed to draw the French government into his financial orbit to salvage his investment.

Aside from a rough road and some unfinished bridges, the only important asset of Benjamin's company was the concession from the Mexican government of Juárez of the right-of-way across the isthmus.[44] Benjamin and Dubois de Saligny decided to try to sell this right-of-way for three million dollars to a new company that they hoped would be formed by the French emperor and any other "protecting parties," such as the British or American government, that wished to join.[45] Thus would Benjamin and his associates in New Orleans relieve themselves of their accumulated indebtedness and transfer to the new entrepreneurs their financial obligations and problems of construction. To Dubois de Saligny would fall the indispensable role of engaging the cooperation of the emperor. The minister's reward (or at least one of them) in the event of success was to be in the form of a real estate negotiation by which Benjamin would buy at double their going price some unpromising tracts of land in Galveston, Texas, that the Frenchman had unwisely acquired in 1842.[46]

One of Dubois de Saligny's first official acts as minister to Mexico (and while he was still in Paris) was the submission of a memorandum to his government in June 1860 citing Benjamin as "one of the most eminent and influential men in the [American] Union" and recommending the formation of an international company guaranteed by France to assume the assets and liabilities of Benjamin's Louisiana-Tehuantepec Company.[47] The memorandum offers a nearly classic example of what the French call *affairisme*—intrusion of business into politics. Unfortunately, it was to be only one of several such combinations that divided Dubois de Saligny's loyalties between service to France and service to mammon.

To follow up this great *affaire* Dubois de Saligny had need of an agent to travel to Washington and New Orleans to negotiate with Benjamin, who had returned to the United States, and his American associates. Who could be better qualified than another old friend, the Marquis of Radepont, who appeared in Paris in the autumn of 1859 on his mission of urging French intervention in behalf of these "unfortunate French" with claims against the Mexican government? In acute financial distress and possessed of a gambler's mentality, Radepont readily fell in with the plan. In return for acting as Dubois de Saligny's "alter ego" in negotiations with the officials of the Louisiana-Tehuantepec Company, he would receive a commission of 5 percent of the purchase price of the right-of-way.[48] Believing that his luck had turned at last, Radepont set out across the Atlantic in the summer of 1860 while Dubois de Saligny postponed his departure to Mexico in order to argue Benjamin's case in Paris.

Radepont and Dubois de Saligny had still another financial iron in the fire: the pressing of claims of French subjects against the Mexican government. If less ingenious than the Tehuantepec scheme, the claims were potentially as profitable. When Gabriac had dispatched Radepont to Paris in 1859 he had turned over to his emissary the dossiers of a few large and select claimants, along with the privilege of pleading their cases in Paris. Before his departure Radepont had struck a bargain with these claimants by which he would receive his traveling expenses and a commission of 10 percent of any monies redeemed through his efforts.[49] Prominent among these clients was Jecker, who was still tenaciously professing himself a French subject. His claim was later fixed at approximately $1,200,000 by a mixed commission on reparations. From this dossier alone Radepont stood to collect $120,000, a fair fortune at the time.[50]

But how could Radepont serve the interests of these clients while he was following the Tehuantepec affair in the United States? This difficulty was surmounted when Dubois de Saligny offered, "for a consideration," to take over the precious cargo of claims. From his vantage point in the legation he was ideally located to press for their collection.

The future for both French *affairistes* looked bright as Dubois de Saligny arrived at his post late in 1860. If the emperor agreed to the idea of a road or canal across the isthmus, he and Radepont would profit from the transaction with Benjamin. If Dubois de Saligny could charm or bully the Mexican government into satisfying the claims of French subjects they would both receive a percentage of the reparations paid. "Saligny has arrived miraculously in the nick of time," exulted Radepont. "If he manages to have my claims indemnified, he will do wonders."[51]

Once in Mexico Dubois de Saligny chanced upon still a third bonanza that he could work to his personal profit through his position as minister of France. This was the affair, later notorious, of the Jecker bonds, a claim of fifteen million dollars against the Mexican government entirely separate from the Jecker dossier entrusted to Radepont. It had arisen from a bond conversion arranged late in 1859 between the penniless Miramón government and the then nearly bankrupt Jecker bank. In an act of desperation for both parties, Miramón issued bonds to the face value of fifteen million dollars in return for less than one million dollars cash and more or less worthless paper from Jecker. Jecker agreed to guarantee payment of 3 percent interest on the new bonds for a period of five years. In return, he was allowed 15 percent of the face value of each new bond at the moment of conversion of an old bond for a new one. Not long after this transaction Jecker's bank went bankrupt and the Miramón government, defeated in battle, lost control of the capital in December 1860. The notoriety of the transaction arose not so much from its terms, which were not out of the ordinary for the time and the place. The credit of the Mexican treasury had long been so poor that the government had been obliged to assume astronomical indebtedness to obtain small sums of cash. Rather it lay in Jecker's later claim to the full, or nearly full, face value of the bonds, to which he had no right. He was the agent, not the holder, of the bonds. Juárez, of course, refused to recognize the legitimacy of the claim. Not only was it spurious, but it was a demand for compensation for money that had been raised to combat him and would indebt his government to the amount of fifteen million dollars plus interest.[52]

Dubois de Saligny had known of the claim before leaving Paris and had discussed it with Jecker's Swiss brother-in-law, Xavier Elsesser, whose wife's fortune was tied up in the bank. But beyond stating, apparently in passing, his opinion that foreign governments, even the United States, would honor the Jecker bonds, he offered no encouragement.[53] Naturally he had no instructions on the subject from the Foreign Ministry, which could not be expected to support so inflated a claim against the Mexican government by a Swiss national, even if his bank had in the past received protection from the French legation.

Yet not long after he arrived in Mexico, Dubois de Saligny began to press the claim forcefully and for reasons that can now be related with considerable precision. When Elsesser had come to Paris in the autumn of 1860 to see what could be done to salvage the family bank, he had not only chatted with Dubois de Saligny but had bethought himself of Morny. The count could not have been a holder of the bonds to any considerable amount, as has been later erroneously alleged, since only a very small fraction of them had been sold. But, heavily invested in Mexico, he was one of Jecker's chief creditors; hence he had a real interest in saving him. Through Morny's confidential agent, M. de Marpon, in charge of the count's Mexican affairs, Elsesser struck a bargain. Morny and his agents would exert their influence in behalf of the Jecker contract in return for a commission of 30 percent of whatever amounts were redeemed.[54]

How was Morny to go about so delicate an operation? How could he obtain the backing of the French government for this claim? He could scarcely approach the emperor and ask him to place the armed might of France behind a spurious claim that would fatten the purse of his half brother.[55] No more could Morny explain the facts of the matter to the French foreign minister, Thouvenel, a career diplomat with an impeccable record of integrity. Thouvenel admitted that he had never read Jecker's contract with Miramón and felt incapable of making a judgment on it.[56]

The solution to his problem was remarkably simple after all. Morny had but to grease the hands of Dubois de Saligny to obtain the official support of the French legation. To this end his man of business dispatched to Mexico a young relative, Count Eugène de Pierres, who was also promised a cut in the boodle.[57] Leaving France in December, he arrived in Mexico in January 1861 and went immediately to the legation. How much was passed under the counter is not and probably never will be known. But it sufficed to convert Dubois de Saligny into an unremitting champion of the claim. Jecker himself later related that no sooner had Pierres arrived and an "arrangement" made than he was "perfectly supported" by the French minister in Mexico.[58]

The Mission of Dubois de Saligny: An Affairiste at Work

Only with this financial network in mind can the conduct of Dubois de Saligny in Mexico in 1861 be understood, because virtually none of it was prompted by the French Foreign Ministry. The early months of his mission were devoted single-mindedly to the care and development of his many combinations.

His arrival at the capital early in January 1861 coincided almost exactly with the triumph of Juárez and the eviction of Miramón. The change in regime meant that Franco-Mexican relations were suspended, because France had recognized the Miramón government as the legitimate one. The circumstance gave Dubois de Saligny a tactical advantage that he was quick to exploit. By withholding recognition from the constitutional government and threatening it with all manner of dire consequences, he might bring it to yield to his many demands.

He launched on this plan of action in February with a multipronged offensive designed to impress Juárez with his vigor and firmness. Adopting a tone of outraged moral indignation, he protested in swift succession a number of acts of the Mexican government that were of small concern to France and for which he had no instructions: the

Duke of Morny

expulsions of the Spanish minister and the papal nuncio, and a search by the Mexican army of the convent of the Sisters of Charity for concealed valuables.[59] His totally unauthorized threats in regard to the sisters later earned him a reprimand from Thouvenel;[60] but his bluff served his purpose at the time by leading the Mexicans to believe that he possessed the confidence of the emperor and was not a man to be trifled with. Judging that he had become "master of the

Jean B. Jecker, Swiss banker in Mexico
who claimed French citizenship and the protection
of the French legation for his monetary claims

situation,"[61] he began to press the Jecker contract and Radepont's dossier of claims with the same audacity. Again without instructions, he presented Francisco Zarco, Mexican foreign minister, a schedule of payments that, he asserted, was the "only one" with a "chance of success." He advised immediate compliance. "If you refuse," he added, "then prepare yourself for the disasters that I have done my best to spare you and the responsibility for which . . . will fall entirely on your government."[62]

Apparently the Mexicans were duly impressed. Juárez, who had

Alphonse Dubois de Saligny,
French minister plenipotentiary to Mexico,
1860–1863

inherited a country in ruins from the unfinished war, could not afford an open rupture with France. Late in March Zarco yielded to the point of signing a claims convention with Dubois de Saligny regulating Mexican indebtedness to French subjects. It was, boasted the triumphant French minister to Radepont, "much more advantageous than any other ever concluded with this country."[63]

The convention was certainly nothing if not flexible. It defined Mexican indebtedness so broadly as to encompass even the flimsiest of French claims.[64] The sum total of these was not stipulated in the document. But the figures the minister had in mind may be divined from his later ultimatum to the Mexican government (January 1862) that demanded over twenty-four million dollars: half for French claims in general, half for the Jecker bonds[65]—and this at a time when the sum owed on the French convention debt could not have been much in excess of six million dollars.[66]

Dubois de Saligny likewise made encouraging progress in the affair of the Jecker bonds. If he did not succeed in making acceptance of the claim the sine qua non of French recognition (his original plan), he at least obtained in March what he declared to be Mexican acknowledgment "in principle" of the Jecker contract and presented his credentials the same month.[67]

But Dubois de Saligny soon learned that it was one thing to have claims acknowledged and regulated, even in writing, and quite another to obtain payment. After the apparent victories of February and March came a series of setbacks. They arose, of course, from the empty treasury that Juárez was helpless to replenish. No less than 77 percent of the Veracruz customs duties were earmarked for foreign creditors (over one-half of them British).[68] The bureaucrats and soldiers of the army were clamoring for their pay. And outside the capital a reactionary army held the mountains of Querétaro while bands of guerrillas roamed at large in the central provinces.

Dubois de Saligny was thus unable to make further headway in the affair of the Jecker bonds. Certainly he did his best to bully Zarco into submission. "Jecker feels he can *demand everything* knowing himself supported by France," he told the Mexican. If Juárez did not accept his terms immediately the result would be "a rupture that will spell the ruin of your Country. . . . So then," he concluded ominously, "reflect well and decide quickly."[69] Yet all that he met was evasion and procrastination. By June the Congress had failed to act on the question of the bonds. Nor had it been willing even to consider ratification of the Zarco-Saligny convention. Although duly signed, it remained inoperative.

The Tehuantepec affair, whose prospects had appeared so bright in 1860, likewise encountered unexpected difficulties in the spring of 1861. In Paris a banking scandal had broken around the Jewish banker Jules Mirès, a protégé of Morny,[70] that rendered French capitalists wary of speculative ventures. Moreover, the Civil War in the United States and the blockade of the Southern ports had generated a widespread fiscal instability. The emperor therefore turned cold on the project and informed Radepont indirectly in May and June that he wished to hear no more of it for the time being, at least. By the end of June Radepont, who had run completely out of money, informed Dubois de Saligny that he was suspending operations.[71]

As Dubois de Saligny's difficulties mounted, his willingness to negotiate diminished. By late April and early May he was thinking in terms of gunboat diplomacy and recommended the dispatch to Mexico of a naval squadron to insure respect for the "dignity and rights of France."[72] In May, frustrated by the refusal of the Mexican Congress to ratify his convention, he reiterated the call for naval action.[73] By June he had a number of fresh "outrages" about which to complain, among them a default of forty thousand dollars owed on the second Levasseur convention. His indignation reached a climax on 17 July when he learned that the Mexican government, goaded to desperation by the insatiable demands of France, England, and Spain on the empty treasury, issued a decree formally suspending all payment on the foreign debt. "No need to add that it is all up with the convention signed by myself and M. Zarco, with the Jecker claim, and with all the other claims as well," he reported.[74] Although without instructions for such a contingency, he ruptured diplomatic relations and proposed to Thouvenel a tripartite naval expedition to seize and control Mexican customshouses.

The time to smash windows had arrived. The debt suspension provided him a seemingly legitimate opportunity to call for deployment of force. After all, the British minister, Sir Charles Wyke, had also reacted vigorously to the decree and had suspended (but not severed) relations with Mexico. If Dubois de Saligny had been unable to plunder Mexico through his own efforts he would summon the might of France to do it for him. In the months following 17 July he submitted a series of provocative reports designed to trigger intervention. Mexico, he wrote, was a land of anarchy crying out for law and order. The Juárez government was utterly without principles or scruples, and its collapse was imminent. A "real social decomposition" had set in. The police and soldiers were no better than bandits, having been recruited from "servants, léperos, and ragamuffins off the street." (He said nothing of the French guns and munitions with which they were armed.) The lives of French subjects and their property were in constant danger. In August he claimed that he himself had been fired upon, although he could produce no evidence or witness of the alleged attempt at assassination.[75]

Many of his arguments were those he had employed earlier on Louis Philippe while in Texas. Others he tailored to fit the circumstances of the 1860s. The themes of Yankee rapacity and Mexican impotence were thoroughly replayed. England, too, was seen as circling around the dying prey. He reported a rumor of a treaty by which the London bondholders would receive twenty or forty million dollars (he did not know which) via the United States, which would purchase Lower California and Sonora for those amounts. To forestall such nefarious schemes, should not France move to take "this wretched country" under her "direct and effective protection"? [76] Repeatedly he emphasized the ease with which France might occupy the country and enforce her will. Resistance would melt away at the sight of a French squadron. By early autumn he had passed from recommendation of seizure of the customshouses to a call for a march on the capital. "With each passing day," he reported, "I am more inclined to believe that nothing could prevent a corps of 4,000 to 5,000 European soldiers from marching right to Mexico City without encountering the slightest resistance." [77]

In the European Courts

While Dubois de Saligny was following the low road of financial speculation to a French intervention in Mexico, the emperor was approaching it from the higher ground of his European diplomacy. That their paths should have met just at the moment when conditions for intervention were the most auspicious was not one of the lesser tragedies of the nineteenth century.

The emperor's European diplomacy was geared to the attainment of what is often called the Grand Design. If the designation seems vague, it is not more so than the specific aims of its author, whose complex personality permitted him to pursue several different and even incompatible aims simultaneously. But if common denominator there were to his policies, it lay in his desire to upset the treaties of 1815 that had destroyed the French empire created by Napoleon I.

This desire had taken him across the Alps in 1859 to fight a war against Austria and had involved him in acrimonious postwar negotiations in which he usually sided with the Sardinians against the Austrians. But by the opening of the 1860s he became aware of the need to mend his fences in Vienna if he were ever to face up to the greater challenge of remaking the map on his eastern frontier. An alliance with Austria was the sine qua non of a confrontation with Prussia in the Rhineland over French acquisition of her "natural frontiers."

But if the road to the Rhine and to other cherished goals of the emperor's foreign policy lay through Vienna, it was at the moment blocked by obstacles placed there by the emperor himself. Greatest of these was the vexatious "Venetian Question," born in the Italian War and the bane of his diplomatic life ever since. Its origin lay in the emperor's failure to live up to his pledge to the Sardinians to "free Italy from the Alps to the Adriatic," i.e., to take from Austria her provinces of Lombardy and Venetia. Instead, he had drawn up short after seizing Lombardy and signed a peace leaving Venetia in Austrian hands. But, feeling his honor at stake, he had since that time tried numerous stratagems to induce the Austrians to surrender in peace what he had failed to wrest from them in war. In the spring and early summer of 1861 he dangled before them his latest proposition: Austrian cession of Venetia in return for blows struck at Italian unity by restoration of the pope and the Bourbon monarchy in the center and south, respectively.[78] But in vain. His compulsive efforts to detach Venetia from Austria were the perfect foil for his desire for an Austro-French rapprochement.

Arrived at this impasse in the summer of 1861, the emperor began to perceive the possibility of tacking far around his Venetian obstacle to win through to the Austrian alliance. He would adopt as his candidate for a throne in Mexico the Archduke Ferdinand Maximilian, younger brother of the Austrian emperor, Franz Joseph. A plum in the shape of a Mexican crown might help bring the two countries together.[79] Napoleon learned from inquiries made by the ever persistent Gutiérrez de Estrada in July 1861 that the Austrians had listened to his arguments and had left the door invitingly ajar for further proposals.[80]

By September the French emperor was ready to press his suit in Vienna. The archduke possessed qualities, argued Napoleon, well suited for this work of regeneration. He came "from a Great Power that is not a Maritime Power," and hence would not offend the "susceptibilities" of England or Spain. He was married to the daughter of the King of the Belgians, uncle of Queen Victoria, thus providing a "natural bond" between France and England. Also, the emperor thought it "in good taste" to propose a candidate from Austria, a country with which France had been at war so recently.[81] Eager to obtain the consent of Franz Joseph, he assured him that France would never expect any favor in return for the proffered throne. The enterprise, he explained, was for the benefit of Mexican and French interests.[82]

The French emperor's proposal had an undeniable appeal to the Austrian royal family and government. To the archduke and his young wife, Carlota, a throne in Mexico promised both an escape from the dull routine of their existence and an opportunity to enter on a useful and active life in glamorous surroundings. Franz Joseph and his foreign minister, Count Rechberg, were pleased with the idea of asserting the principle of monarchy in the New World and of combating the gathering forces of republicanism. Nor was there any denying the fact that the elevation of an Austrian archduke to a throne in Mexico would lend new luster to the dynasty.[83]

On the other hand, Franz Joseph and Rechberg were suspicious of Napoleon's motives. Why should the Emperor of the French go out of his way to do a favor for an Austrian prince? Only two years had passed since he had tried to evict the Austrians from Italy by armed force. Since then he had recognized Victor Emmanuel as King of Italy and further eroded Austria's position in the peninsula. Was it not axiomatic in diplomacy that for every favor extended there must be a quid pro quo? What was he expecting in return? Napoleon could have chosen a number of other candidates. There was no shortage of princes in the *Almanach de Gotha*.

In effect, Napoleon's *arrière pensée* was only too easily perceived in diplomatic circles. Ferdinand Maximilian had been viceroy of Lombardy-Venetia before the Italian War. Not much depth of penetration was required to visualize Mexico as compensation for this loss. Across Europe, from Turin to Brussels to London, the offer was seen as at least a partial consolation to Austria for the sacrifice to be asked of her on the Adriatic. Even Thouvenel, although he disclaimed a request for a quid pro quo for Mexico, could be brought to admit that some day in the future Mexico would be placed in the diplomatic scales against Venetia.[84] Empress Eugénie was frankest of all in confessing that "in my husband's thought," elevation of an Austrian archduke to a throne in Mexico would serve as an argument to obtain Venetia for Italy. "With this turn in events," she later declared, "the program of 1859 would be fully realized: Italy would henceforth be free to the shores of the Adriatic."[85]

Eugénie disliked the idea of giving the Italians still another province, but she had long been one of the strongest proponents in the French court of a monarchical intervention in Mexico. In the 1850s she had spun a number of fanciful intrigues to place crownless European princes on thrones in the New World. One had been a scheme to establish the Carlist claimant to the Spanish throne, Don Juan de Borbón, in Mexico in 1857.[86] Another in the spring of 1861 would have seen the Spanish general, Don Joaquin Elío, a blood relation of the empress and a prominent Carlist, lead an army to Mexico in behalf of the Duke of Modena, who had lost his duchy in the Italian War.[87] By the summer of 1861 she had switched her allegiance to Ferdinand Maximilian.[88] Herself an ardent austrophile, she saw in the archduke the ideal candidate not only to realize her monarchical dreams in the New World but to lead her sometimes errant husband away from the camp of the anticlerical Italianissimes to the safe, conservative refuge of the Austrian alliance.

For years Eugénie had provided a hospitable reception in her court to Mexican diplomats and émigrés. She had enjoyed the opportunities to converse in her native tongue and had accepted unquestioningly their arguments in favor of monarchy. At heart a Legitimist with a deep reverence for traditional royalty, she had long sympathized with the Carlist cause in Spain. Since the Mexicans spoke Spanish and worshiped in Catholic churches, in her book they were all Spaniards. From this premise it followed that the empress, a Spaniard, was herself an authority on the proper—i.e., monarchical—governance of Mexico.[89]

In the opinion of the empress the most deserving and attractive of the Mexicans in court was Don José Manuel Hidalgo y Esnaurrizar. Although born in Mexico, he felt himself more Spanish than Mexican and to the scorn of Mexican patriots renounced his Mexican citizenship in 1861 in favor of his Spanish "fatherland."[90] As a legation secretary in Madrid he had been a frequent guest in the salon of Eugénie's mother, Countess of Montijo. Transferred to Paris, he quickly became a court favorite and followed its seasonal preregrinations from Saint-Cloud to Fontainebleau, from Biarritz to Compiègne. From this vantage point he gained access to the emperor and with his facile tongue reminded the ruler almost daily of the nobility of his *grande pensée*.

Friends and foes of the empress have generally agreed in assigning to her an important role in the origin of the Mexican venture. Denial of her influence would be difficult, inasmuch as the empress herself admitted her responsibility. The Austrian ambassador in Paris, Prince Richard von Metternich, often commented on the feverish anxiety with which she followed events in Mexico and on the crushing sense of guilt that oppressed her when the empire failed.[91] In 1867, after the death of Ferdinand Maximilian before a firing squad at Querétaro, the fundamental honesty of her character prompted her to confess, "For me the most painful thing in the world would be to find myself face to face with a brother and a mother [Franz Joseph and Archduchess Sophia] to whose grief I have contributed by the instigation of the Mexican expedition."[92]

Yet it is easy to exaggerate the role of the empress and the émigrés. They were after all preaching to one already long converted. The émigrés themselves and their work have been imperfectly known to historians. Usually the impression is given, especially by European historians unfamiliar with Mexican history, that they had lived in exile for so many years that they had lost touch with their native country and in arguing for monarchy did not know what they were talking about.[93] Much is made of the roles of Gutiérrez de Estrada and Hidalgo. If others are identified they are assumed to have been of the same types. Gutiérrez, who had now lived in Europe for two decades, had by this time become something of a comic figure owing to his pertinacious rounds of the European courts *buscando un rey* and to his bombastic style of speaking and writing. Since, owing to his seniority, he was given the honor of reading the speech offering the crown to the archduke in 1864, he is held to have represented the group as a whole. Hidalgo, the other most prominent émigré, was the protégé of the empress and an easy target of derision. He exemplified "petticoat diplomacy" at its worst. But Hidalgo had been in Europe not as an émigré, but as legation secretary until the arrival of Juárez in power in 1861.[94] The other émigrés had arrived in Europe only very recently, most of them after the victory of the Juaristas, or, like Hidalgo, they had been living there on official business and in constant communication with the Mexican government. Many had served the governments of either Zuloaga or Miramón. Juan Nepomuceno Almonte, the Mexican reputedly best liked by the emperor, had represented Mexico as minister in London and Paris until dismissed by Juárez early in 1861. Ignacio Aguilar, Francisco Javier (Padre) Miranda, Antonio Suárez de Peredo, the Conde del Valle, and Joaquín Velázquez de Leon had held important posts in the conservative governments. Antonio Escandon was building the railroad from

Veracruz to the capital.[95] Gutiérrez de Estrada was the only émigré of long standing, and he was persona non grata with the emperor, the empress, and with Maximilian himself.

Conjonctures: The Decision Is Made

By the autumn of 1861 the emperor was ready to take the final plunge. During the summer a series of *conjonctures* had presented him with singularly fortuitous circumstances for action. Important among them was the progress of the Civil War in the United States. Its outbreak the previous April had relieved him for the moment of the threat of American aggression against Mexico. When the North suffered defeat at the Battle of Bull Run in July he saw that the struggle would be a protracted one. It thus presented him with a perhaps once-in-a-lifetime opportunity too good to be passed up. France need not worry over resistance from the United States should he undertake the introduction of a monarchy into the New World. As Thouvenel remarked, the Americans would have "other fish to fry" until the internecine struggle was settled.[96] The Civil War also meant that, owing to the blockade of the Southern ports, France would need to look elsewhere for a source of raw cotton to supply her textile industry. The emperor believed that Mexico could develop into such a supplier but only, of course, if it could achieve political stability and organize its productive forces.[97]

Meanwhile during this summer, the alarmist and provocative reports of Dubois de Saligny, arriving in Paris at regular intervals, were producing their intended effect. They told the French government again, and in the most urgent tones, what it had heard so often from its legation in Mexico: the necessity of reorganization of Mexican society for the benefit of French and Mexicans alike; the effortless ease with which this intervention could be brought off; the total impossibility of improvement of French commerce or of the welfare of French subjects in Mexico while anarchy prevailed.

These reports arrived just when the emperor was at last in a position to heed the call. The parvenu ruler of 1852 had by now established his dynasty, had fought two apparently successful wars, had revitalized the entente with England, and had presided over ten years of unprecedented industrial and commercial expansion within France. Not only was he relatively free, but he had good reason to think that the offer of a Mexican crown to Ferdinand Maximilian would help him obtain the Austrian alliance and advance him toward the goals of his Grand Design.

The intervention would likewise be an excellent manifestation of his Saint Simonian economic goal of stimulating European industry through promotion of international trade. Napoleon III did as much to build French commerce as Napoleon I had done to destroy it. The combined value of French imports and exports nearly trebled under the Second Empire. By the early 1850s, for example, Bordeaux commerce was back to the volume of 1786 and it continued to expand at an increasingly rapid rate. In the first ten years of his reign Napoleon III had all but completed the major network of French railroads so that the principal ports were now linked to their domestic sources of supply. In 1851 he had presided over the founding of the government-subventioned Messageries Maritimes, which had become the chief rivals of the British packet ships in carrying mails and passengers. Operating from Bordeaux, they sailed regularly to Brazil and La Plata in 1860 and in 1861 added New York to their schedule.[98] If the regeneration of Mexico was executed as planned, they would sail on a regular basis to Veracruz as well.

The intervention would also permit him to bar the Americans from the Isthmus of Tehuantepec and to proceed eventually with the construction of a canal. Despite the disarray in international banking in 1861 that had caused him to cease his parleys with Radepont, the canal was a project still very much in his mind.[99] When Michel Chevalier was later charged with writing an explanation and defense of the Mexican expedition, he emphasized the canal as a vital component of the *grande pensée*. By intervening in Mexico France would command a position "astride the two oceans, and at the crossroads of world commerce."[100] By opening a trade route across the isthmus, the emperor planned to bring to Europe the rich trade from the Orient and prevent the United States from monopolizing trade with Central America.

By the late summer of 1861 only the trigger or pretext for intervention was lacking. It arrived late in August with the report of Dubois de Saligny announcing the Mexican suspension of payment on foreign debt and the rupture of Franco-Mexican diplomatic relations. Here were the "legitimate grounds," as Napoleon phrased it,[101] needed to justify intervention in the eyes of public opinion and to obtain the collaboration of Great Britain. The independent work of the French minister in Mexico in escalating the modest French claims beyond the possibility of negotiation had played directly into the emperor's hands at precisely the moment when he could exploit it to the fullest. On the orders of the emperor, Thouvenel immediately wrote Dubois de Saligny that "the government of the emperor" fully approved of his conduct and demanded the establishment of European commissioners in Mexican ports to assure regular allocation of customs revenues for payment of foreign debt. Should Mexico refuse, Dubois de Saligny and the British minister could count on the support of the naval forces of the two countries for their demands.[102] As the last statement implied, the emperor already knew that the British government was unwilling to tolerate another, prolonged interruption of payment on their formidable debt. Thus, Juárez's action of 17 July became the launching pad of the negotiations that led to the Tripartite Convention of 31 October among England, France, and Spain, stipulating collective naval action to demand from Mexico protection of their subjects and fulfillment of its financial obligations.

The Tripartite Convention of course made no mention of the establishment of a monarchy in Mexico and even bound the contracting parties "not to exercise in the internal affairs of Mexico any influence of a nature to prejudice the right of the Mexican nation to choose . . . the form of its Government."[103] For England and Spain it was the prelude to another of those sterile episodes of gunboat diplomacy whose only merit lay in their short duration.

For the emperor the convention was the opening wedge for the entry of his princely protégé and the prelude to reorganization of the country. By the time the agreement had been negotiated, he had not only his pretext for action but also his princely candidate. Early in October he learned from Vienna that Archduke Ferdinand Maximilian would not refuse a crown offered by the Mexican "nation," and that, under certain conditions, the Austrian emperor would place no obstacles in the way of his acceptance.[104] With the archduke's conditional acceptance, the last tessera in the broad and intricate mosaic that was the *grande pensée* had fallen into place. Although the emperor was subsequently to hesitate, to twist and turn, even at times to desire an escape from the responsibilities he had incurred, he had now committed himself to the most tragic adventure of his reign.

7

In Retrospect

This [strong and rational] government for the latin races, is it possible except under a monarchy? I think not, and everyone assures me that all honest and sensible people in Mexico think the same.—Thouvenel to Fla-hault, 1861

The stoics affirmed a fatal, unchangeable concatenation of causes, reaching even to the illicit acts of man's will.—*South*

When viewed from the vantage point of the twentieth century, the Napoleonic intervention in Mexico appears to have had a high degree of inevitability in it. As in a Greek drama the protagonists seemed to move ineluctably toward the fateful moment of decision, impelled by forces or events in large part outside their control: the anarchy and civil war in Mexico, the machinations of the *affairistes*, the vicis-situdes of the emperor's European diplomacy, and the outbreak of the Civil War in the United States. When the news of the Mexican suspension of payment on foreign debt reached Paris in September 1861, the elaborate stage was set, the cast assembled. The denoue-ment, i.e., the decision to intervene, never seemed in doubt.

Yet to many contemporaries of the emperor his decision to place an archduke on a Mexican throne was anything but inevitable or predictable. To Karl Marx, writing from the vantage point of a seat in the British Museum, Napoleon's role in the expedition was a simple example of military adventurism. For him the venture origi-nated not in the head of the emperor, but in British financial circles. The London bondholders, British shipowners, and merchants were pulling the strings of their puppet, Palmerston, in the British govern-ment. "It is well known that the original impulse for the expedition to Mexico came from the English Cabinet and not from the Tui-leries," wrote Marx in 1862.[1] Marxist historians continue to write in this vein even in the twentieth century, despite their difficulty in explaining why the emperor went on with the operation after the British withdrew in 1862.[2]

But Marx was correct in perceiving that the emperor's Mexican policy was not a response to imperatives within his own country. Neither the pressures of bankers and merchants nor the public in general had dictated his initiative. He did not consult the French people before launching his expedition and when they did learn of it later, after it had run into difficulties, they were almost unanimous in denouncing it.[3] From time to time in the late 1850s the chambers of commerce of the Atlantic ports had petitioned the emperor to make use of his navy to facilitate their trade and to collect their claims.[4] Yet French exports to Mexico represented such a tiny fraction of French overseas trade in general, and the Mexican "debt" to French subjects, even if Dubois de Saligny's estimates were accepted as valid, was so small, that redress of economic grievances was neither a vital political nor economic necessity for the emperor. They could easily have been disregarded if he had wished, especially given the dismal record of armed intervention in the past.

Napoleon was justifiably proud of the takeoff of the French economy in the 1850s, a decade often referred to by economists as that of France's first industrial revolution. Undeniably the long-range goals of the Mexican intervention were seen by the emperor as lending further stimulation to French commerce and industry. Moveover, the fivefold increase in French exports to Mexico in 1864, when French soldiers occupied much of the country, was evidence of what even the promise of stability could do for French trade.[5] But in 1861 French merchants and industrialists were not clamoring for an armed invasion of Mexico in behalf of their interests. In July 1862 a *procureur général* reporting on public opinion in Bordeaux wrote in a report typical of most, "The Mexican expedition, badly understood in the beginning, has been, I must affirm it, as a matter of principle very unpopular in this area."[6] By 1865 the Bordeaux Chamber of Commerce was bemoaning the prolongation of the enterprise and petitioning the emperor to bring it to an end.[7] Nor were the deputies in the Legislative Body, be they from industrial or commercial constituencies, arguing for intervention. One may search in vain in the *Archives parlementaires* of 1861 (the first year under the Second Empire in which the proceedings were published) for any mention at all of French interests in Mexico. Only later, after the British and Spanish withdrawals and after the humiliating check of the French army before Puebla did the intervention become a subject of debate in the lower house; and then the government was hard pressed to justify its action in sending a French army into the interior.[8]

Nonetheless, although the emperor was later to repent his decision, there was a good deal of logic behind it. None of his nineteenth-century predecessors had achieved a successful Mexican policy. The Bourbons had dealt patronizingly and insultingly with the Mexican republic and might well have tried to install a monarchy in Mexico had they possessed the means and had they overcome the opposition of Great Britain. Charles X was on the verge of war with Mexico when he lost his throne. Orleanist "policy," which alternated between cross-grained indifference and mean vituperation, deteriorated into gunboat diplomacy in 1838. After the fiasco of the "Pastry War," the king had just sense enough to avoid further entanglement; but his ill humor and the fantastic diplomats he permitted to represent him badly served French subjects and commerce and deepened Mexican distrust of French intentions.

The experience of decades had shown that French interests in Mexico could not thrive in a republic constantly afflicted by civil disorder. The claims arising out of commerce were a chronic source of friction. France had been unable to negotiate a treaty guaranteeing her subjects either freedom from forced loans or the right to engage in retail trade. Although by the 1850s the French had long ago given up on a treaty, and although Mexico had in general ceased harassment of foreigners by prohibitions of retail trade, conditions for the conduct of the kinds of enterprises carried on by the French colony of urban little men were never worse. The emperor understood the futility of gunboat diplomacy. It exacerbated Mexico's ills and increased the likelihood of future forced loans or other impositions on foreign capital. These in turn generated fresh claims, evasions, debt suspensions, and ultimata. Even Gabriac had a moment of true insight when he reported in 1856 that "the pressure of the great powers on their [Mexican] finances is one of the principal causes of their [Mexican] demoralization and anarchy."[9] And Mexican "demoralization and anarchy" lay precisely at the roots of the difficulties of the French community of merchants and craftsmen.

Consequently, although the grievances of the French in Mexico did not of themselves suffice to trigger the invasion and monarchical experiment, they were an essential ingredient in the decision to intervene. French subjects not only supplied the emperor with the

immediate, albeit ostensible, reason for action but also, by their decades of troubles, underscored and dramatized Mexico's need for
social reorganization. Dubois de Saligny was only the last of a long
line of diplomats to argue for the introduction of European civilization as the only hope of salvation. Others before him had almost
invariably arrived at the same conclusion.

It was only after the failure of Maximilian to establish his empire
and the ignominious retreat of the French army at the virtual dictation of the government of the United States that the public, politicians, and, subsequently, historians began to upbraid the emperor for
what they called his folly. Whether they believed his motives to have
been quixotic or meanly avaricious, his critics have blamed his ignorance as the basic cause of the tragedy. Instead of informing himself
accurately on the true conditions in Mexico, the familiar argument
runs, he allowed himself to be hoodwinked by a handful of self-
serving émigrés and deluded by the clerical enthusiasms of his wife.
"Without a shred of evidence," wrote a prominent British historian
of the Second Empire, he persuaded himself of the existence of a
strong monarchist movement that would welcome a prince as libera-
tor.[10] "He was badly informed because he did nothing to inform
himself well," concluded the foremost French authority on the origins of the expedition.[11] Hence he failed to recognize what now
seems self-evident: that a foreign monarchy could not have taken
root on the American continent and that the experiment must inevitably have led to disaster.

Such views misjudge totally the climate of opinion in which the
emperor lived. As a nineteenth-century statesman, he could not be
expected to have seen anything inherently unworkable in the imposition of a prince of one nationality on a people of another. Who better
than his Hapsburg protégé could have been expected to face such a
contingency with equanimity? Transfers of princes from throne to
throne and country to country were a commonplace in Europe in the
first half of the century. The settlement of 1815, which had ignored
national sentiment, was holding up remarkably well, all things considered. The decades following it had seen numerous interventions
by the powers either in defense of beleaguered monarchs or in expeditions to implant a ruler of their choice in a troubled area. The
examples of Greece in the 1820s and Belgium in 1830 come immediately to mind. In Brazil, when Napoleon III began his reign, a Bra-
ganza seemed securely seated on his throne.

The point is perhaps so obvious that it has been overlooked: nationalism had not yet developed into the potent force that it was soon
to become, and what force it had achieved was not yet fully recognized. In the case of Mexico this oversight is the more understand-
able, since one of the standard comments by British and French
diplomats was the deplorable absence of any sense of national identity or patriotism in Mexico that would enable the country to defend
itself against a foreign aggressor. Mexican factionalism in the face of
the French bombardment of 1838–39 and the successive encroachments of the United States seemed to prove the correctness of their
evaluation.

It was not only French diplomats in Mexico who urged a monarchical solution. British and Spanish representatives blamed what they
regarded as Mexican ineptitude and weakness as the source of the
country's problems. From there it was but a short step to recommendation of monarchy as a cure. "A Foreign Intervention or even
Conquest would be a matter of very easy accomplishment, the great
Body of the Nation including almost all the wealthy classes, are
favorably inclined to such a change," wrote the British minister in
1858.[12] Of the seven British ministers and chargés d'affaires in Mexico
between 1830 and 1861 only one, George B. Mathew, a chargé d'affaires of brief tenure, had any tolerance whatsoever for the men who
governed Mexico.[13]

The loose, pseudosociological jargon on the deficiencies of the
Mexican "race" and its incompatibility with republican institutions
used by the diplomats was likewise present in contemporary published works dealing with Mexico. Many books were written by
European adventurers, scholars, and colonists who flocked to Mexico
in the first half of the century. French travel literature was the most
abundant of all, since the French colony in Mexico outnumbered the
residents of any other European country except Spain. At least
twenty-five travel accounts were published either by French subjects
or in the French language between 1830 and 1860.[14] Being a popular
literary form at the time, these books found a wide audience in the
literate public, and even the least meritorious of them often ran to
second and third editions.

Looked at superficially, these books would appear to have had
little in common. Their authors were men of letters, scientists, merchants, adventurers, diplomats, and many others. J. C. Beltrami, for
example, was an Italian who had been a civil servant in Napoleon I's

Kingdom of Italy; he was also an incurable romantic and inveterate roamer.[15] Mathieu de Fossey had been a colonist in Tehuantepec in 1829 and had been one of the few to stay on in Mexico, where he prospered mildly for the next twenty-five years.[16] His book was almost encyclopedic in nature and used as a reference work by European diplomats and prospective settlers in Mexico. Eugène Duflot de Mofras had been a young attaché in the French legation in Mexico with a mission from the Orleanist government to explore the West Coast of America as far north as the Russian settlements. His resulting book was published by official order.[17] Yet despite the heterogeneity of these writers, many of their reactions to the Mexican scene were remarkably similar, and their reflections and observations were often repetitive. Certain themes are easily recognized: the inexhaustible natural wealth of Mexico as contrasted with the poverty of its people, the continuous political instability of the country, the peril posed to Mexico by the "Anglo-American race" to the north, and the inability of the Mexicans to solve their own problems. Almost inevitably, the authors recommended European aid as a solution and, especially after the Mexican loss of Texas, New Mexico, Arizona, and California, they called specifically for French intervention in behalf of a European prince.[18]

These books were only saying what the French and other European representatives in Mexico had been saying for years in stronger and more specific language. And the emperor had heard the same arguments from a host of respected Mexicans as well. Small wonder that he did not doubt the feasibility of his *grande pensée*. In sponsoring a European prince in 1861 he was taking an action that had long been urgently recommended by intelligent, highly placed, and experienced men on both sides of the Atlantic. Thouvenel, although European-oriented and of pragmatic disposition, was completely indoctrinated into this line of thinking. "This [strong and rational] government for the latin races, is it possible except under a monarchy?" he questioned rhetorically in a private letter to the French ambassador in London, Count Auguste Flahault, in 1861. "I think not," he answered his own question, "and everyone assures me that all honest and sensible people in Mexico think the same."[19]

The loose rhetoric of race that pervaded European thinking and writing on Mexico inevitably left its mark on French policy and underscored the need for intervention. For some, the widely accepted inferiority of the Mexicans could be attributed to deficiencies in their "blood," i.e., to their anatomical or physiological inheritance. For others the "racial" deficiency derived from a regrettable Spanish legacy compounded by geographical isolation. In either case the cure lay in the infusion of European peoples and civilization.

Still another racial hypothesis making the rounds was the belief (accepted, for example, unquestionably by Thouvenel) in the existence of a select fraternity of *races latines*, of which both France and Mexico were members. Bound by ties primarily of religion (Roman Catholic) and secondarily of language (romance), the latin races allegedly responded to the same stimuli and required the same governance.[20] Under the influence of this afflatus the French could be more confident than ever that the introduction of a European monarchy was the correct solution to Mexico's problems. If even the enlightened and civilized latin nations of Europe (of which France was the leader) were in need of the stabilizing influence of a throne, how could the Mexicans, childlike and ignorant, hope to survive without its discipline? By mid-century the monarchist thesis had become a truism to be repeated, not a hypothesis to be tested. Without fear of controversion, the *Annuaire des deux mondes*, a compendium of informed French thinking, could assert in 1850, "Luxury-loving and disorderly . . . the Mexican is neither by taste nor habit adapted to republican austerity. Under the stable government of a monarchy . . . Mexico could have avoided ten revolutions that have impoverished, devastated, and dismembered it."[21]

How thoroughly the emperor had absorbed the monarchist thesis may be seen in his instructions, also addressed to his ambassador in London, intended for the edification of Lord Palmerston and written in October 1861 just as he made the decision to take action. In it he explained his motives for intervention and directed the ambassador to convey them to the prime minister. His arguments in favor of a monarchy read like a précis of the documents and literature, published and unpublished, on Mexico of the previous decades. He noted the "anarchy" and "approaching ruin" in Mexico, the need for an "insurmountable barrier to the encroachments of North America," the advantages offered by Mexico to European commerce, and the desire of "important persons" in Mexico for a monarchy. All this convinced him of the need for a "stable government" in "one of the finest countries of the world." Consequently, he concluded, redress of grievance would be merely the ostensible purpose of the intervention; for he would be less than honest, he confessed, knowing the

Mexicans and the state of their affairs, to engage himself not to support a change in government that he desired with all his heart, "because it is in the interest of civilization in general." [22]

Implicit in the monarchist thesis were the convictions that a nation's character determined the type of government it must have and that a nation's vices or virtues had their roots more in heredity than in environment or in historical past. The French, of course, were not alone in holding such beliefs. The historian George M. Fredrickson, for example, has found the same type of prejudgments in the debate then taking place in the New World on the character of the Blacks and their destined place on the American continent. His conclusion was that by mid-century "democracy itself was beginning to be defined as racial in origin and thus realizable perhaps only by people with certain hereditary traits." [23]

The belief that Mexico was ungovernable except by monarchy can thus be seen as racist at bottom. The *grande pensée* was to a large degree a plan of action to realize the destinies of *les races latines*. [24] It was neither the first nor the last ideology to promote adventurism overseas. Hannah Arendt has said in *The Origins of Totalitarianism*, "The fact that racism is the main ideological weapon of imperialistic politics is so obvious that it seems as though many students prefer to avoid the beaten path of truism." [25] In the hands of the emperor that weapon was used to persuade him of the beneficence and the nobility of his plan to place a European prince on a Mexican throne. And for a visionary and well-intentioned ruler like Napoleon III, such an ideology was the prerequisite for action.

But ideology was not the only reason for the general acceptance of the monarchist thesis. The continuous political turbulence in the Latin American republics appeared as prima facie evidence of its truth. In any case, it might be argued that monarchy never had a real test in Mexico. Maximilian proved a severe disappointment to the supporters of monarchy, both French and Mexican, who were usually political reactionaries. As emperor he tried (in vain) to attract the support of the liberals and very soon alienated the church, on which the reactionaries relied for support. His policies were completely at variance with the principles formerly enunciated in monarchist newspapers such as *El Tiempo* and by earlier reactionaries such as Lucas Alamán. [26] Those who had worked for his reign felt a bitter sense of betrayal at his liberal course. In his council of state in 1864 only one of its members, Teodosio Lares, was of the reactionary monarchist party. He would have nothing to do with the ultraconservative Gutiérrez de Estrada and, after tolerating Hidalgo as his minister in Paris for a time owing to his popularity with Eugénie, he dismissed him from his post when he realized how badly his ideas were being represented at the French court.[27]

For that matter it could also be argued that the empire of Maximilian was fatally compromised before the archduke stepped ashore by the personalities and misdeeds of the French ministers plenipotentiary. For decades they had tarnished the image of France by their arrogance. Too often chosen for reasons that had nothing to do with their qualifications, they were the products of a system in which special interest and patronage frequently weighed more heavily than merit. Ironically, the two worst of a poor lot were the representatives of Louis Napoleon, despite his good beginning and good will. The partisan conduct of Gabriac identified the legation with the forces of reaction. With Dubois de Saligny came the stench of *affairisme*. The French emperor belatedly recognized the man for what he was and brought him home in disgrace in 1863. But the foul odor of his corruption remained to permeate the empire of Maximilian and to insure his isolation. Since that time historians writing of the French intervention have often tended to see no farther than Dubois de Saligny and the Jecker bonds and have in consequence written off the entire *grande pensée* as little more than a sordid financial scheme.

But at the onset of intervention and during its early stages rare was the voice raised in protest. In the French government Thouvenel cooperated readily with his master. Walewski had overcome his earlier reluctance and even facilitated the private negotiations that led to the archduke's acceptance.[28] Although the British government was unwilling to involve itself in an invasion of Mexico, both Palmerston and Sir Charles Wyke, British minister in Mexico in 1861, believed that monarchy was the correct solution for the country.[29] Leopold, the Coburg King of the Belgians, although cautious as usual, did not discourage his son-in-law from considering the Mexican throne when his advice was asked. Mexico was best suited for a monarchy, he wrote, and "the elements of political unity exist."[30] In the Austrian government, Rechberg was of course concerned lest the archduke's acceptance lead to a French demand for a quid quo pro; but he could not deny that the prince's elevation would lend "a new distinction" to the Hapsburgs.[31] Metternich, in Paris, was skeptical from the first. However, exposed daily to the empress's naive plans for disposing of excess royalty in the New World—especially Carlists—he tended to regard the venture as an example of female foolishness.[32] This view has persisted. The empress's strong advocacy of the venture, her abysmal ignorance of Latin America, whose people she thought were the same as "the Spanish race,"[33] combined to accentuate the later belief that monarchy had been romantic nonsense from the outset.

In 1861 and 1862, when an occasional objector spoke out, he could usually be written off as acting out of self-interest or spite. The most serious early protest came from Marshal Prim, commander of the Spanish expeditionary force in Mexico, who wrote the emperor an earnest and, as it turned out, uncannily prophetic letter warning of the absence of a large monarchical party in Mexico.[34] Yet since Prim was widely believed to have aspired himself to the throne of Mexico, his arguments could be disregarded.

The emperor may certainly be excused for believing in the reality of the threat posed to Mexico by the United States. If any truth were held self-evident in European foreign ministries in the mid-nineteenth century it was that Mexico, if left without succor, would disappear entirely from the map. An unnatural gift of prophecy would have been required for the emperor to foresee how the struggle between the North and South over the question of slavery would halt the expansionist movement of the United States on its southern borders.

Why then, it may fairly be asked, did the emperor persist in his plans after his army encountered unexpected resistance and after popular support for a monarchy failed to materialize? The explanation is too complicated to be given fully here, but it is not to be found in a refusal to face reality. During the spring and summer of 1863 the emperor came very close to throwing up the game.[35] But escape was by no means easy. His soldiers, his flag, the honor of France had been engaged. "I realize that I have gotten myself into a tight corner," he told Wyke, "but the affair has to be liquidated."[36] When he decided to continue, his reasons were very different from those that had prompted his initiative in 1861. By 1864 his plan was to terminate French sacrifices of men and money and to foist off on the archduke the burdens of the crown that he had created. By requiring Mexico to pay France an indemnity and to bear all expenses of the occupying troops, he could recoup his losses. Nor had he forgotten the reputedly inexhaustible mineral wealth of Mexico; his plan was to force Maximilian to concede to France the product of the mines of Sonora.[37] By then he was less interested in the future of the Mexican throne than he was in his own, which had been shaken in France by public hostility to the venture and in Europe by the rejection by Austria of his proposed alliance in 1863. Offended by the Austrian rebuff and disappointed in his failure to turn the Mexican expedition to the advantage of his European diplomacy, he offered Maximilian no more than a military occupation of three years—the minimal support to induce him to accept the crown and to depart.[38] He neither guaranteed the territorial integrity of the Mexican empire nor promised to defend it against the United States. As the prospects of the French emperor had deteriorated in both Europe and Mexico, the archduke, persisting in his ambition, became the victim.

If the French emperor as head of state must still be held accountable for the catastrophe, he cannot be held to have been more gullible and less informed than the men around him. It was not that he did not seek information; rather, the information he received led him farther down the dangerous path. The French intervention in Mexico was not a sudden inspiration, nor was it a harebrained scheme. It was not even an aberration in French thinking about Mexico. Rather, it was the logical outgrowth of the French experience in Mexico over a period of decades. Its implementation had been urged upon him and his predecessors for years. But whereas others had talked, he would act. His intelligence and character combined in just the right degrees those qualities that made the experiment irresistible to him: a generous dash of humanitarian liberalism, a faith in a strong government to perform wonders, and a family penchant for enterprises of great risk. His intention was good; the result was disaster. But in the atmosphere breathed by the emperor, everyone knew, or thought he knew, that a monarchy was a necessity for *les races latines*. He and his contemporaries had fallen victims to the conventional wisdom and unexamined sociological truisms of the day.

As a phenomenon in modern French history the Napoleonic intervention in Mexico was unique. Earlier in the nineteenth century, when the Bourbons desired a monarchical solution in Mexico, France was too weak and too precariously situated vis-à-vis Europe to embark on such an expedition. By the end of the century, the emergence of the United States as a power of the first rank and the consolidation of the Mexican republic spelled an end to European interference in the internal affairs of a North American nation. Napoleon III appeared on the scene at a time of transition in which, for a few brief years, it seemed still possible for France to extend her system to the Western Hemisphere. The Frenchman's confidence in the cultural and material superiority of the Old World over the New was as yet unshaken. His faith in the institution of monarchy was still strong. When the Civil War broke out in the United States contemporaries very naturally believed that republicanism was doomed to destruction. They could as yet not see that the great age of Europe was approaching its end and that the traditional hierarchies were eroding. With the advent of universal suffrage and industrial capitalism, leadership of the Western world passed to the American giant. The new era relegated the *grande pensée* to the dustbin of history. In the Archduke Ferdinand Maximilian, Mexico saw the last of the *conquistadores*.

Appendix

French Exports, 1827–1864
(Commerce spécial expressed in millions of francs [a])

Year	To all Countries	To Mexico	Year	To all Countries	To Mexico
1825		14.1	1845	848	10.3
1826		12.0	1846	852	8.3
1827	507	13.6	1847	720	2.5
1828	511	7.8	1848	690	10.8
1829	504	7.7	1849	938	18.5
1830	453	18.3	1850	1,068	16.0
1831	484	16.9	1851	1,158	18.5
1832	507	9.7	1852	1,257	14.9
1833	559	11.4	1853	1,542	15.9
1834	510	9.0	1854	1,414	18.2
1835	577	13.0	1855	1,558	17.1
1836	629	7.5	1856	1,893	19.5
1837	514	8.2	1857	1,866	17.8
1838	659	6.5	1858	1,887	11.3
1839	677	9.2	1859	2,266	12.9
1840	695	10.4	1860	2,277	12.3
1841	761	10.0	1861	1,926	13.5
1842	644	8.5	1862	2,243	16.1
1843	687	9.4	1863	2,643	16.4
1844	790	12.0	1864	2,924	57.3

[a]Commerce spécial refers to products originating within France, either from her soil or her industries. From Statistique de la France: commerce extérieur (Paris, 1838); Tableau décennal du commerce de la France, 1827 à 1836; Tableau général du commerce, published annually 1837 to 1847; Annales du commerce. . . . Faits commerciaux, nos. 46 à 59.

Abbreviations Used in the Notes and Bibliography

AEM	Archivos de la Embaja Mexicana
AHDM	*Archivo Histórico Diplomático Mexicano*
AHSRE	Archivo Histórico de la Secretaría de las Relaciones Exteriores
AMAE	Archives du Ministère des Affaires Étrangères
CC	Correspondance Commerciale in AMAE
CP	Correspondance Politique in AMAE
HHSA	Haus-, Hof-, und Staatsarchiv
HKM	Hausarchiv Kaiser Maximilians von Mexico
L.	Legajo in AEM
MD	Mémoires et Documents in AMAE
PRO:FO	Public Record Office, Foreign Office
RDHM	*Relaciones Diplomáticas Hispano-Mexicanas*
RFM	*Relaciones Franco-Mexicanas*, edited by Luis Weckmann
RP	Radepont Papers

Notes

Notes to Chapter 1

1. Alexandre Jehan Henri de Clercq, ed., *Recueil des traités de la France*, 1:81–88.
2. Etienne Pasquier to Augustin Lagarde, Paris, 6 Nov. 1821, AMAE,CP:Espagne, vol. 714, cited in William Spence Robertson, *France and Latin-American Independence*, p. 201.
3. Louis Desgraves and Georges Dupeux, *Bordeaux au XIXe siècle*, p. 47; see also Camille Jullian, *Histoire de Bordeaux depuis les origines jusqu'en 1895*, p. 717.
4. Camacho to Villèle, Paris, Apr. 1827, AEM, L.VII, *RFM*, 1:131–32, no. 2081.
5. Robertson, *France and Latin-American Independence*, pp. 202–14.
6. Harold Temperley, "French Designs on Spanish America in 1820–1825," p. 35.
7. Polignac to Chateaubriand, London, 12 Dec. 1823, AMAE,CP:Angleterre, vol. 617, unnumbered.
8. Guillaume de Bertier de Sauvigny, *The Bourbon Restoration*, pp. 57–59.
9. Jean-Baptiste Guillaume Joseph, Comte de Villèle, *Mémoires et correspondance du Comte de Villèle*, 4:188–201.
10. Ibid., pp. 239–40.
11. François Auguste René, Vicomte de Chateaubriand, *Voyages en Amérique, en Italie, au Mont-Blanc*, 6:220.
12. Ibid., p. 221.
13. This statement, drawn up by Canning and signed by Polignac, is known as the Polignac Memorandum. See AMAE,MD:Amérique, vol. 35. For a discussion of the effect of British opposition, see Temperley, "French Designs on Spanish America," pp. 41–53.
14. Chateaubriand, *Voyages en Amérique*, 6:221.
15. Carlos E. Muñoz Oraá, "Pronóstico de la independencia de América, y un proyecto de monarquías en 1781," pp. 439–73.
16. Egon Caesar, Count Corti, *Maximilian and Charlotte of Mexico*, 1:14.
17. For a summary of French official attitudes toward Mexico in this period, see "Mémorandum sur les révolutions du Mexique," AMAE,CP:Mexique, vol. 1.
18. Chateaubriand, *Voyages en Amérique*, 6:214.
19. See, among many examples, Talaru to Chateaubriand, 17 Aug. 1823, AMAE, CP:Espagne, vol. 723.
20. Corti, *Maximilian and Charlotte*, 1:14.
21. Chateaubriand to Talaru, Paris, 31 Mar. 1824, AMAE,CP:Espagne, vol. 724, cited in Robertson, *France and Latin-American Independence*, p. 288.
22. Robertson, *France and Latin-American Independence*, p. 255.
23. Murphy, Sr., to Rocafuerte, Bagnères de Bigorre, 14 Aug. 1825, AEM, L.II, *RFM*, 1:56–57, no. 461. Murphy referred to the decision of 1822.

24. "Instructions données aux personnes envoyées au Mexique," 17 Dec. 1823, AMAE,CP:Mexique, vol. 2. Samouel was the agent selected for Mexico (Samouel to Donzelot, 15 Sept. 1824, copy, ibid., unnumbered).

25. See Camacho to Duperré, Mexico, 11 May 1826, AEM, L.II, *RFM*, 1:51, no. 355. Camacho reviews Murphy's reception in Camacho to Murphy, Sr., Mexico, 13 May 1826, ibid., 1:47, no. 311.

26. Murphy, Sr., to Rocafuerte, Paris, 3 and 4 Sept. 1825, ibid., 1:46, nos. 292, 293; DeLaunay to Murphy, Havre, 15 Sept. 1826, ibid., 1:59, no. 486; Murphy to Rocafuerte, Bordeaux, 26 Sept. 1826, ibid., 1:60, no. 492. The original reports of Rocafuerte and copies of Murphy's reports may be found in AHSRE, Francia, Relaciones con México, 2-5-2635, 1825–26.

27. Late in 1825 Martin was designated as agent in Mexico under the authority of the French minister of the navy (Murphy, Sr., to Rocafuerte, Paris, 26 Dec. 1825, AEM, L.II, *RFM*, 1:50, no. 350). In 1826 he received his title of "Inspector" and was made subordinate to the Foreign Ministry (Murphy, Sr., to Mexican foreign minister, Paris, 23 Oct. 1826, ibid., 1:51, no. 357; dossier personnel of Alexandre Victor Martin, AMAE).

28. Murphy, Sr., to Rocafuerte, Paris, 9 Jan. 1826, ibid., 1:60, no. 510; "Report on Mexico by M. Cuvillier, capitaine de vaisseau, commander of French naval station in Havana," 1826, AMAE,MD:Mexique, vol. 40.

29. *Le Constitutionnel*, 30 Jan. 1825. See table of French exports, 1826–64, p. 193. For the years before 1826 one must rely on estimates made by Mexican officials. Sebastian Camacho, Mexican foreign minister, asserted that 49 French merchant ships came to Mexico during 1826. Other French merchandise entered Mexico in that year via merchant ships of the United States (Camacho to Villèle, Paris, Apr. 1827, AEM, L.VII, *RFM*, 1:131–32, no. 2081). For volume of trade with Mexico from the major French ports of Bordeaux, Marseilles, Nantes, and Le Havre, see ibid., 1, passim, for the reports of Mexican agents in those ports.

30. *Statistique de la France: Commerce extérieur*, 6:147.

31. Murphy, Sr., to Rocafuerte, draft, Paris, 20 June 1826, AEM, L.I, *RFM*, 1:25–26, no. 60.

32. Desgraves and Dupeux, *Bordeaux au XIXe siècle*, p. 47.

33. Martin to Damas, Mexico, 25 Dec. 1827, AMAE,CC:Mexico, vol. 1, no. 9, ff. 247–48; same to same, 30 Nov. 1827, AMAE,CP:Mexique, vol. 3, no. 24.

34. Desgraves and Dupeux, *Bordeaux au XIXe siècle*, pp. 38–39, 51; Bertier de Sauvigny, *The Bourbon Restoration*, pp. 24–26; *Nouvelle biographie générale depuis les temps les plus reculés jusqu'à nos jours*, 18:914.

35. Murphy, Sr., to Mexican Foreign Ministry, Paris, 23 Oct. 1826, AEM, L.II, *RFM*, 1:51, no. 357; Murphy to Rocafuerte, 23 Oct. 1826, AHSRE, Francia, Relaciones con México, 2-5-2635, 1825–26.

36. Rocafuerte to Murphy, London, 19 Oct. 1825, AEM, L.II, *RFM*, 1:47, no. 303; Rocafuerte to Mexican Foreign Ministry, London, 11 Apr. 1826, no. 61, AHSRE, Francia, Relaciones con México, 2-5-2635, 1825–26.

37. Camacho to Espinosa de los Monteros, London, 20 Dec. 1826, AEM, L.V, *RFM*, 1:102, no. 1439.

38. Camacho to Villèle, Paris, Apr. 1827, ibid., L.VII, *RFM*, 1:131–32, no. 2081.

39. "Extracto de la conferencia privada habida con el Sor. Conde de Villèle en la noche del 4 de Mayo de 1827," draft, ibid., 1:132, no. 2082. For Damas's reaction to Camacho's proposed treaty, see Damas to Camacho, Paris, draft, 8 May 1827, AMAE,CC:Mexico, vol. 1, ff. 193–204.

40. "Declaraciones cambiadas en París, el 8 de Mayo de 1827, entre el Señor Baron de Damas, . . . y el Señor Camacho . . . ," *Tratados y convenciones celebrados y no ratificados por la República Mexicana*, in *Derecho Internacional Mexicano*, Pt. 2, pp. 254–67. The terms are summarized in *RFM*, 1:138, notes.

41. Murphy, Sr., to Mexican Foreign Ministry, Paris, 10 May 1827, AEM, L.VII, *RFM*, 1:133, no. 2093.

42. Damas to Martin, Paris, 1 Dec. 1827, AMAE,CP:Mexique, vol. 3, no. 1, ff. 140–45.

43. J. Houdaille, "Les Français au Mexique et leur influence politique et sociale (1760–1800)," pp. 144–45.

44. Ibid., p. 196.

45. Martin to Damas, Mexico, 28 Mar. 1828, AMAE,CP:Mexique, vol. 3, no. 6. See also Abel Chatelain, "Les Migrations françaises vers le Nouveau Monde aux XIXe et XXe siècles," p. 55. For the early French movement into Spain, see Olwen H. Hufton, *The Poor of Eighteenth-Century France 1750–1789*, pp. 87–90, 105–6.

46. Houdaille, "Les Français au Mexique," pp. 198–233. For an impressionistic account of some of these early French in Mexico, see Auguste Génin, *Les Français au Mexique du XVIe siècle à nos jours*, passim. Génin, a Frenchman established in Mexico in the twentieth century, has undertaken no archival research and can cite only isolated examples.

47. Martin to Damas, Mexico, 15 Mar. 1827, AMAE,CP:Mexique, vol. 3, no. 8.

48. The history of French emigration to foreign lands is very imperfectly known. Except for a few countries such as England or the United States, reliable statistics are almost impossible to compile. See Michel Huber, Henri Bunle, and Fernand Boverat, *La Population de la France*, pp. 285–86; and Louis Chevalier, "L'Emigration française au XIXe siècle," p. 127.

49. Martin to Damas, Mexico, 30 Nov. 1827, AMAE,CC:Mexico, vol. 1, no. 14, ff. 231–32; Circular of Murphy, Sr., to all agents, Paris, 27 Apr. 1827, AEM, L.VI, *RFM*, 1:114, no. 1713; Murphy to Jacques Galos, commercial agent in Bordeaux, Paris, 30 Jan. 1827, AHSRE, Francia, Expediente H/112.4 (44-0), 1826–31.

50. Cochelet to French foreign minister, Mexico, 18 Feb. 1832, AMAE, CP:Mexique, vol. 7, no. 10. This figure represents a sharp increase over the 102 French subjects that Houdaille established were living in Mexico around 1810 (Houdaille, "Les Français au Mexique," p. 233).

51. At least five and perhaps six ships loaded with passengers sailed from Le Havre to Coatzacoalcos during these years. The figures 500 to 600 are a conservative estimate based on reports by Félix Carrère, vice-consul in Veracruz (Carrère to French foreign minister, Veracruz, 30 Jan. 1831, AMAE,CC:Veracruz, vol. 1, ff. 33–41; same to same, 1 Mar. 1831, ibid.; same to same, 7 Apr. 1831, ibid., no. 39, ff. 85–91). Giordan, on the other hand, maintained that there were 700 colonists in the first three ships alone (F. Giordan to M. Gaullieuse Hardy, copy, no date, but probably Feb. 1831, ibid., ff. 30–31). In the autumn of 1831 the French government dispatched a ship that repatriated 73 of the colonists (Carrère to Molé, Veracruz, 7 Oct. 1831, ibid., no. 53, ff. 171–72).

52. Martin to La Ferronnays, Mexico, 26 Apr. 1828, AMAE,CP:Mexique, vol. 3, no. 9.

53. Cochelet to French foreign minister, Mexico, 15 Oct. 1829, AMAE,CC: Mexico, vol. 2, no. 17, ff. 454–58.

54. Same to same, 29 Mar. 1831, ibid., vol. 8, no. 8, ff. 242–44; same to same, 6 Feb. 1832, ibid., no. 2, ff. 179–87.

55. Mathieu de Fossey, *Le Mexique*, pp. 15–23, 55–57; M. A. Brissot, *Voyage au Goazacoalcos* [sic], *aux Antilles, et aux Etats-Unis*, p. 16; Laisné de Villevêque to French foreign minister, 25 Mar. 1831, AMAE,CC:Veracruz, vol. 1, ff. 81–84; see also Laisné de Villevêque to Molé, Paris, Chambre des Députés, Questure, 23 Oct. 1830, ibid., ff. 166–68.

56. Bertier de Sauvigny, *Bourbon Restoration*, pp. 238–67. See André Armengaud, *La Population française au XIXe siècle*, pp. 86–93, for general trends in French emigration in this period.

57. Cochelet to French foreign minister, Mexico, 22 Jan. 1832, AMAE,CP:Mexique, vol. 7, no. 6; same to same, 7 Feb. 1832, ibid., no. 9; Lucas Alamán, *Historia de Méjico desde los primeros movimientos que prepararon su independencia en el año de 1808, hasta la época presente*, 4:607.

58. Alleye de Cyprey to Guizot, Mexico, 12 July 1845, AMAE,CP:Mexique, vol. 32, unnumbered, ff. 77–79; *RDHM*, 2:342n.

59. J. C. Beltrami, *Le Mexique*; see, for example, 1:ix–xiii, an essay entitled "Aux Mexicains."

60. Martin to La Ferronnays, Mexico, 6 Oct. 1828, AMAE,CP:Mexique, vol. 3, no. 29. Giordan claimed he left France owing to the persecution of the Bourbon government (F. Giordan to M. Gaullieuse Hardy, copy, no date, but probably Feb. 1831, AMAE,CC:Veracruz, vol. 1, ff. 30–31).

61. Martin to Damas, Mexico, 10 Apr. 1828, AMAE,CP:Mexique, vol. 3, no. 7.

62. Houdaille, "Les Français au Mexique," pp. 157–59.

63. David M. Pletcher, *The Diplomacy of Annexation*, pp. 44–47.

64. French foreign minister to Gros, Paris, 6 Oct. 1831, AMAE,MD:Amérique, vol. 41, ff. 214–51; Cochelet to La Ferronnays, Mexico, 30 May 1829, AMAE,CP: Mexique, vol. 4, no. 5. By mid-century some 82 percent of the French population were either skilled craftsmen or traders. See *Registre de la Population Française au Mexique*, drawn up by André Levasseur, French minister in Mexico, 30 Apr. 1849, AMAE,MD:Mexique, vol. 7. Génin, *Les Français au Mexique*, pp. 353–444, gives many case histories. He greatly exaggerates the importance of the emigration from Barcelonnette. For activity of the French in New Mexico, see Robert Ryal Miller, trans. and ed., "New Mexico in Mid-Eighteenth Century," pp. 168, 173. See also Jean Meyer , "Les Français au Mexique au XIXe siècle," pp. 58–59; and F. Arnaud, *Les Barcelonnettes au Mexique*, passim.

65. Murphy, Jr., to Mexican Foreign Ministry, Paris, 22 Aug. 1828, AEM, L.IX, *RFM*, 1:162, no. 2736; same to same, 23 Nov. ibid., L.II, *RFM*, 1:52, no. 362.

66. Martin to La Ferronnays, Mexico, 30 Oct. 1828, AMAE,CP:Mexique, vol. 3, no. 31; French foreign minister to Martin, Paris, 28 June 1828, ibid., unnumbered; dossier personnel of Alexandre Victor Martin, AMAE. Cochelet to French Foreign Ministry, Mexico, 13 July 1829, AMAE,CP:Mexique, vol. 4, no. 9; dossier personnel of Adrien Cochelet, AMAE; M. A. Laisné de Villevêque to his father, extract, Mexico, 19 Aug. 1829, AMAE,CP:Mexique, vol. 4, ff. 185–89.

67. French foreign minister to Martin, Paris, 12 Apr. 1827, AMAE,CC:Mexico, vol. 1, ff. 185–87; Cochelet to La Ferronnays, Mexico, 25 July 1829, AMAE,CP: Mexique, vol. 4, no. 15; "Mémorandum," Oct. 1829, ibid. (this is a position paper of the Foreign Ministry that reviews the situation of the French consuls in Mexico and French relations with Mexico); Cochelet to French Foreign Ministry, Mexico, 5 Nov. 1830, AMAE,CC:Mexico, vol. 3, no. 36, ff. 190–92.

68. Minister of navy to Rayneval, minister of foreign affairs, Paris, 23 Sept. 1828, AMAE,CP:Mexique, vol. 3; Martin to La Ferronnays, Mexico, 26 Sept. 1828, ibid., no. 25; Foreign Ministry to Martin, Paris, 11 Dec. 1828, ibid., no. 7; Martin to La

Ferronnays, Mexico, 13 Jan. 1829, ibid., vol. 4, no. 5; minister of navy to minister of foreign affairs, Paris, 20 Aug. 1829, ibid., unnumbered; Cochelet to French foreign minister, Mexico, 11 Nov. 1829, ibid., no. 41; same to same, 27 Jan. 1830, ibid., vol. 5, no. 8; same to same, 20 Feb. 1830, ibid., no. 15; same to same, 28 June 1830, ibid., no. 50.

69. Minister of finances to foreign minister, Paris, 22 Jan. 1829, AMAE,CC: Paquebots, no number; "Instruction sur le service des paquebots, remises à M. Cochelet, 11 février 1829, signé par M. le Cte de Portales [foreign minister par interim]," ibid.

70. "Observations sur Tableau du service de paquebots," no date, Cochelet to Foreign Ministry, Mexico, 18 Aug. 1829, ibid.

71. Balguerie and Co. to French foreign minister, Bordeaux, 20 July 1830, ibid.

72. Martin to La Ferronnays, Mexico, Chancellerie, 30 June 1828, AMAE,CC: Mexico, vol. 1, ff. 311–12.

73. Foreign Ministry to Carrère, Paris, 15 Feb. 1830, draft, AMAE,CC:Paquebots.

74. Complaints of Mexican fear or hatred of foreigners were legion. See, for example, Fossey, Le Mexique, p. 81; M. A. Laisné de Villevêque to his father, extract, Mexico, 19 Aug. 1829, AMAE,CP:Mexique, vol. 4; French subjects to Alleye de Cyprey, Monterey, 21 Oct. 1843, ibid., vol. 26, ff. 46–50; Pakenham to Palmerston, Mexico, 3 June 1831, PRO:FO 50/66, no. 35; Pakenham to Alamán, copy, Mexico, 11 Apr. 1832, ibid., 50/72.

75. Cochelet to French foreign minister, Mexico, 12 Aug. 1829, AMAE,CP:Mexique, vol. 4, no. 12.

76. Same to same, 9 Sept. 1829, ibid., no. 28. Cochelet's entire correspondence is permeated with such sentiments. See, for example, same to same, 17 Sept. 1829, ibid., no. 30; and 27 Jan. 1830, ibid., vol. 5, no. 8. The correspondence of M. Athanase Laisné de Villevêque, vice-consul in Mexico, with his father, cuestor of the Chamber of Deputies, is also typical of this type of reporting. See extracts in ibid., vol. 4, 29 Aug. 1829, and 18 Sept. 1829. For samples of French published accounts displaying similar attitudes, see Fossey, Le Mexique, p. 249; Gabriel Ferry, Scènes de la vie mexicaine, passim; Eugène Duflot de Mofras, Exploration du territoire de l'Orégon, des Californies, et de la mer Vermeille, exécutée pendant les années 1840, 1841, et 1842, 1, chap. 1. British and Spanish diplomats held similar views. For a summarization, see my "Monarchy in Mexico," pp. 51–68; and my "Voyageurs Français au Mexique, fourriers de l'intervention (1830–1860)," pp. 1–19.

77. Polignac to Cochelet, Paris, 4 May 1830, AMAE,CP:Mexique, vol. 5, no. 2.

78. French foreign minister to Gros, Paris, 6 Oct. 1831, AMAE,MD:Amérique, vol. 41, ff. 214–51.

79. Martin to French foreign minister, Mexico, 19 Dec. 1828, AMAE,CP:Mexique, vol. 3, no. 39.

80. Martin to La Ferronnays, Mexico, 10 Dec. 1828, ibid., no. 37; Hubert Howe Bancroft, History of Mexico, 5:43, gives a standard description.

81. See table of French exports. A dialogue between the Mexican chargé d'affaires in Paris and the commercial house of Chaviteau and Co. in 1833 gives a convenient summary of many of the obstacles in the way of the development of Franco-Mexican trade (7 Mar. 1833, AEM, L.XV, RFM, 1:247–48, nos. 4871–72).

82. French foreign minister to Gros, Paris, 6 Oct. 1831, AMAE,MD:Amérique, vol. 41, ff. 214–51. The foreign minister was reviewing the problems of French trade with Mexico in the 1820s.

83. Cochelet to French foreign minister, Mexico, 15 Jan. 1830, AMAE,CC: Mexico, vol. 2, ff. 567–71, no. 2.

84. Most of the French merchants themselves recognized the impossibility of establishing the extent of their damages and of obliging the Mexican government to pay an indemnity "that can only be fictitious" (Cochelet to French Foreign Ministry, Mexico, 12 June 1830, AMAE,CP:Mexique, vol. 5, no. 46).

85. Cochelet to La Ferronnays, Mexico, 6 June 1829, ibid., vol. 4, no. 4; same to same, 6 July 1829, ibid., no. 10; "Mémorandum," Jan. 1830, ibid. This last is a position paper of the Foreign Ministry reviewing the French position in Mexico under the regime of the "démocrates les plus exagérés."

86. Murphy, Jr., to Mexican Foreign Ministry, reserved (res.), Paris, 12 May 1829, AEM, L.IX, RFM, 1:160, no. 2702; same to same, res. Paris, 31 May 1829, ibid., 1:164, no. 2774; Report of Alamán to the Mexican Congress, 12–13 Feb. 1830, copy, AMAE,MD:Mexique, vol. 41.

87. Murphy, Jr., to Mexican Foreign Ministry, res., Paris, 19 Aug. 1829, AEM, L.VIII, RFM, 1:142, no. 2273; same to same, 27 Jan. 1830, ibid., 1:165, no. 2781.

88. Cochelet to French foreign minister, Mexico, 17 July 1829, AMAE,CP:Mexique, vol. 4, no. 13; same to same, 25 July 1829, ibid., no. 15. See also Lorenzo de Zavala, Ensayo histórico de las revoluciones de México, 2:181–85.

89. "Lettre de M. Lai[s]né de Villevêque vice-consul de France au Mexique à son père, Mexico," 24 Jan.–3 Feb. 1830, AMAE,CP:Mexique, vol. 5, ff. 26–42.

90. Cochelet to La Ferronnays, Mexico, 19 July 1829, ibid., vol. 4, no. 14; same to same, 25 July 1829, ibid., no. 15.

91. "Extrait d'une lettre de M. Le Coupé, Commandant la Themis et la station de Cuba à S. E. M. le Ministre de la marine," Havana, 8 July 1829, ibid., ff. 146–48; Foreign Ministry to Baron Hyde de Neuville, minister of the navy, Paris, confidential, 4 Aug. 1829, ibid., ff. 169–70; minister of navy to minister of foreign affairs, Paris, confidential, 20 Aug. 1829, ibid., f. 190; same to same, 31 Aug. 1829, ibid., ff. 196–97.

92. Cochelet to French foreign minister, Mexico, 3 Sept. 1829, ibid., no. 13; same to same, 11 Sept. 1829, ibid., no. 14.

93. Martin to La Ferronnays, Mexico, copy, 30 Apr. 1828, AMAE,CC:Mexico, vol. 1, ff. 291–95; foreign minister to Cochelet, Paris, 10 Feb. 1829, ibid., vol. 2, no. 18; Alamán to Cochelet, copy, Mexico, 30 July 1830, AEM, L. VII, RFM. 1:135, no. 2129. A copy of this letter in French translation and dated 29 July 1830 is in AMAE, CC:Mexico, vol. 2, ff. 730–36.

94. "Observaciones" (no date, but most likely Feb. 1828, in response to the king's address from the throne of 5 February 1828, in which no mention of the Declarations of 1827 was made), AEM, L.VII, RFM, 1:134, no. 2120; Murphy, Jr., to Mexican Foreign Ministry, Paris, 19 Dec. 1827, ibid., L.V, RFM, 1:104, no. 1463; Murphy, Jr., to La Ferronnays, Paris, 7 Feb. 1828, ibid., L.IX, RFM, 1:163, no. 2755; Cañedo to Murphy, Jr., Mexico, 24 Apr. 1828, ibid., no. 1761; Murphy, Jr., to Mexican Foreign Ministry, Paris, 23 Nov. 1828, ibid., L.II, RFM, 1:52, no. 362; same to same, res., 17 Jan. 1829, ibid., L.VIII, RFM, 1:141–42, no. 2265; Cochelet to French Foreign Ministry, Mexico, 6 Mar. 1830, AMAE,CP:Mexique, vol. 5, no. 20.

95. Murphy, Jr., to Mexican foreign minister, Paris, 25 June 1829, AEM, L. IX, RFM, 1:164–65, no. 2775; Zavala, Ensayo histórico, 2:12–13; José María Tornel, Breve reseña histórica de los acontecimientos más notables de la Nación Mexicana desde el año de 1821 hasta nuestros días, pp. 57–58.

96. French Foreign Ministry to Cochelet, Paris, 10 Feb. 1829, AMAE,CC:Mexico, vol. 2, no. 18.

97. Murphy, Jr., to Mexican Foreign Ministry, Paris, 27 Sept. 1829, AEM, L.IX, *RFM*, 1:154, no. 2778, Cochelet to French foreign minister, Mexico, 27 Jan. 1830, AMAE,CP:Mexique, vol. 5, no. 8.

98. Cochelet to French foreign minister, Mexico, 10 Feb. 1830. AMAE,CP:Mexique, vol. 5, no. 13.

99. Cochelet to French Foreign Ministry, Mexico, 27 Jan. 1830, ibid., no. 8.

100. Polignac to Cochelet, Paris, 4 May 1830, ibid., no. 2.

101. Cochelet to French foreign minister, Mexico, 23 Mar. 1830, ibid., no. 25; same to same, 6 Apr. 1830, ibid., no. 29; Alamán to Murphy, Jr., Mexico, 27 Mar. 1830, AEM, L.XII, *RFM*, 1:199, no. 3573.

102. Polignac to Cochelet, Paris, draft, 24 June 1830, AMAE,CP:Mexique, vol. 5, no. 3; same to same, 23 July 1830, ibid., no. 4; Murphy, Jr., to Mexican foreign minister, res., Paris, 26 Apr. 1830, AEM, L.IX, *RFM*, 1:161–62, no. 2717; same to same, 27 July 1830, ibid., 1:165, no. 2787.

103. Cochelet to Alamán, copy (au sujet du pillage dans le port de la Lagune, du Brick français, la *Bonne Laure*), 22 Jan. 1830, AMAE,CP:Mexique, vol. 5, ff. 24–25.

104. Cochelet to French foreign minister, Mexico, 25 Mar. 1830, ibid., no. 25; same to same, 24 June 1830, ibid., no. 49; Cochelet to Alamán, copy, Mexico, 22 June 1830, AEM, L.XIII, *RFM*, 1:226, no. 4132; Alamán to Murphy, Jr., Mexico, 23 June 1830, ibid., 1:225, no. 4131.

105. Polignac to Cochelet, Paris, 4 May 1830, AMAE,CP:Mexique, vol. 5, no. 2; Cochelet to French foreign minister, Mexico, 28 July 1830, ibid., no. 56.

106. Cochelet to French foreign minister, Mexico, 24 July 1830, ibid., no. 55; Alamán to Cochelet, copy, 30 July 1830, AEM, L.VII, *RFM*, 1:135, no. 2129; Pakenham to Aberdeen, Mexico, 10 June 1830, PRO:FO 50/61, no. 46.

107. Cochelet to French foreign minister, Mexico, 28 June 1830, AMAE,CP:Mexique, vol. 5, no. 50.

Notes to Chapter 2

1. Murphy to Alamán, Paris, 11 Aug. 1830, AEM, L.VIII, *RFM*, 1:143, no. 2280, reproduced in part by D. Jorge Flores, *Lorenzo de Zavala y su misión diplomática en Francia (1834–1835)*, *AHDM*, 8:68–69.

2. Gorostiza to Alamán, Paris, 10 Aug. 1830, Flores, *Lorenzo de Zavala*, p. 72.

3. For a discussion of Lafayette's role in the Paris revolution, see David Pinkney, *The French Revolution of 1830*, pp. 160–64 and 358. See also Thomas E. B. Howarth, *Citizen-King*, p. 152; and S. Charléty, *La Monarchie de Juillet (1830–1848)*, pp. 22–23.

4. Marie, Marquis de Lafayette, *Mémoires, correspondance et manuscrits*, 6:315, from a speech by Lafayette in the Chamber of Deputies, 9 July 1829.

5. Lafayette to Murphy, Jr., Paris, 7 Dec. 1830, ibid., 6:480.

6. "Memorandum," 24 Aug. 1830, AMAE,CP:Colombie, vol. 7, reproduced in part by William Spence Robertson, *France and Latin-American Independence*, pp. 526–28; Murphy, Jr., to Mexican Foreign Ministry, Paris, 27 Sept. 1830, AEM, L.IX, *RFM*, 1:167, no. 2794.

7. Pinkney, *Revolution of 1830*, pp. 298–99, 304–6; Baron Antoine Louis Deffaudis, *Questions diplomatiques et particulièrement des travaux et de l'organisation du ministère des affaires étrangères*, p. 77.

8. Molé to French minister of finances, Paris, 17 Sept. 1830, AMAE,CP:Mexique, vol. 6, ff. 39–40; Murphy, Jr., to Mexican Foreign Ministry, Paris, 27 Sept. 1830,

AEM, L.XII, *RFM*, 1:212, no. 3819; Murphy, Jr., to Molé, Paris, 5 Oct. 1830, ibid., L.IX, *RFM*, 1:167, no. 2797; Molé to Murphy, Jr., Paris, 8 Oct. 1830, ibid., L.XII, *RFM*, 1:212, no. 3823; Ternaux to Murphy, Jr., Paris, 20 Oct. 1830, ibid., no. 3829; Alamán to Murphy, Jr., Mexico, 30 Nov. 1830, ibid., L.IX, *RFM*, 1:168, no. 2804.

9. "Memorandum," AMAE,MD:Amérique, vol. 36, reproduced in part in Robertson, *France and Latin-American Independence*, pp. 528–29.

10. 1 Sept. 1830, Chambre des Députés, *Archives parlementaires*, 2d ser., 63:365–66; *Le Moniteur*, 5 Sept. 1830.

11. Molé to Murphy, Jr., Paris, 30 Sept. 1830, AEM, L.IX, *RFM*, 1:167, no. 2795.

12. Deffaudis, *Questions diplomatiques*, p. 77.

13. The quotations are from Cochelet to French foreign minister, Mexico, 5 Nov. 1830, AMAE,CC:Mexico, vol. 3, ff. 188–92, no. 36.

14. Carrère to French inhabitants of Veracruz, 25 Nov. 1830, AMAE,CP:Mexique, vol. 6, ff. 91–92; Cochelet to Department, Mexico, 5 Nov. 1830, AMAE,CC:Mexico, vol. 3, 1830–31; Carrère to French minister of navy and colonies, Veracruz, 7 Nov. 1830, AMAE,CP:Mexique, vol. 6, ff. 85–86; Cochelet to Department, Mexico, 21 Feb. 1831. AMAE,CC:Mexico, vol. 3; Cochelet to French foreign minister, Mexico, 5 Nov. 1830, ibid., ff. 190–92, no. 36.

15. Alamán to Cochelet, copy, Mexico, 29 Nov. 1830, AMAE, CP:Mexique, vol. 6, f. 89, emphasis mine; Cochelet to French foreign minister, Mexico, 8 Dec. 1830, ibid., no. 79.

16. Cochelet to French foreign minister, Mexico, 2 Jan. 1831, ibid., no. 1.

17. For Alamán's reactions to the July Revolution, see Cochelet to French foreign minister, Mexico, 8 Dec. 1830, ibid., no. 79; same to same, 26 Dec. 1830, ibid., no. 81; same to same, 4 Aug. 1831, ibid., no. 29.

18. Same to same, 15 Feb. 1831, ibid., no. 5; same to same, 15 Feb. 1831, AMAE, CC:Mexico, vol. 3, no. 5, ff. 228–31.

19. Gros to French foreign minister, Mexico, 5 Apr. 1832, AMAE,CP:Mexique, vol. 7, no. 10, cypher; same to same, 30 Aug. 1832, ibid., no. 5.

20. The above argument is well developed by Pinkney, *Revolution of 1830*, pp. 274–95, with extensive bibliographical references to the historical debate on the "bourgeois" monarchy. See especially Patrick-Bernard Higonnet, "La Composition de la Chambre des Députés de 1827 à 1831," pp. 354, 361–64, 371; Adeline Daumard, *La Bourgeoisie parisienne de 1815 à 1848*, pp. 479–84; Charles H. Pouthas, "Les Ministères de Louis-Philippe," pp. 108–11; and René Rémond, *The Right Wing in France from 1815 to de Gaulle*, pp. 113–17. The most recent analysis of the impact of the Revolution of 1830 is the quantitative study by Thomas D. Beck, *French Legislators, 1800–1834*. His conclusions (pp. 132–45) refine and to some extent revise the work of Pinkney but, like Pinkney's, hold that the Revolution of 1830 did not signify the arrival in power of a new class of capitalist entrepreneurs.

21. Louis Desgraves and Georges Dupeux, *Bordeaux au XIXe siècle*, p. 65; Balguerie to Sébastiani, Bordeaux, 5 Feb. 1831, AMAE,CC:Paquebots; same to same, 2 Aug. 1831, ibid.

22. Pinkney, *Revolution of 1830*, p. 358; Lafayette, *Mémoires*, 6:489–513; S. Charléty, *La Monarchie de juillet (1830–1848)*, pp. 22–23.

23. Murphy, Jr., to Mexican foreign minister, Paris, 28 July 1831, AEM, L.XI, *RFM*, 1:190, no. 3413. For Villevêque's self-justification see Laisné de Villevêque to French foreign minister, copy, Paris, 25 Mar. 1831, AMAE,CC:Veracruz, vol. 1, ff. 81–84.

24. *Nouvelle biographie générale depuis les temps les plus reculés jusqu'à nos jours*, 18: 914.

25. Flores, *Lorenzo de Zavala*, pp. 80–89.

26. Ibid., pp. 98–102; for the correspondence between Zavala and his government during his mission in France, see ibid., pp. 121–204.

27. *Tratados y convenciones celebrados y no ratificados por la República Mexicana*, in *Derecho internacional mexicano*, Pt. 2, pp. 269–77.

28. Cochelet to French foreign minister, Mexico, 12 Dec. 1830, AMAE,CC: Mexico, vol. 3, no. 40, ff. 210–18.

29. "Declaracion y Contra-Declaracion," *Tratados y convenciones celebrados y no ratificados*, p. 277.

30. Sébastiani to Gros, Paris, 6 Oct. 1831, AMAE,MD:Amérique, vol. 41, ff. 214–51.

31. Cochelet to French foreign minister, Mexico, 25 Nov. 1831, AMAE,CP:Mexique, vol. 6, no. 33; same to same, 15 Dec. 1831, ibid., no. 34. For the report on the Mexican congressional committee that studied the treaty, see AEM, L.XII, *RFM*, 1:208, no. 37777, 20 Oct. 1831.

32. For executed and unexecuted treaties between Mexico and other powers at this time, see *Tratados y convenciones concluidos y ratificados por la República Mexicana desde su independencia hasta el año actual, acompañados de varios documentos que les son referentes*, passim, and *Tratados y convenciones celebrados y no ratificados*, passim. The correspondence between Pakenham and Palmerston affords many details on the controversies over the British and other treaties. See those of 3 May 1831, PRO:FO 50/65, no. 32; 1 July 1831, ibid., 50/66, no. 49; 2 Aug. 1831, ibid., no. 51; 6 Oct. 1831, ibid., no. 61; 11 Oct. 1832, ibid. 50/73, no. 68; 11 Dec. 1832, ibid., no. 79; 12 Mar. 1833, ibid., 50/79, no. 13; and 11 June 1833, ibid., no. 26.

33. Cochelet to French foreign minister, Mexico, copy, 25 Oct. 1831, AMAE,CC: Mexico, vol. 3, no. 32, ff. 367–72; for the reaction of the French government to Mexico's action, see "Note sur le traité avec le Mexique," Mexique (notes), 1831, AMAE,MD:Mexique, vol. 9, ff. 13–16; see also Cochelet to French foreign minister, 2 Jan. 1832, AMAE,CP:Mexique, vol. 7, no. 2.

34. Sébastiani to Gros, Paris, 4 Mar. 1832, AMAE,CP:Mexique, vol. 7, no. 2; Gros to French foreign minister, Mexico, 5 Apr. 1832, ibid., no. 10, cypher.

35. Dossier personnel of Baron Jean-Baptiste Louis Gros, AMAE.

36. Sébastiani to Gros, Paris, 6 Oct. 1831, AMAE,MD:Amérique, vol. 41, ff. 214–51.

37. Gros to French foreign minister, Mexico, 20 Apr. 1832, AMAE,CC:Mexico, vol. 4, no. 1, f. 13.

38. *El Diario*, Mexico, 11 Apr. 1832. This article is reproduced in report of Pakenham to Palmerston, Mexico, 26 Apr. 1832, PRO:FO 50/72, in the original Spanish, and in AMAE,CP:Mexique, vol. 7, ff. 153–55 in French translation. See also Gros to French foreign minister, Mexico, 14 Apr. 1832, AMAE,CP:Mexique, vol. 7, no. 13; and Pakenham to Alamán, copy, Mexico, 11 Apr. 1832, PRO:FO 50/72.

39. Gros to French foreign minister, Xalapa, 19 Feb. 1832, AMAE,CP:Mexique, vol. 7, no. 2, cypher; Pakenham to Palmerston, Mexico, 2 Apr. 1832, PRO:FO 50/72, no. 23.

40. Carrère to French foreign minister, Veracruz, 2 Feb. 1832, AMAE,CP:Mexique, vol. 7, no. 61; Gros to Carrère, copy, Mexico, 10 Mar. 1832, ibid., ff. 110–11; Carrère to French foreign minister, Veracruz, 9 Apr. 1832, ibid., no. 70, ff. 157–61.

41. Gros to French foreign minister, Mexico, 30 Mar. 1832, ibid., no. 9, cypher.

42. Same to same, Xalapa, 19 Feb. 1832, ibid., no. 2, cypher.

43. *Archives du commerce, recueil de tous les documents officiels, renseignements, faits et avis, pouvant intéresser les négociants, fondé et dirigé par M. P. Henrichs*, 9 (1835):79.

44. See table of French exports, p. 193.

45. Gros to French foreign minister, Xalapa, 19 Feb. 1832, AMAE,CP:Mexique, vol. 7, no. 2, cypher; see also same to same, Mexico, 1 Mar. 1832, ibid., no. 3; same to same, 21 Apr. 1832, AMAE,CC:Mexico, vol. 4, no. 2, ff. 14–16; Carrère to French foreign minister, Veracruz, 8 May 1832, AMAE,CP:Mexique, vol. 7, no. 71, ff. 200–203; Hersant to Sébastiani, Tampico, 23 Apr. 1832, ibid., no. 16, ff. 178–79.

46. Gros to French foreign minister, Mexico, 22 Mar. 1832, cypher, AMAE,CP: Mexique, vol. 7, no. 8.

47. Gros to Casimir Périer, Mexico, 16 Mar. 1832, ibid., no. 7; Gros to French foreign minister, Mexico, 20 Oct. 1832, ibid., no. 16; Gros to Fagoaga, copy, 19 Nov. 1832, ibid., f. 377; Gros to Sébastiani, Mexico, 24 Nov. 1832, ibid., no. 19.

48. Hersant to Sébastiani, Tampico, 23 Apr. 1832, ibid., no. 16, ff. 178–79.

49. Gros to French foreign minister, Mexico, 5 Nov. 1832, ibid., no. 17; same to same, 1 Dec. 1832, ibid., no. 20, cypher.

50. Carrère to French foreign minister, Veracruz, 8 May 1832, ibid., no. 71, ff. 200–203; Hersant to Sébastiani, Xalapa, 7 Dec. 1832, ibid., no. 22, ff. 410–11.

51. Rigny to French foreign minister, Paris, 7 July 1832, ibid., nos. 277–78.

52. Gros to French foreign minister, Mexico, 5 May 1832, AMAE,CC:Mexico, vol. 4, no. 3, ff. 16–26; same to same, 5 June 1832, AMAE,CP:Mexique, vol. 7, no. 18.

53. Treaty of 15 October 1832, *Tratados y convenciones celebrados y no ratificados*, pp. 277–97.

54. Gros to French foreign minister, Mexico, 31 Dec. 1832, AMAE,CP:Mexique, vol. 7, no. 27.

55. Same to same, 25 Jan. 1833, ibid., vol. 8, no. 29.

56. Murphy, Jr., to Mexican Foreign Ministry, Paris, 27 Sept. 1830, AEM, L.IX, *RFM*, 1:167, no. 2794.

57. Dossier personnel of Baron Antoine Louis Deffaudis, AMAE; Henri Contamine, *Diplomatie et diplomates sous la restauration 1814–1830*, p. 147.

58. Deffaudis to Broglie, Mexico, 31 July 1833, AMAE,CP:Mexique, vol. 8, no. 16, ff. 90–93.

59. Same to same, 15 May 1833, AMAE,CC:Mexico, vol. 4, no. 5; same to same, 1 June 1833, ibid., no. 6; same to same, 21 Aug. 1833, ibid., no. 16; same to same, 28 Apr. 1833, AMAE,CP:Mexique, vol. 8, no. 9. Many other examples could be cited.

60. Deffaudis to Broglie, Mexico, 15 July 1833, AMAE,CC:Mexico, vol. 4, no. 7, ff. 129–32.

61. Same to same, 6 May 1833, AMAE,CP:Mexique, vol. 8, no. 10.

62. Same to same, 9 Sept. 1833, ibid., no. 18.

63. Same to same, 28 Aug. 1833, ibid., no. 7; same to same, 10 Sept. 1833, ibid., no. 19; Pakenham to Palmerston, Mexico, 11 Sept. 1833, PRO:FO 50/80, no. 50; same to same, 5 Oct. 1833, ibid., no. 55.

64. Broglie to Gros, Paris, 1 Feb. 1833, AMAE,CP:Mexique, vol. 8, no. 10. Deffaudis also was obliged to obey these instructions until they were replaced by new ones.

65. Broglie to Deffaudis, Paris, 26 Dec. 1833, ibid., no. 17.

66. Deffaudis to Broglie, Mexico, 6 May 1833, ibid., no. 10; same to same, 9 Sept. 1833, ibid., no. 18.

67. Pakenham to Palmerston, Mexico, 9 Aug. 1833, PRO:FO 50/80, no. 46; Deffaudis to Broglie, Mexico, 9 Sept. 1833, AMAE,CP:Mexique, vol. 8, no. 18.

68. Deffaudis to Broglie, Mexico, 28 Aug. 1833, AMAE,CP:Mexique, vol. 8, no. 17.

69. Same to same, 10 Sept. 1833, ibid., no. 19; same to same, 1 Oct. 1833, ibid., no. 20; same to same. 20 Apr. 1834, ibid., no. 29; same to same, 14 Aug. 1835, ibid., vol. 9, no. 57.

70. Same to same, 1 Oct. 1833, ibid., vol. 8, no. 20.

71. Peyronnel (commander of Gulf naval station) to Deffaudis, Veracruz, 10 Apr. 1833, ibid., f. 43; Deffaudis to Peyronnel, Mexico, copy, 17 Apr. 1833, ibid., ff. 46–49; Deffaudis to Broglie, Mexico, 28 Apr. 1833, ibid., no. 9.

72. The station was not reestablished until the spring of 1837. See Rosamel to Molé, Paris, 29 Mar. 1837, ibid., vol. 11, ff. 70–71; French foreign minister to French minister of navy, Paris, 3 Apr. 1837. ibid., ff. 102–3; Rosamel to Molé, 25 Nov. 1837, ibid., vol. 12, ff. 36–40.

73. French minister of finances to French foreign minister, Paris, 12 July 1832, AMAE,CC:Paquebots; Humann (French minister of finances) to French foreign minister, Paris, 9 Nov. 1832, ibid.

74. Rigny (French minister of navy) to French foreign minister, Paris, 2 Aug. 1833, ibid.; Deffaudis to Broglie, Mexico, 21 Aug. 1834, AMAE,CC:Mexico, vol. 4, no. 16; same to same, 23 Jan. 1836, ibid., no. 35.

75. French foreign minister to Gros, 6 Oct. 1831, AMAE,MD:Amérique, vol. 41, ff. 214–51. A decision to establish a consulate on the Pacific coast was not implemented. Deffaudis to Broglie, Mexico, 1 June 1833, AMAE,CC:Mexico, vol. 4, no. 6; same to same, 21 Aug. 1834, ibid., no. 16; French foreign minister to Deffaudis, Paris, 26 June 1834, ibid., no. 14; Deffaudis to Broglie, Mexico, 23 Jan. 1836, ibid., no. 35, ff. 315–20.

76. Deffaudis to Broglie, Mexico, 2 May 1833, AMAE,CC:Mexico, vol. 4, no. 3.

77. Deffaudis to French foreign minister, Mexico, 15 July 1834, AMAE,CP:Mexique, vol. 8, no. 34. For reasons explained later in above paragraph of the text, Deffaudis failed to report the action of the Congress at the time it took place.

78. Deffaudis to Lombardo, copy, confidential, 3 Feb. 1834, ibid., ff. 180–81; "Projet de convention entre le Mexique et la France" is reproduced in ibid., f. 183.

79. Deffaudis to French foreign minister, Mexico, 15 July 1834, ibid., no. 34.

80. Pouthas, "Les Ministères de Louis-Philippe," p. 113; Charléty, La Monarchie de juillet, pp. 112–16. For a discussion of ministerial instability in France in the 1830s, see Douglas Johnson, Guizot. Aspects of French History, 1787–1874, pp. 155–76.

81. Deffaudis to Rigny, Mexico, 5 Mar. 1835, AMAE,CP:Mexique, vol. 9, no. 47; same to same, 26 May 1835, ibid., no. 52; Deffaudis to Broglie, Mexico, 29 July 1835, ibid., no. 55; Broglie to Deffaudis, Paris, Sept. 1835, ibid., no. 25.

82. Deffaudis to Rigny, Mexico, 1 Feb. 1835, ibid., no. 43.

83. Same to same, 3 Mar. 1835, ibid., no. 46. Scholars do not agree upon the significance of the hostility displayed by certain administrations to foreign commerce and industry. Some have said that these men were reacting against the "European" sector of the criollo "bourgeoisie" that deliberately chose the path of underdevelopment of Mexico and dependence on Europe. See, for example, André Gunder Frank, Lumpenbourgeoisie: Lumpendevelopment, p. 57; and Barbara A. Tenenbaum, "Straightening Out Some of the Lumpen in the Development," pp. 3–14.

84. Gutiérrez de Estrada to Mangino, Mexico, 9 Mar. 1835, AEM, L.XII, RFM, 1:209, no. 3786; Deffaudis to Rigny, Mexico, 28 Feb. 1835, AMAE,CP:Mexique, vol. 9, no. 45, ff. 33–36.

85. Gutiérrez de Estrada to Deffaudis, printed, Mexico, 3 Mar. 1835, AEM, L.XII, *RFM*, 1:209, no. 3788. This exchange is not to be found in the French documents. Perhaps Deffaudis did not want his government to see it.

86. Deffaudis to Rigny, Mexico, 24 May 1835, AMAE,CP:Mexique, vol. 9, no. 51, ff. 120–22; same to same, 25 Apr. 1835, ibid., no. 49, ff. 81–84; the "Law on Foreigners" of 24 March 1835 is reproduced in French in ibid., ff. 58–60.

87. Pakenham to Gutiérrez de Estrada, copy, Mexico, 25 Apr. 1835, PRO:FO 50/92.

88. Pinkney, *Revolution of 1830*, pp. 241–43; Gros to F. Fagoaga, copy, Mexico, 12 Nov. 1832, AMAE,CP:Mexique, vol. 7, ff. 369–72.

89. Deffaudis to Broglie, Mexico, 26 Oct. 1835, AMAE,CP:Mexique, vol. 9, f. 4.

90. Deffaudis to Rigny, Mexico, 3 Mar. 1835, ibid., no. 46, ff. 37–41.

91. Same to same, 31 Mar. 1835, ibid., no. 48, ff. 69–74; AEM, L.XXI, *RFM*, 1:297–98, nos. 7290–96; Deffaudis to Mexican foreign minister, Mexico, 31 Aug. 1835, ibid., 1:305, no. 7342; Deffaudis to Broglie, Mexico, 1 Sept. 1835, AMAE,CP: Mexique, vol. 9, no. 59, ff. 153–55; same to same, 25 Oct. 1835, AMAE,CC:Mexico, vol. 4, no. 33 , ff. 303–4; same to same, 15 Aug. 1835, AMAE,CP:Mexique, vol. 9, no. 57, ff. 150–53.

92. Broglie to Deffaudis, Paris, 1 Aug. 1835, AMAE,CP:Mexique, vol. 9, no. 24, ff. 146–47. Broglie's note to Mangino is missing from the archives. Mangino's reply to it, in which he promises to refer the case to his government, is 22 July 1835, ibid., ff. 138–39.

93. Deffaudis to Broglie, Mexico, 1 Feb. 1836, ibid., vol. 10, no. 75, ff. 13–17; same to same, 31 Dec. 1835, ibid., vol. 9, no. 72, ff. 209–12.

Notes to Chapter 3

1. See, for example, Henry Bamford Parkes, *A History of Mexico*, p. 206; F. Weymuller, *Histoire du Mexique*, p. 90; Carlos Pereyra, *De Barradas á Baudin*, pp. 212–32.

2. 11 Mar. 1837, Chambre des Députés, *Archives parlementaires*, 108:306; 18 June 1839, ibid., 126:64; 21 June 1838, ibid., 124:146; Jacques Penot, "L'Expansion commerciale française au Mexique et les causes du conflit franco-mexicain de 1838–1839," p. 180; Ashburnham to Palmerston, Mexico, 5 May 1838, PRO:FO 50/114, no. 24; Le Ray to Baudin, Sacrificios, 8 Nov. 1838, AMAE,CP:Mexique, vol. 14, ff. 142–47.

3. André Levasseur, *Registre de la Population Française au Mexique*, 30 Apr. 1849, AMAE,MD:Mexique, vol. 7. For an analysis of this document, see chap. 5, pp. 123–31.

4. For an analysis of the foreign populations resident in Mexico, see chap. 5, pp. 123–31.

5. Deffaudis to Molé, Mexico, 26 Feb. 1837, AMAE,CP:Mexique, vol. 11, no. 123, ff. 30–33; same to same, 5 July 1837, ibid., no. 148, ff. 198–201.

6. Same to same, 15 June 1837, ibid., no. 141, ff. 148–53. For the detailed reporting on the alleged grievances, see vol. 11 for the year 1837, passim.

7. See table of French exports, p. 193.

8. Deffaudis to Vermote, captain of brig *Palinure*, copy, Mexico, 27 Feb. 1836, AMAE,CP:Mexique, vol. 10, ff. 27–29.

9. Deffaudis to Broglie, Mexico, 2 Jan. 1836, ibid., no. 73, ff. 4–7; Pakenham to Palmerston, Mexico, 6 Jan. 1836, PRO:FO 50/98, no. 3.

10. Hubert Howe Bancroft, *History of Mexico*, 5:179, 183–84; Vicente Riva Palacio, ed., *México a través de los siglos*, 4:362–63.

11. Gloux to Thiers, Veracruz, 12 Oct. 1836, AMAE,CC:Veracruz, vol. 1, no. 69, ff. 420–26.

12. Pakenham to Palmerston, Mexico, 1 July 1836, PRO:FO 50/99, no. 47; same to same, 14 Feb. 1837, ibid., 50/105, no. 3; Deffaudis to Thiers, Mexico, 15 July 1836, AMAE,CP:Mexique, vol. 10, no. 92, ff. 104–9.

13. Broglie to Deffaudis, Paris, 7 Feb. 1836, AMAE,CC:Mexico, vol. 4, no. 17, ff. 331–38. The instructions, although issued in Broglie's name, had been drawn up in the commercial division of the Foreign Ministry.

14. Thiers to Deffaudis, Paris, 19 Mar. 1836, AMAE,CP:Mexique, vol. 10, no. 27, ff. 40–41.

15. Same to same, 27 Apr. 1836, ibid., no. 28, ff. 58–60; same to same, 6 July 1836, ibid., no. 30, ff. 94–95.

16. Deffaudis to Broglie, Mexico, 20 Apr. 1836, AMAE,CC:Mexico, vol. 4, ff. 366–67; same to same, 18 Apr. 1836, AMAE,CP:Mexique, vol. 10, no. 85, ff. 52–54.

17. Ortiz Monasterio to Deffaudis, Mexico, 20 Apr. 1836, AEM, L.XII, *RFM*, 1:210, no. 3805; Ortiz Monasterio to Cuevas, Mexico, 20 Apr. 1836, ibid., no. 3802; Deffaudis to Ortiz Monasterio, Mexico, 20 Apr. 1836, ibid., no. 3804; Deffaudis to Broglie, Mexico, 21 Apr. 1836, AMAE,CC:Mexico, vol. 4, no. 39, ff. 369–71.

18. Deffaudis to Thiers, Mexico, 20 Oct. 1836, AMAE,CP:Mexique, vol. 10, no. 110, ff. 199–201.

19. Deffaudis to Broglie, Mexico, 30 Jan. 1834, AMAE,CC:Mexico, vol. 4, no. 12, ff. 162–65.

20. Deffaudis to Thiers, Mexico, 31 Aug. 1836, AMAE,CP:Mexique, vol. 10, no. 102, ff. 159–64. This report describes the petition from the merchants in the capital. See also merchants from Zacatecas to Deffaudis, Zacatecas, 18 Oct. 1836, ibid., f. 195; merchants in Tampico to Deffaudis, Tampico, 15 Oct. 1836, ibid., f. 193; and French merchants to Deffaudis, Mexico, 18 Oct. 1836, ibid., f. 194.

21. Pakenham to Palmerston, Mexico, 6 Sept. 1836, PRO:FO 50/100, no. 62; Deffaudis to Thiers, Mexico, 18 Aug. 1836, AMAE,CP:Mexique, vol. 10, no. 99, ff. 140–43; same to same, 16 July 1836, AMAE,CC:Mexico, vol. 4, no. 46, ff. 403–6.

22. Deffaudis to Ortiz Monasterio, copy, 14 July 1836, AMAE,CP:Mexique, vol. 10, ff. 96–99; same to same, 15 July 1836, ibid., ff. 100–104; Deffaudis to Thiers, Mexico, 20 July 1836, ibid., no. 93, ff. 109–11; AHSRE, Francia-Mexico, L-E-1917 (I).

23. Molé to minister of navy, Paris, 28 Oct. 1836, AMAE,CP:Mexique, vol. 10, ff. 209–10; French minister of navy to Rear Admiral de la Bretonnière, at Brest, copy, 2 Nov. 1836, ibid., ff. 210–11.

24. Molé to French minister of navy, Paris, 14 Nov. 1836, AMAE,CP:Mexique, vol. 10, f. 222; "Memorandum on Mexico," 19 Nov. 1836, ibid., ff. 231–32. The latter is a position paper drawn up, or at least approved, by Molé.

25. Molé to Deffaudis, Paris, 7 Nov. 1836, AMAE,CP:Mexique, vol. 10, no. 31, ff. 213–16. The subsequent quotations in the paragraph are all from this document. It is summarized and quoted in part in AEM, L.XXI, *RFM*, 1:299, no. 7299.

26. Deffaudis to Molé, Mexico, 27 Feb. 1837, AMAE,CP:Mexique, vol. 11, no. 124, ff. 41–44; same to same, 16 Mar. 1837, ibid., no. 127, ff.47–50; Deffaudis to Ortiz Monasterio, confidential, Mexico, 26 Feb. 1837, AEM, L.XXI, *RFM*, 1:299, no. 7298.

27. Deffaudis to Molé, Mexico, 16 Mar. 1837, AMAE,CP:Mexique, vol. 11, no.

127, ff. 47–50; same to same, 25 Mar. 1837, AMAE,CC:Mexico, vol. 5, no. 66, ff. 111–13.

28. Bretonnière to Deffaudis, Havana, on board the *Didon*, 8 Mar. 1837, AMAE, CP:Mexique, vol. 11, f. 74.

29. Deffaudis to Bretonnière, copy, Mexico, 22 Mar. 1837, ibid., ff. 75–76.

30. Molé to Deffaudis, Paris, 4 Apr. 1837, ibid., no. 33, ff. 103–10; same to same, 13 June 1837, ibid., no. 34, f. 147; minister of navy to Molé, Paris, 22 Nov. 1837, ibid., vol. 10, f. 233; S. Charléty, *La Monarchie de juillet 1830–1848*, pp. 143–45.

31. Deffaudis to Molé, Mexico, 18 Apr. 1837, AMAE,CP:Mexique, vol. 11, no. 134, ff. 104–8; Ashburnham to Palmerston, Mexico, 1 May 1837, PRO:FO 50/106, no. 5; Deffaudis to Molé, Mexico, 25 May 1837, AMAE,CP:Mexique, vol. 11, no. 138, ff. 133–36; same to same, 2 Apr. 1837, ibid., no. 133, ff. 96–98; Cuevas to Garro, Mexico, 5 June 1837, AEM, L.XXI, *RFM*, 1:305, no. 7355; AHSRE, Francia-Mexico, L-E-1917 (I).

32. Deffaudis to Molé, Mexico, 29 Mar. 1837, AMAE,CP:Mexique, vol. 11, no. 130, ff. 72–74; same to same, 18 June 1837, ibid., no. 145, ff. 186–88.

33. Note from Deffaudis to Monasterio, copy, Mexico, 13 Apr. 1837, ibid., ff. 122–24.

34. Deffaudis to Molé, Mexico, 20 Aug. 1837, ibid., no. 155, ff. 219–20.

35. Same to same, 28 June 1837, ibid., no. 146, ff. 188–91; Cuevas to Garro, Mexico, 28 June 1837, AEM, L.XXI, *RFM*, 1:298, no. 7297; same to same, 6 Aug. 1837, ibid., p. 302, no. 7314; Mexican foreign minister to Garro, Mexico, D.F., 28 Dec. 1837, AHSRE, Garro, Máximo, L-E-395.

36. Molé to Deffaudis, Paris, 20 Aug. 1837, AMAE,CP:Mexique, vol. 11, f. 218; Deffaudis to Molé, Mexico, 23 Aug. 1837, ibid., no. 156, ff. 225–28.

37. Molé to Deffaudis, Paris, 11 Sept. 1837, ibid., no. 35, ff. 238–39.

38. "Rapport au Roi," draft, Paris, [by Molé], 1 Oct. 1837, ibid., vol. 12, ff. 4–8.

39. Molé to Deffaudis, Paris, 23 Oct. 1837, ibid., vol. 12, no. 36, f. 13; same to same, 3 Nov. 1837, ibid., no. 37, f. 15; same to same, 10 Nov. 1837, AMAE,CC: Mexico, vol. 5, no. 27, ff. 182–85; Garro to Mexican foreign minister, Paris, 14 Nov. 1837, AHSRE, Garro, Máximo, L-E-395.

40. *Archives parlementaires de 1787 à 1860*, 2d ser., 18 Dec. 1837, 114:325.

41. The petition itself has not been located. Deffaudis, however, learned of it and spoke of it to Pakenham (Pakenham to Palmerston, Mexico, 2 Apr. 1836, PRO:FO 50/99, no. 22).

42. Molé to Deffaudis, 9 Dec. 1837, AMAE,CP:Mexique, vol. 12, no. 39, f. 62; *Archives parlementaires*, Chambre des Députés, 11 Mar. 1837, 108:306.

43. Deffaudis to Broglie, Mexico, 21 Nov. 1835, AMAE,CP:Mexique, vol. 9, no. 68, f. 192.

44. *Archives parlementaires*, Chambre des Députés, 11 Mar. 1837, 108:306–8.

45. Deffaudis learned of the discussion of Mexico in the Chamber via Duport and expressed his annoyance that the Paris newspapers of that date (which he received) made no mention of it (Deffaudis to Molé, Mexico, 25 May 1837, AMAE,CP:Mexique, vol. 11, no. 138, ff. 133–36).

46. *Archives parlementaires*, Chambre des Pairs, 3 Jan. 1838, 114:465; ibid., Chambre des Députés, 8 Jan. 1838, 114:525.

47. Molé to Deffaudis, Paris, 31 Dec. 1837, AMAE,CP:Mexique, vol. 12, no. 41, ff. 71–72. Molé had refused to discuss the French quarrel with Garro and had met his notes with "extraordinary silence" (Garro to Mexican Foreign Ministry, res., 12 Jan. 1835, AEM, L.XXII, *RFM*, 1:325–26, no. 7701).

48. Deffaudis to Molé, 24 July 1837, AMAE,CP:Mexique, vol. 11, no. 151; same to same, 17 Aug. 1837, ibid., no. 154; same to same, 29 Sept. 1837, ibid., no. 158. Charles Ashburnham, British chargé d'affaires in Mexico, believed that Deffaudis desired an armed invasion of the interior to seize the capital (Ashburnham to Palmerston, Mexico, confidential, 30 Nov. 1837, PRO:FO 50/108, no. 63).

49. There is never the slightest hint of a desire to reorganize Mexican society or to go beyond the limits of the demands submitted to the Mexican government anywhere in the archives of the Foreign Ministry or the public statements of the king and Molé. See also Marquis de H. G. H. Noailles, ed., *Le Comte Molé, 1781–1855,* 6:38–39; François Ferdinand Philippe Louis Marie d'Orléans, Prince de Joinville, *Vieux souvenirs 1818–1848,* p. 149; Jurien de la Gravière, *Les Gloires maritimes de la France, L'Amiral Baudin,* pp. 118–19.

50. See, for example, Deffaudis to Molé, Mexico, 29 Mar. 1837, AMAE,CP:Mexique, vol. 11, no. 130; same to same, 18 June 1837, ibid., no. 142; same to same, 25 June 1837, ibid., no. 144.

51. "Rapport au Roi," draft, Paris, 1 Oct. 1837, AMAE,CP:Mexique, vol. 12, ff. 4–8; E. H. Jenkins, *A History of the French Navy from Its Beginnings to the Present Day,* p. 290.

52. Charléty, *La Monarchie de juillet,* pp. 145–46, 151–52; Noailles, *Le Comte Molé,* p. 16.

53. Noailles, *Le Comte Molé,* pp. 37–39; Nancy Nichols Barker, ed. and trans., *The French Legation in Texas,* 1:37–112. In November 1837 the French government conducted a general review of its relations with the Latin American republics ("Note sur l'état des Rapports de la France avec le Mexique et les nouveaux Etats de l'Amérique du Sud," AMAE,CP:Mexique, vol. 12, ff. 50–59). For intervention in Argentina, see John F. Cady, *Foreign Intervention in the Río de la Plata, 1838–1850,* chaps. 2 and 3.

54. Charléty, *La Monarchie de juillet,* p. 145.

55. Garro to Mexican Foreign Ministry, res., London, 6 June 1839, AEM, L.XXI, *RFM,* 1:317, no. 7560.

56. Same to same, res., Paris, 25 Mar. 1845, AEM, L.XIX, *RFM,* 1:281, no. 6837; same to same, 30 May 1845, ibid., L.XXIV, *RFM,* 2:26, no. 8588; see also same to same, 30 Oct. 1844, ibid., 2:32, no. 8724.

57. Deffaudis to Molé, Mexico, 28 Dec. 1837, AMAE,CP:Mexique, vol. 12, no. 169, ff. 67–68; same to same, 29 Dec. 1837, ibid., no. 170, ff. 68–70; DeLisle to Molé, 2 Jan. 1838, ibid., no. 1, ff. 74–78; Gloux to Molé, Veracruz, 28 Jan. 1838, AMAE, CC:Veracruz, vol. 2, no. 82, ff. 1–3.

58. Bazoche to captain of *Laurier,* copy, 9 Jan. 1838, AMAE,CP:Mexique, vol. 12, f. 98; Bazoche to Deffaudis, copy, 9 Jan. 1838, ibid., ff. 100–101; Deffaudis to Molé, Sacrificios, 26 Jan. 1838, ibid., no. 171, ff. 101–7.

59. Molé to Deffaudis, draft, Paris, 3 Nov. 1837, ibid., no. 37, f. 15; same to same, 10 Nov. 1837, ibid., ff. 26–28; same to same, 10 Nov. 1837, AMAE,CC:Mexico, vol. 5, no. 27, ff. 182–85; "Affaire du Mexique, 1838," AMAE,CP:Mexique, vol. 12, ff. 82–88.

60. Deffaudis to Molé, Sacrificios, 26 Jan. 1838, AMAE,CP:Mexique, vol. 12, no. 171, ff. 101–7.

61. Gloux to Molé, Veracruz, 6 Mar. 1838, ibid., no. 85, ff. 176–79; Deffaudis to Molé, Sacrificios, 23 Mar. 1838, ibid., no. 173, ff. 190–96; "Affaire du Mexique, 1838," ibid., ff. 82–88. A summary of the terms may be found in Bancroft, *History of Mexico,* 5:190, n. 14; and in William Spence Robertson, "French Intervention in

Mexico in 1838," pp. 228–29; see also P. Blanchard and A. Dauzats, *San Juan de Ulùa* [sic], *ou relation de l'expédition française au Mexique, sous les ordres de M. le contre-amiral Baudin*, pp. 229–50.

62. Antonio de la Peña y Reyes, ed., *La primera guerra entre México y Francia*, pp. 58–61; DeLisle to Molé, Mexico, 1 Apr. 1838, AMAE,CP:Mexique, vol. 12, no. 9, ff. 217–22; same to same, 4 Apr. 1838, ibid., no. 11, ff. 240–43; Ashburnham to Palmerston, Mexico, 4 Apr. 1838, PRO:FO 50/113, no. 21; Eugène Maissin, *The French in Mexico and Texas (1838–1839)*, pp. 25–29.

63. Cuevas to Garro, Mexico, 4 Apr. 1838, AEM, L.XXI, *RFM*, 1:308–9, no. 7493; Garro to Molé, Paris, 26 May 1838, AMAE,CP:Mexique, vol. 13, ff. 33–35.

64. Among others, the British chargé d'affaires noted the general belief in Mexico in French monarchical designs (Ashburnham to Palmerston, Mexico, 5 May 1838, PRO:FO 50/114, no. 24; same to same, confidential, 24 May 1838, ibid., no. 39). The French made vigorous but vain efforts to combat this belief. See Deffaudis to DeLisle, copy, Sacrificios, 22 Mar. 1838, AMAE,CP:Mexique, vol. 12, no. 2, ff. 196–99; De-Lisle to Cuevas, Mexico, 20 Mar. 1838, AEM, L.XXI, *RFM*, 1:309–10, no. 7498. Deffaudis ordered the French consul in Veracruz, A. Gloux, to enter on a correspondence that would give the lie to monarchical rumors and to arrange for its publication. When Gloux proceeded to do so, the Mexican government expelled him from the country (Deffaudis to Molé, Sacrificios, 25 May 1838, AMAE,CP:Mexique, vol. 13, no. 182, ff. 22–26; Gloux to Molé, on board *Herminie*, 1 June 1838, AMAE,CC:Veracruz, vol. 2, no. 1; Ashburnham to Palmerston, Mexico, 24 May 1838, PRO:FO 50/114, no. 36). Deffaudis also corresponded with agents in Washington, D.C., to refute monarchical charges (Garro to Molé, Paris, 36 May 1838, AMAE,CP:Mexique, vol. 13, ff. 33–35). The French government formally denied any desire to invade and conquer Mexico in the pages of the *Journal des débats* (31 July 1838).

65. Deffaudis to Molé, Sacrificios, 6 May 1838, AMAE,CP:Mexique, vol. 12, no. 180, ff. 284–90.

66. Same to same, 25 May 1838, ibid., vol. 13, no. 182, ff. 22–26; Parseval (captain of *Iphigénie*) to Rosamel (French minister of navy), copy, Havana, 31 Mar. 1838, ibid., vol. 12, ff. 213–16; Bazoche to Deffaudis, Sacrificios, copy, 10 June 1838, ibid., vol. 13, f. 136; DeLisle to Molé, Mexico, 31 June 1838, ibid., no. 14, ff. 82–87; same to same, 26 July 1838, ibid., no. 16, ff. 119–23.

67. Deffaudis to Molé, Sacrificios, 16 May 1838, ibid., vol. 13, no. 181, ff. 4–6.

68. DeLisle to Molé, Sacrificios, 23 June 1838, ibid., no. 14, ff. 82–87; Deffaudis to Molé, Brest, 5 Aug. 1838, ibid., no. 183 "et dernier," ff. 127–36; Rosamel to Baudin, copy, Paris, Aug. 1838, ibid., ff. 154–59; Delisle to Molé, Sacrificios, 18 Aug. 1838, ibid., no. 17, ff. 163–65; same to same, 25 Aug. 1838, ibid., no. 18, ff. 180–82; Gloux to Molé, 27 Sept. 1838, ibid., ff. 193–94.

69. Rosamel to Louis Philippe, copy, Paris, 10 Aug. 1838, ibid., ff. 142. This report is annotated "Approuvé" and signed "Louis Philippe." It mentions four mortar ships, two of which for some reason did not take part in the later action. See the official list of ships as of 3 January 1839 in Blanchard and Dauzats, *San Juan de Ulùa* [sic], p. 439. For Baudin, see *Nouvelle biographie générale depuis les temps les plus reculés jusqu'à nos jours*, 4:774; Loyall Farragut, *The Life of David Glasgow Farragut*, p. 133; and Gravière, *Les Gloires maritimes de la France*, passim.

70. Rosamel to Baudin, copy, Paris, Aug. 1838, AMAE,CP:Mexique, vol. 13, ff. 154–59; Molé to Baudin, Paris, draft, 23 Aug. 1838, ibid., vol. 14, ff. 18–20; Molé to DeLisle, draft, 22 Aug. 1838, ibid., vol. 13, no. 46, f. 65.

71. Gutiérrez de Estrada to Garro, Paris, 10 Sept. 1838, AEM, L.XXI, *RFM*, 1.313-14, no. 7521.

72. Le Ray to Baudin, Mexico, 1 Nov. 1838, AMAE,CP:Mexique, vol. 14, ff. 120-21; Cuevas to Baudin, 3 Nov. 1838, ibid., ff. 124-29; Baudin to Cuevas, copy, *Néréide*, 7 Nov. 1838, ibid., ff. 138-40; AHSRE, Francia-Mexico, L-E-1917 (I).

73. DeLisle to Molé, Sacrificios, 26 July 1838, AMAE,CP:Mexique, vol. 13, no. 16, ff. 119-23. Luis Cuevas later estimated that five million pesos were lost in the blockade during its entirety (Luis Gonzaga Cuevas, *Exposición del Ex-Ministro que la suscribe, sobre las diferencias con Francia*, p. 51).

74. Le Ray to Baudin, Sacrificios, 8 Nov. 1838, AMAE,CP:Mexique, vol. 14, ff. 142-47; Bancroft, *History of Mexico*, 5:189.

75. Baudin to Molé, *Néréide*, 24 Nov. 1838, AMAE,CP:Mexique, vol. 14, no. 8, ff. 236-41. For the French proposals and Mexican counterproposals, see ibid., ff. 166-72, 195-99, 220-23; see also Peña y Reyes, *La primera guerra entre México y Francia*, pp. 120-60; and Blanchard and Dauzats, *San Juan de Ulúa* [sic], pp. 266-91; AHSRE, Francia-Mexico, L-E-1917 to L-E-1931.

76. Alleye de Cyprey to Guizot, Mexico, 27 Sept. 1843, AMAE,CP:Mexique, vol. 25, no. 188, ff. 21-27.

77. Pakenham to Palmerston, Mexico, 2 Aug. 1831, PRO:FO 50/66, no. 51; see also same to same, 3 May 1831, ibid., no. 32; same to same, 1 July 1831, ibid., no. 49; Doyle to Watson and Co., copy, 17 Oct. 1832, ibid., 50/165.

78. Gloux to Alleye de Cyprey, Veracruz, 22 Apr. 1844, AMAE,CC:Veracruz, vol. 2, no. 300, ff. 91-92; same to same, extract, 27 Apr. 1844, AMAE,CP:Mexique, vol. 26, f. 242; Gloux to Guizot, Veracruz, 25 May 1841, AMAE,CC:Veracruz, vol. 2, ff. 83-86, unnumbered; Guizot to Count Louis Sainte-Aulaire, copy, Paris, 10 June 1844, AMAE,CP:Mexique, vol. 27, no. 42, ff. 21-22; Molé to Deffaudis, draft, Paris, 10 Nov. 1837, AMAE,CC:Mexico, vol. 5, no. 27, ff. 182-85; Baudin to Ray, copy, Sacrificios, 27 Oct. 1838, AMAE,CP:Mexique, vol. 14, ff. 90-101; *RDHM*, 3:xi.

79. Baudin to Rincon, *Néréide*, copy, 27 Nov. 1838, AMAE,CP:Mexique, vol. 15, f. 7, 2:00 p.m.

80. Baudin to Molé, *Néréide*, 30 Nov. 1838, ibid., no. 12, ff. 20-27.

81. Jenkins, *History of French Navy*, pp. 290-91; E. Chevalier, capitaine de vaisseau, *Histoire de la marine française de 1815 à 1870*, p. 86; Bancroft, *History of Mexico*, 5:192-93.

82. Chevalier, *Histoire de la marine française*, p. 87.

83. Joinville, *Vieux souvenirs*, p. 147; Gravière, *Les Gloires maritimes de la France*, p. 119.

84. Baudin to Molé, *Néréide*, 30 Nov. 1838, AMAE,CP:Mexique, vol. 15, no. 12, ff. 20-27; Blanchard and Dauzats, *San Juan de Ulúa* [sic], pp. 320-24.

85. "Convention, entre . . . Baudin . . . Rincon," 28 Nov. 1838, AMAE,CP:Mexique, vol. 15, ff. 17-19; Baudin to Molé, *Néréide*, copy, 28 Nov. 1838, ibid., ff. 16-17; Baudin to Bustamante, copy, 3 Dec. 1838, ibid., ff. 338-40; Carlos María Bustamante, *El Gabinete mexicano durante el segundo período de la administración del exmo. señor presidente D. Anastasio Bustamante, hasta la entrega del mando al exmo, señor presidente interino, D. Antonio López de Santa Anna*, 1:125-37.

86. Bustamante, *Gabinete mexicano*, 1:137-39; Ashburnham to Palmerston, separate, 4 Dec. 1838, PRO:FO 50/116; same to same, 10 Dec. 1838, ibid., no. 100.

87. Baudin to Molé, *Néréide*, 9 Dec. 1838, AMAE,CP:Mexique, vol. 15, ff. 60-61;

Pakenham to Sir Charles Paget, copy, H.M.S. *Pique*, Sacrificios, 31 Dec. 1838, PRO: FO 50/123; Jenkins, *History of French Navy*, p. 291.

88. Baudin to Molé, *Néréide*, 9 Dec. 1838, AMAE,CP:Mexique, vol. 15, ff. 60–61; Joinville, *Vieux souvenirs*, pp. 165–66; Chevalier, *Histoire de la marine française*, p. 98; Ashburnham to Palmerston, Mexico, 31 Dec. 1838, PRO:FO 50/116, no. 115; Pakenham to Sir Charles Paget, copy, H.M.S. *Pique*, Sacrificios, 31 Dec. 1838, PRO/FO 123, unnumbered.

89. Baudin to Don José Urréa, *Néréide*, copy, 22 Dec. 1838, AMAE,CP:Mexique, vol. 15, ff. 88–90, reproduced in Spanish translation in *Diario del Gobierno*, 9 Jan. 1839; Urréa to Baudin, Tampico, 27 Dec. 1838, AMAE,CP:Mexique, vol. 15, ff. 93–94; Maissin, *French in Mexico and Texas*, p. 45.

90. Baudin to Molé, *Néréide*, 30 Dec. 1838, AMAE,CP:Mexique, vol. 15, no. 14, ff. 109–13; Joinville, *Vieux souvenirs*, p. 167; Ashburnham to Palmerston, confidential, Mexico, 24 May 1838, PRO:FO 50/114, no. 39; same to same, 31 Dec. 1838, ibid., 50/116, no. 115; Pakenham to Palmerston, separate and confidential, H.M.S. *Pique*, Sacrificios, 3 Jan. 1839, ibid., 50/123; Maissin, *French in Mexico and Texas*, p. xx.

91. Baudin to Molé, *Néréide*, 15 Dec. 1838, AMAE,CP:Mexique, vol. 15, ff. 75–76.

92. Garro to Mexican Foreign Ministry, res., Mexico, 14 Nov. 1838, AEM, L.XXI, *RFM*, 1:315, no. 7533.

93. Molé to Baudin, Paris, 20 Sept. 1838, AMAE,CP:Mexique, vol. 14, ff. 56–62.

94. Pakenham to Palmerston, H.M.S. *Pique*, Sacrificios, 3 Jan. 1839, PRO:FO 50/123, no. 4; Douglas to Baudin, translation, Sacrificios, 11 Jan. 1839, AMAE,CP: Mexique, vol. 15, f. 160; Baudin to Molé, *Néréide*, 14 Jan. 1839, ibid., no. 21, ff. 170–73; Maissin, *French in Mexico and Texas*, pp. 33–37. Documents on the British mediation in AHSRE may be found in Francia-Mexico, L-E-1925 (III) and L-E-1928 (VI).

95. Pakenham to Gorostiza, copy, Mexico, 17 Jan. 1839, PRO:FO 50/123; Gorostiza to Pakenham, Mexico, 18 Jan. 1839, AMAE,CP:Mexique, vol. 15, ff. 206–8; Pakenham to Baudin, private, copy, 20 Jan. 1839, PRO:FO 50/123; Pakenham to Palmerston, Mexico, 26 Jan. 1839, ibid., no. 11; Pakenham to Gorostiza, copy, Mexico, 29 Jan. 1839, ibid.; Pakenham to Palmerston, 23 Feb. 1839, ibid., no. 16.

96. Gorostiza to Garro, res., Mexico, 31 Dec. 1838, AEM, L.XXI, *RFM*, 1:315, no. 7536.

97. Pakenham to Palmerston, Mexico, 26 Jan. 1839, PRO:FO 50/123, no. 11; Bancroft, *History of Mexico*, 5:200–203.

98. *Tratados y convenciones concluidos y ratificados por la República Mexicana desde su independencia hasta el año actual, acompañados de varios documentos que les son referentes*, pp. 415–23. For the correspondence accompanying the negotiations, see Peña y Reyes, *La primera guerra entre México y Francia*, pp. 337–43.

99. *Diario del Gobierno de la República Mexicana*, 15 Mar. 1839. See AMAE,CP:Mexique, vol. 16, ff. 122–27 for the French translation of this speech.

100. Baudin to Gorostiza, *Néréide*, 22 Mar. 1839, AMAE,CP:Mexique, vol. 16, ff. 168–73.

101. Pakenham to Baudin, Mexico, translation, 23 Mar. 1839, ibid., ff. 174–77; Gorostiza to Baudin, Mexico, translation, 21 Mar. 1839, ibid., ff. 159–60.

102. Baudin to Molé, *Néréide*, 9 Apr. 1839, AMAE,CP:Mexique, vol. 16, no. 34, ff. 249–52.

103. Baudin to Gorostiza, copy, *Néréide*, 23 Apr. 1839, ibid., ff. 262–63; Baudin to

Molé, 27 Apr. 1839, ibid., no. 35, ff. 272–73; Pakenham to Palmerston, Mexico, 11 May 1839, PRO:FO 50/124, no. 28.

104. Pakenham to Palmerston, Mexico, 11 May 1839, PRO:FO 50/124, no. 28.

105. Garro to Mexican Foreign Ministry, res., London, 15 June 1839, AEM, L.XXI, *RFM*, 1:317, no. 7561.

106. Dalmatia to Garro, Paris, 10 June 1839, AEM, L.XXI, *RFM*, 1:319, no. 7598; *Tratados y convenciones concluidos y ratificados*, pp. 419 and 422.

107. Gorostiza to Pakenham, Mexico, 21 Feb. 1839, AEM, L.XXI, *RFM*, 1:318, no. 7582; Gorostiza to Baudin, 21 Mar. 1839, ibid., no. 7581.

108. *Diario del Gobierno de la República Mexicana*, 15 Mar. 1839.

109. For Mexican views of the claims, see Cuevas, *Exposición del Ex-Ministro*, pp. 40–42; Bancroft, *History of Mexico*, 5:204, n. 40. In 1848 the French foreign minister admitted that part of the indemnity (without specifying how much) remained to be distributed, owing to the difficulty of substantiating the credentials of the claimants (French foreign minister to Goury du Roslan, draft, Paris, 23 Sept. 1848, AMAE, CP:Mexique, vol. 37, no. 7, f. 43).

110. Ashburnham to Palmerston, confidential, Mexico, 24 May 1838, PRO:FO 50/114, no. 39; AHSRE, Francia-Mexico, L-E-1917 to L-E-1931 contains miscellaneous documents on the blockade.

111. *Archives parlementaires*, Chambre des députés, 26 June 1839, 126:333.

112. Baudin to Dalmatia, Brest, 9 Aug. 1839, AMAE,CP:Mexique, vol. 16, ff. 298–99; "Extrait d'une dépêche de l'Amiral Baudin, datée du mois d'avril [1839] et publiée par le consul de France à la Nouvelle-Orleans," *Le Courrier des deux mondes*, Oct. 1839, Mexico. Pakenham enclosed a copy of this article in his report to Palmerston of 18 May 1840, PRO:FO 135, no. 48.

113. Dalmatia to DeLisle, Paris, draft, 11 July 1839, AMAE,CP:Mexique, vol. 17, no. 47, ff. 172–73.

114. Dalmatia to Alleye de Cyprey, Paris, draft, 31 Oct. 1839, ibid., vol. 18, no. 1, ff. 22–47; "Mémorandum" [on the results of the expedition to Mexico], 25 Dec. 1839, ibid., f. 76.

115. The words quoted in the previous sentence are those of the Mexican bishop, Moralès in his address on the occasion of the presentation of the cross (DeLisle to Dalmatia, Mexico, 21 June 1839, ibid., vol. 17, no. 29, ff. 149–52). For further evolution of the myth, see Bancroft, *History of Mexico*, 5:200. Santa Anna's version of his heroism is earnestly related by Bustamante, *Gabinete mexicano*, 1:141–45.

116. DeLisle to Dalmatia, Mexico, 12 Sept. 1839, AMAE,CP:Mexique, vol. 17, no. 36, ff. 220–23; Pakenham to Admiral Sir Thomas Harvey, copy, Mexico, 20 July 1839, PRO:FO 50/126.

117. The figures are in dispute. The bombardment of the fortress and attack on Veracruz are said to have caused fewer than 100 casualties (Jenkins, *History of the French Navy*, p. 291). See Bancroft, *History of Mexico*, 5:199, n. 30, for varying estimates. DeLisle's reports to Molé from Sacrificios in August 1838 give an impressionist idea of the incidence of the fever among the crews on the blockading vessels (18 Aug. 1838, AMAE,CP:Mexique, vol. 13, no. 17, ff. 163–65; and 25 Aug. 1838, ibid., ff. 180–82).

118. The government asked the Chamber to vote two supplementary credit bills amounting to 7,075,915 francs for the expeditions to Mexico and Buenos Aires of 1838–39. It also requested a special credit of 4,912,800 francs for future expenses in protecting French commerce in America. (The franc was worth approximately one-fifth of a peso or dollar.) *Archives parlementaires*, 1 June 1839, 125:257; ibid., 18 June

1839, 126:63; ibid., 13 July 1839, 127:544–46. The expenses of the two expeditions are not listed separately, but that to Mexico must have been the more expensive, since it involved over one-third more ships than the one to Buenos Aires (Jenkins, *History of French Navy*, p. 291).

119. DeLisle to Dalmatia, Mexico, 1 Oct. 1839, AMAE,CP:Mexique, vol. 17, no. 38, ff. 240–41.

120. Ibid.; see also same to same, 26 July 1838, ibid., vol. 13, no. 16, ff. 119–23; French minister of navy and colonies to French foreign minister, Paris, 12 Apr. 1839, ibid., vol. 17, f. 75; Laisné de Villevêque to DeLisle, Mexico, 4 Dec. 1838, ibid., vol. 15, ff. 44–53; Baudin to Molé, *Néréide*, 14 Dec. 1838, ibid., vol. 15, no. 11, ff. 71–73; same to same, 30 Dec. 1838, ibid., no. 14, ff. 109–13; Dalmatia to Alleye de Cyprey, Paris, draft, 31 Oct. 1839, AMAE,CP:Mexique, vol. 18, no. 1, ff. 22–47; Ashburnham to Palmerston, Mexico, 10 Dec. 1838, PRO:FO 50/116, no. 100.

121. Dalmatia to Alleye de Cyprey, draft, Paris, 31 Oct. 1839, AMAE,CP:Mexique, vol. 18, no. 1, ff. 22–47.

Notes to Chapter 4

1. Pakenham to Palmerston, Mexico, 7 Oct. 1840, PRO:FO, 50/137, no. 87; same to same, 9 Feb. 1840, ibid., no. 21; DeLisle to Dalmatia, Mexico, 28 Dec. 1839, AMAE,CP:Mexique, vol. 18, no. 47, f. 77; Clayton Charles Kohl, *Claims as a Cause of the Mexican War*, pp. 30–34, 38–39; Agustín Cué Cánovas, *Historia social y económica de México*, 2:349–53; Edgar Turlington, *Mexico and Her Foreign Creditors*, pp. 4, 6, 16–21, 27–30; Jan Bazant, *Historia de la deuda exterior de México (1823–1946)*, chap. 1.

2. Pakenham to Palmerston, Mexico, 22 Oct. 1839, PRO:FO, 50/126, no. 86; same to same, 3 Jan. 1840, ibid., 50/134, no. 5; Pakenham to Aberdeen, 6 Jan. 1842, ibid., 50/153, no. 6; DeLisle to Dalmatia, Mexico, 31 Dec. 1839, AMAE,CP:Mexique, vol. 18, no. 48, ff. 80–84; Calderón de la Barca to Pérez de Castro, Mexico, 3 Nov. 1840, *RDHM*, 1:172–73, no. 56.

3. Pakenham to Palmerston, Mexico, 9 Feb. 1840, PRO:FO 50/134, no. 21.

4. Dubois de Saligny to Dalmatia, New Orleans, 4 May 1840, AMAE,CP:Texas, no. 13, published in English translation in Nancy Nichols Barker, ed. and trans., *The French Legation in Texas*, 1:137. Examples of this attitude are legion. See, for example, "Memorandum on Texas" [for Count Louis Mathieu Molé], Paris, 8 May 1838, ibid., pp. 39–47.

5. Deffaudis to Thiers, Mexico, 1 Sept. 1836, AMAE,CP:Mexique, vol. 10, no. 103, ff. 164–67; Alleye de Cyprey to Guizot, 11 Aug. 1841, ibid., vol. 20, no. 72, ff. 279–81; Dubois de Saligny to Dalmatia, New Orleans, 4 May 1840, Barker, *French Legation*, 1:138.

6. Gutiérrez's "Carta" to the president is reproduced in French translation in AMAE,CP:Mexique, vol. 19; see f. 283 for the main statement of his thesis. For commentary by the European diplomats, see Calderón de la Barca to Pérez de Castro, 16 Nov. 1840, *RDHM*, 1:167, no. 54; Pakenham to Palmerston, Mexico, 26 Oct. 1840, PRO:FO 50/137, no. 95; Alleye de Cyprey to French foreign minister, Mexico, 27 Oct. 1840, AMAE,CP;Mexique, vol. 19, no. 29, ff. 232–34; Alleye de Cyprey to Thiers, 30 Nov. 1840, ibid., no. 32, ff. 256–62; Ortiz Monasterio to Garro, Mexico, 26 Oct. 1840, AEM, L.XX, *RFM*, 1:294, no. 7260; Manuel Rivera Cambas, *Historia de la intervención Europea y Norte-Americana en México y del imperio de Maximiliano de Hapsburgo*, 1:78–85.

7. DeLisle to Dalmatia, Mexico, 1 Oct. 1839, AMAE,CP:Mexique, vol. 17, no. 38, f. 237.

8. Dalmatia to Alleye de Cyprey, Paris, 31 Oct. 1839, ibid., vol. 18, no. 1, ff. 22–47.

9. Garro to Mexican Foreign Ministry, res., Paris, 17 Sept. 1839, AEM, L.XXIII, RFM, 2:9, no. 8089; same to same, Paris, Oct. 1839, L.XIX, RFM, 1:280, no. 6822; same to same, Paris, res., 13 Oct. 1839, L.XXIII, RFM, 2:10, no. 8099; same to same, Paris, res., 14 May 1840, L.XXIV, RFM, 2:17, no. 8349.

10. Memorandum presented to Congress by Cañedo, Jan. or Feb. 1840, ibid., L.XXIII, RFM, 2:10, no. 8107; Alleye de Cyprey to Dalmatia, Mexico, 18 May 1840, AMAE,CP:Mexique, vol. 18, no. 14, ff. 238–39.

11. Dalmatia to Garro, Paris, 12 Oct. 1839, AEM, L.XXIII, RFM, 2:9, no. 8097; draft of note in AMAE,CP:Mexique, vol. 17, f. 226.

12. Dalmatia to Dubois de Saligny, draft, Paris, 16 Oct. 1839, AMAE,CP:Texas, no. 1, in English translation in Barker, French Legation, 1:107–11.

13. For a short biography of this elusive diplomat, see Barker, French Legation, 1:17–35; and Nancy Nichols Barker, "France Disserved," pp. 25–43. Because Dubois de Saligny falsified the records of his dossier personnel in the Foreign Ministry and traveled under several different names, his career has long remained a mystery. I am indebted to the remarkable research of Me Maurice Paz, Avocat à la Cour de Paris honoraire in Paris, which enabled me to track down Dubois de Saligny's birth, marriage, and death certificates, which established his true identity and helped to fill in some of the many gaps of knowledge of his career.

14. Dubois de Saligny to Dalmatia, New Orleans, 4 May 1840, AMAE,CP:Texas, no. 13, Barker, French Legation, 1:136–42; for recent accounts of Dubois de Saligny's proposals and their fate, see Nancy Nichols Barker, "In Quest of the Golden Fleece," pp. 253–62; and Nancy Nichols Barker, "From Texas to Mexico" pp. 15–18.

15. Dubois de Saligny to Dalmatia, New Orleans, 4 May 1840, AMAE,CP:Texas, no. 13, Barker, French Legation, 1:137.

16. Thiers to Dubois de Saligny, Paris, 6 Sept. 1840, AMAE,CP:Texas, no. 2, ibid., 1:162.

17. The story is told by Dubois de Saligny in his reports to the French Foreign Ministry in the autumn of 1840 and spring of 1841 (ibid., pp. 163–242).

18. Ashbel Smith, Reminiscences of the Texas Republic, p. 34; Guizot to Dubois de Saligny, Paris, 18 Aug. 1841, no. 4, AMAE,CP:Texas, no. 4, Barker, French Legation, 1:257–59.

19. Dossiers personnels of Deffaudis and Alleye de Cyprey, AMAE.

20. Charles Durand to French minister of interior, Frankfurt, undated, dossier personnel of Alleye de Cyprey, AMAE; minister of interior to minister of foreign affairs, Paris, 20 Jan. 1834, ibid.

21. Bustamante's speech to Congress on 1 January 1840 is reproduced in Spanish and translation in Pakenham to Palmerston, Mexico, 9 Feb. 1840, PRO:FO 50/134, no. 10; Cañedo presented a memorandum to Congress on the subject of Texas in either January or February 1840, AEM, RFM, L.XXIII, 2:10, no. 8107; DeLisle to Molé, Mexico, 8 May 1839, AMAE,CP:Mexique, vol. 17, no. 25, ff. 109–11; Pakenham to Palmerston, Mexico, 11 May 1839, PRO:FO 50/124, no. 30; DeLisle to Dalmatia, Mexico, 27 July 1839, AMAE,CP:Mexique, vol. 17, no. 32, ff. 182–84; same to same, 1 Oct. 1839, ibid., no. 38, ff. 238–40; same to same, 23 Nov. 1839, ibid., vol. 18, no. 45, ff. 51–55; same to same, 19 Dec. 1839, ibid., no. 46, ff. 70–72.

22. Calderón de la Barca to Pérez de Castro, Mexico, 15 Feb. 1840, RDHM, 1:31–33, no. 12; Alleye de Cyprey to Dalmatia, Veracruz, 3 Feb. 1840, AMAE,CP:

Mexique, vol. 18, no. 1, ff. 133–35; Gloux to Dalmatia, Veracruz, 6 Feb. 1840, AMAE,CC:Veracruz, vol. 2, ff. 28–29, unnumbered; Fanny Calderón de la Barca, *Life in Mexico*, p. 689, n. 16, and p. 704, n. 6.

23. Mathieu de Fossey, *Le Mexique*, p. 285; Calderón de la Barca to Pérez de Castro, Mexico, 1 Apr. 1840, *RDHM*, 1:52, no. 21; Alleye de Cyprey to Dalmatia, Mexico, 25 Feb. 1840, AMAE,CP:Mexique, vol. 18, no. 2, ff. 160–65.

24. Calderón de la Barca to Pérez de Castro, Mexico, 1 Apr. 1840, *RDHM*, 1:52, no. 21; same to same, 2 June 1840, ibid., 1:73–74, no. 29.

25. For Alleye de Cyprey's version of the cathedral incident, see his report to Thiers, Mexico, 25 June 1840, AMAE,CP:Mexique, vol. 19, no. 8, ff. 4–13. For other versions, see Calderón de la Barca, *Life in Mexico*, pp. 248–49, 720–21, n. 5; the reports of Calderón de la Barca to Pérez de Castro, Mexico, 2 June 1840, *RDHM*, 1:72–73, no. 29; and 29 June 1840, ibid., 1:99–100, no. 35; Pakenham to Palmerston, Mexico, 5 July 1840, PRO:FO 50/136, no. 62.

26. Cañedo to Garro, res., Mexico, 2 July 1840, *RFM*, 2:5, no. 8030.

27. Alleye de Cyprey to Thiers, Mexico, 25 June 1840, AMAE,CP:Mexique, vol. 19, no. 8, ff. 4–13.

28. Alleye de Cyprey to Thiers, Mexico, 11 Aug. 1840, ibid., no. 14, ff. 125–33; same to same, 29 Sept. 1840, ibid., no. 22, ff. 182–86; Cañedo to Garro, res., Mexico, 1 Oct. 1840, AEM, L.XXIII, *RFM*, 2:13, no. 8233; Pakenham to Palmerston, Mexico, 9 Oct. 1840, PRO:FO 50/137, no. 90. For other examples of Alleye de Cyprey's irascibility, see Alleye de Cyprey to Monasterio, Mexico, 17 Mar. 1841; Alleye de Cyprey to Camacho, 4 June 1841; and Alleye de Cyprey to Bocanegra, 30 Dec. 1841, AHSRE, Francia-Mexico, L-E-1931 (V).

29. This quotation and the one in the previous paragraph are from Alleye de Cyprey to Thiers, Mexico, 13 July 1840, AMAE,CP:Mexique, vol. 19, no. 11, ff. 77–85.

30. Ibid., and same to same, 28 Sept. 1840, ibid., no. 20, f. 175.

31. Thiers to Alleye de Cyprey, Paris, 4 Sept. 1840, ibid., no. 7, ff. 155–56; Guizot to Alleye de Cyprey, 9 Nov. 1840, ibid., no. 8, f. 249.

32. Guizot to Alleye de Cyprey, Paris, 7 July 1841, ibid., vol. 20, no. 11, f. 216; Alleye de Cyprey to Guizot, Mexico, 17 Jan. 1841, ibid., no. 36, ff. 20–24.

33. Alleye de Cyprey to Guizot, 4 Jan. 1842, ibid., vol. 21, no. 91, ff. 187–89; Gómez Pedraza to Garro, res., Mexico, 2 Nov. 1841, AEM. L.XXIV, *RFM*, 2:20–21, no. 8496; Pakenham to Aberdeen, Mexico, 31 Jan. 1842, PRO:FO 50/153, no. 15 and same to same, Mexico, 2 May 1842, ibid., no. 33.

34. Alleye de Cyprey to Guizot, Mexico, 25 Feb. 1842, AMAE,CP:Mexique, vol. 21, no. 96, ff. 238–43; and same to same, 11 May 1842, ibid., vol. 22, no. 104, ff. 32–35; the prohibition decree is reproduced in AEM, L.XII, and summarized in *RFM*, 1:206, no. 3718. For the English translation, see that date in PRO:FO 50/163.

35. Alleye de Cyprey to Guizot, Mexico, 27 Sept. 1843, AMAE,CP:Mexique, vol. 25, no. 188, ff. 21–27; Doyle to Aberdeen, Mexico, 29 Sept. 1843, PRO:FO 50/164, no. 76.

36. Alleye de Cyprey to Bocanegra, copy, Mexico, 25 Sept. 1843, *RFM*, 1:199, no. 3580; a copy also in AMAE,CP:Mexique, vol. 25.

37. Alleye de Cyprey to Guizot, Mexico, 16 Mar. 1844, AMAE,CP:Mexique, vol. 26, no. 226, ff. 141–48.

38. Alleye de Cyprey, "Mémoire sur la situation du Mexique en mars 1844," ibid., ff. 168–87. See also Alleye de Cyprey to Guizot, 18 Mar. 1844, ibid., no. 228, ff. 166–67; and Alleye de Cyprey to Desages, private, 19 Mar. 1844, AMAE,MD:Pa-

piers Desages, vol. 36; same to same, 31 Mar. 1844, ibid.; and same to same, 30 May 1844, ibid.

39. Guizot to Alleye de Cyprey, Paris, 25 May 1844, AMAE,CP:Mexique, vol. 26, no. 44, f. 319.

40. *Archives parlementaires*, Chambre des Députés, 24 Jan. 1844; *Moniteur universel*, 25 Jan. 1844; Garro to Mexican foreign minister, reserved, Paris, 29 Jan. 1844, AEM, L.XXVI, *RFM*, 2:59, no. 9312; Garro to Guizot, Paris, 30 Jan. 1844, AMAE,CP:Mexique, vol. 26, ff. 52–56.

41. Two good studies of the diplomatic relations between France and the United States are Henry Blumenthal, *A Reappraisal of Franco-American Relations, 1830–1871*; and Lynn M. Case and Warren F. Spencer, *The United States and France*. For the question of the annexation of Texas, see especially David M. Pletcher, *The Diplomacy of Annexation*, pp. 113–226.

42. Guizot to Sainte-Aulaire (French ambassador in London), Paris, 14 June 1844, *Minute*, AMAE,CP:Mexique, vol. 27, no. 44, ff. 23–24. Sainte-Aulaire was instructed to communicate this message to Aberdeen.

43. Alleye de Cyprey to Guizot, Mexico, 28 June 1844, ibid., no. 261, ff. 200–204; Alleye de Cyprey to Desages, private, Mexico, 28 June 1844, AMAE,MD:Papiers Desages, vol. 36; same to same, 27 Aug. 1844, ibid.

44. Alleye de Cyprey to Guizot, Mexico, 28 Apr. 1844, AMAE,CP:Mexique, vol. 26, no. 240, ff. 231–32; Garro to Guizot, Paris, 25 May 1844, ibid., ff. 305–9; Alleye de Cyprey to Guizot, Mexico, 26 June 1844, ibid., vol. 27, no. 259, ff. 185–86; same to same, 29 June 1844, ibid., unnumbered, ff. 204–6; same to same, 29 Aug. 1844, ibid., vol. 28, no. 275, ff. 229–30; same to same, 27 Sept. 1844, ibid., vol. 29, no. 278, ff. 81–83.

45. PRO:FO 50/175, passim; AMAE,CP:Mexique, vols. 27 and 28, passim, especially Alleye de Cyprey to Guizot, 25 June 1844, vol. 27, no. 258, ff. 171–73 and "Extrait d'une lettre de Tabasco," 15 June 1844, ibid., f. 174; Oliver to Spanish foreign minister, Mexico, 30 Apr. 1844, *RDHM*, 3:51–52, no. 257; and same to same, 24 Nov. 1844, ibid., 3:117, no. 296; Oliver to Bocanegra, 22 June 1844, AEM, L.XXV, *RFM*, 2:51, no. 9169; Alleye de Cyprey to Bocanegra, 22 June 1844, ibid., 2:50, no. 9165; Bankhead to Bocanegra, 24 June 1844, ibid., 2:51, no. 9171; Génin, *Les Français au Mexique du XVIe siècle à nos jours*, pp. 206–7; Pletcher, *Diplomacy of Annexation*, p. 151.

46. Alleye de Cyprey to Guizot, Mexico, 12 Aug. 1844, AMAE,CP:Mexique, vol. 28, no. 268, ff. 9–25.

47. Sainte-Aulaire to Guizot, extrait, London, 2 Nov. 1844, AMAE,CP:Mexique, vol. 29, ff. 173–75.

48. Guizot to Alleye de Cyprey, Paris, 26 Oct. 1844, ibid., no. 48.

49. Same to same, 27 Nov. 1844, ibid., vol. 30, no. 49, ff. 45–47.

50. Guizot to Sainte-Aulaire, confidential, Paris, 26 Oct. 1844, ibid., vol. 29, ff. 214–16; Sainte-Aulaire to Guizot, London, 2 Nov. 1844, ibid., ff. 273–75; same to same, 15 Nov. ibid., f. 301.

51. Guizot to Dubois de Saligny, Paris, 17 Jan. 1845, AMAE,CP:Texas, no. 3, Barker, *French Legation*, 2:610–12. A "P. S." is dated 20 January [?]. Guizot to Alleye de Cyprey, Paris, 26 Feb. 1845, AMAE,CP:Mexique, vol. 30, no. 52, ff. 240–41; Pletcher, *Diplomacy of Annexation*, pp. 186–90.

52. See the dispatches of Dubois de Saligny of March and April 1845, AMAE,CP: Texas, nos. 64–66, Barker, *French Legation*, pp. 637–54. The reports of Charles Elliot to his government are reproduced in Ephraim Douglass Adams, ed., *British Diplo-*

matic Correspondence concerning the Republic of Texas, 1838–1846, pp. 453–72.

53. Alleye de Cyprey to Guizot, Mexico, 27 Apr. 1845, AMAE,CP:Mexique, vol. 31, no. 311, ff. 138–45; same to same, 20 May 1845, ibid., no. 313, ff. 171–78; Bermúdez de Castro to Spanish foreign minister, Mexico, 30 Mar. 1845, *RDHM*, 3:150–52, no. 308.

54. Pletcher, *Diplomacy of Annexation*, cites the major ones. See especially p. 204.

55. From Paris Garro frequently noted the pro-American, anti-English position of the opposition in the Chamber. He believed public opinion in general was pro-American. See Garro to Mexican foreign minister, res., 30 May 1845, *RFM*, 2:26, no. 8588; and same to same, res., 28 June 1845, ibid., 2:55, no. 9259. See also Pletcher, *Diplomacy of Annexation*, pp. 189–90.

56. Alleye de Cyprey to Léontine, Mme de Rivière, Mexico, 29 Sept. 1844, AMAE,CP:Mexique, vol. 29, ff. 120–21.

57. Alleye de Cyprey to Guizot, Mexico, 19 June 1845, ibid., vol. 31, no. 320, ff. 366–84.

58. Alleye de Cyprey to Léontine, Mme de Rivière, Mexico, 29 Sept. 1844, ibid., vol. 29, ff. 120–21.

59. Ibid., vols. 31 and 32, passim, especially Alleye de Cyprey to Cuevas, copy, 25 May 1845, vol. 31, ff. 310–14; Alleye de Cyprey to Guizot, 29 May 1845, 10 June 1845, ibid., vol. 31, no. 316, ff. 305–10 and ff. 359–61; same to same, 10 June 1845, no. 319, ff. 359–61; and same to same, 20 June 1845, vol. 32, no. 320–bis, ff. 26–28. The diplomatic correspondence related to the incident is published in Antonio de la Peña y Reyes, ed., *El Barón Alleye de Cyprey y el Baño de las Delicias*.

60. Alleye de Cyprey to Guizot, Mexico, 19 June 1845, AMAE,CP:Mexique, vol. 31, no. 320, ff. 366–84, last part in cypher.

61. Garro to Mexican Foreign Ministry, res., Paris, 16 July 1845, AEM, L.XXVI, *RFM*, 2:69–70, no. 9513; same to same, 26 July 1845, ibid., 2:70, no. 9515; same to same, 20 Aug. 1845, ibid., no. 9518.

62. Guizot to Alleye de Cyprey, Paris, 17 July 1845, AMAE,CP:Mexique, vol. 32, no. 57, ff. 80–82; same to same, res., 17 July 1845, ibid., ff. 82–87, in cypher.

63. Alleye de Cyprey to Guizot, Mexico, 24 Sept. 1845, ibid., no. 338, ff. 202–5; same to same, res., 25 Sept. 1845, ibid., ff. 205–9.

64. Alleye de Cyprey to Guizot, res., Mexico, 1 Oct. 1845, ibid., ff. 210–12; same to same, res., Veracruz, 24 Oct. 1834, ibid., ff. 220–23; Guizot to Alleye de Cyprey, Paris, 25 Nov. 1845, ibid., f. 240; Bermúdez de Castro to Guizot, Mexico, 27 Oct. 1845. *RDHM*, 4:144–45, no. 3, Appendix; Bermúdez de Castro to Spanish foreign minister, 27 Oct. 1845, ibid., 3:224–28, no. 300.

65. See, for example, *El Tiempo*, Mexico, 22 Feb. 1846; Hubert Howe Bancroft, *History of Mexico*, 5:292–93; *RDHM*, 3:xv–xvii, Prologue; Alleye de Cyprey to Guizot, Mexico, 7 Jan. 1846, AMAE,CP:Mexique, vol. 33, no. 3 (2d ser.), ff. 43–52; Bermúdez de Castro to Guizot, 28 Jan. 1846, ibid., no. 1, ff. 80–81; Bankhead to Aberdeen, Mexico, confidential, 30 Jan. 1846, PRO:FO 50/195; Manuel Camargo to Paredes, 20 Jan. 1845 [should be 1846], Paredes Papers.

66. Bankhead to Aberdeen, Mexico, confidential, 30 Mar. 1846, PRO:FO 50/196, no. 45; see also same to same, 29 Apr. 1846, ibid., no. 58; and same to same, 30 May 1846, ibid., 50/197, no. 72.

67. F. Martinez de la Rosa to Spanish ambassador in Paris res., translation, Madrid, 7 Feb. 1846, AMAE,CP:Mexique, vol. 33, ff. 99–104.

68. "Note sur le Mexique d'après les renseignements fournis par M. le Général Paredes traduits et rédits par M. de Mofras," AMAE,MD:Mexique, vol. 9, ff. 124–

31; *RDHM*, 3:xv–xvii, Prologue; Bankhead to Aberdeen, Mexico, 30 Mar 1846, PRO:FO 50/196, no. 39; same to same, 9 June 1846, ibid., 50/197, no. 77; Goury du Roslan to Guizot, Havana, 27 June 1846, AMAE,CP:Mexique, vol. 34, no. 13, ff. 70–80.

69. Castillo y Lanzas to Garro, Mexico, 23 Mar. 1846, *RFM*, 2&80, no. 9761; Bermúdez de Castro to Guizot, Mexico, 28 Mar. 1846, *RDHM*, 4:158–59, n. 16, Appendix; Castillo y Lanzas to Bermúdez de Castro, 28 Apr. 1846, ibid., 4:176, no. 26. The government designated Ignacio Valdivielso, a monarchist with long residence in Madrid, as minister plenipotentiary to France, but withdrew the appointment before he could take office.

70. Lavergne to Goury du Roslan, Paris, 24 Apr. 1846, extra-officielle, AMAE, CP:Mexique, vol. 33, ff. 265–66; Guizot to Bermúdez de Castro, 28 Apr. 1846, ibid., no. 4, f. 274; Goury du Roslan to Lavergne, Havana, 10 June 1846, ibid., vol. 34, ff. 51–54.

71. Bermúdez de Castro to Guizot, Mexico, 27 Aug. 1846, *RDHM*, 4:193–94, no. 38, Appendix; same to same, 28 Sept. 1840, ibid., 4:205–6, no. 50; same to same, 28 Oct. 1846, ibid., 4:209, no. 52; Bermúdez de Castro to Spanish foreign minister, 24 Sept. 1846, ibid., 3:290–91, no. 353; "Note pour le Ministre," Paris, May 1847, Direction Politique, AMAE,MD:Mexique, vol. 9, ff. 132–33; Goury du Roslan to Bermúdez de Castro, Havana, 8 June 1847, AMAE,CP:Mexique, vol. 35, ff. 219–20; Bermúdez de Castro to Guizot, 3 Aug. 1847, *RDHM*, 4:244, no. 73, Appendix.

72. Goury du Roslan to Guizot, Havana. 8 Aug. 1847, AMAE,CP:Mexique, vol. 35, no. 38, ff. 210–13; same to same, Mexico, Sept. 1847, ibid., no. 40, ff. 305–8; same to same, 13 Feb. 1848, ibid., vol. 36, no. 57, ff. 80–82; L. de la Rosa to Goury du Roslan, private and confidential, Querétaro, 9 Mar. 1848, AEM, L.XXVI, *RFM*, 2:62, no. 9339; L. de la Rosa to Mangino, res., 10 Mar. 1848, ibid., 2:61, no. 9337.

Notes to Chapter 5

1. Goury du Roslan to Lamartine, Mexico, 26 May 1848, AMAE,CP:Mexique, vol. 36, no. 74, ff. 197–99; same to same, 7 June 1848, ibid., no. 75, ff. 211–12. De la Rosa to Mangino, res., Querétaro, 11 Mar. 1848, Rafael Heliodoro Valle, ed., *Un diplomático mexicano en Paris (Don Fernando Mangino, 1848–1851)*, pp. 25–27.

2. Luis de la Rosa to Mangino, Querétaro, 11 May 1848, AEM, L.XXV, *RFM*, 2:56, no. 9269; Luis de la Rosa to Goury du Roslan, Querétaro, 29 Apr. 1848, *RDHM*, 4:247–48, no. 76, Appendix, Annex; Goury du Roslan to Luis de la Rosa, 29 Apr. 1848, ibid., 4:248–49, no. 77.

3. Mangino to Bastide, Paris, 23 June 1848, AMAE,CP:Mexique, vol. 36, f. 227; same to same, 10 July 1848, ibid., ff. 231–34.

4. Dossier personnel of André Nicolas Levasseur, AMAE.

5. For examples, see Levasseur to French foreign minister, Mexico, 6 July 1850, AMAE,CP:Mexique, vol. 38, no. 43; Levasseur to Bastide, Mexico, 6 Dec. 1848, ibid., vol. 37, no. 1, ff. 83–88.

6. Levasseur to Bastide, Mexico, 6 Dec. 1848, ibid.; Cuevas to Mangino, Mexico, 13 Feb. 1849, AEM, L.XXVII, *RFM*, 2:86, no. 9931.

7. Mangino to Mexican Foreign Ministry, Muy res., Paris, 27 Jan. 1849, AEM, L.XIV, *RFM*, 1:237, no. 4432; same to same, res., 29 Jan. 1849, ibid., L.XXVII, 2:86, no. 9930.

8. Daniel Dawson, *The Mexican Adventure*, pp. 42–49; Edward W. Richards, "Louis Napoleon and Central America," p. 179.

9. Mexico, *Memoria del Ministerio de Guerra y Marina. Años 1850–1857*, report of 28 Jan. 1850, pp. 21–22; Lacunza to Mangino, res., 11 Aug. 1849, AEM, L.XXVIII, *RFM*, 2:95, no. 10295; Rondo Cameron, *France and the Economic Development of Europe, 1800–1914*, pp. 36–43; Hubert Howe Bancroft, *History of Mexico*, 5:567–71; Levasseur to French minister of foreign affairs, Mexico, 7 May 1849, AMAE,CP: Mexique, vol. 37, no. 20, ff. 152–55; Corona to Mangino, Paris, 30 Aug. 1850, AEM, L.XXIX, *RFM*, 2:101, no. 10999.

10. French foreign minister to Mangino, Paris, 24 Dec. 1849, AMAE,CP:Mexique, vol. 38, ff. 19–20; same to same, 14 Jan. 1850, ibid., ff. 31–32; same to same, 29 May 1850, AEM, L.XXVIII, *RFM*, 2:97, no. 10737.

11. The records of the purchases are fragmentary; see AEM, L.XXIX, XXX, XXXII. The documents are summarized in *RFM*, 2:118–20, nos. 11445–537; 123–24, nos. 11538–758; 132–33, nos. 12025–70; and 162–63, nos. 12869–955.

12. Levasseur to French foreign minister, Mexico, 9 Apr. 1850, AMAE,CP:Mexique, vol. 38, no. 37, ff. 97–100; French foreign minister to Levasseur, Paris, 31 May 1850, ibid., no. 13; Report of Mexican secretary of war, José F. Correa, Mexico, 22 Jan. 1851, AEM, L.XXVII, *RFM*, 2:86, no. 9949; Yañez to Mangino, Mexico, 3 Feb. 1851, Valle, *Un diplomático mexicano en Paris*, p. 111.

13. Mexico, *Memoria del Ministerio de Guerra y Marina*, Report of 30–31 Jan. 1852, p. 73.

14. Levasseur to French foreign minister, Mexico, 10 Sept. 1849, AMAE,CP: Mexique, vol. 37, no. 26, ff. 201–3; Ortiz Monasterio to Mangino, Mexico, 2 July 1850, AEM, L.XXIX, *RFM*, 2:116, no. 11301; Corona to Mangino, Paris, 30 Aug. 1850, ibid., p. 101 , no. 10999; for some of the Mexican students sent to France, see *RFM*, 2:124–25, nos. 11759–831; Mexico, *Memoria del Ministerio de Guerra y Marina*, Report of 30–31 Jan. 1852, pp. 73–77.

15. French foreign minister to Levasseur, Paris, 31 July 1848, AMAE,CP:Mexique, vol. 36, no. 1, ff. 262–64. Mangino reported French claims to the amount of $1,180,274 extant at the beginning of 1848 (Mangino to Mexican foreign minister, res., Paris, 29 Apr. 1848, Valle, *Un diplomático mexicano en Paris*, p. 58).

16. Goury du Roslan to Bastide, Mexico, 2 Aug. 1848, AMAE,CP:Mexique, vol. 37, no. 82, ff. 3–6; Levasseur to French foreign minister, Mexico, 1 Apr. 1849, ibid., no. 18, ff. 134–43; Bankhead to Palmerston, Mexico, 13 Aug. 1850, PRO:FO 50/ 237, no. 30.

17. French foreign minister to Goury du Roslan, Paris, 3 Nov. 1848, AMAE,CP: Mexique, vol. 37, no. 9, ff. 66–68; Levasseur to French foreign minister, Mexico, 1 Apr. 1849, ibid., no. 18, ff. 134–43; same to same, 12 June 1849, ibid., no. 22, ff. 171–79; French foreign minister to Levasseur, Paris, 3 Aug. 1849, ibid., no. 217 [*sic*], ff. 193–97; same to same, 20 Feb. 1850, ibid., vol. 38, no. 3, ff. 49–50; Levasseur to French foreign minister, Mexico, 2 Aug. 1850, ibid., no. 46, ff. 150–58.

18. Lamartine to A. Pageot (French minister plenipotentiary in Washington, D.C.), Paris, 27 Mar. 1848, AMAE,CP:Etats Unis, vol. 105, no. 63; Lamartime to Mangino, Paris, 26 Apr. 1848, *RFM*. 2:84–85, no. 9901.

19. Levasseur to French foreign mininster, Mexico, 25 Dec. 1851, AMAE,CP: Mexique, vol. 39, no. 91; Doyle to Palmerston, Mexico, 5 Dec. 1851, PRO:FO 50/246, no. 96. The terms of the French convention and those signed by the Mexican government with the British and Spanish representatives are summarized briefly in Bancroft, *History of Mexico*, 5:601–2, n. 17.

20. Dated 30 April 1849, the *Registre* is found in AMAE,MD:Mexique, vol. 7. To my knowledge the only other reference to the *Registre* in a published work (other

than my own) is the brief (and inaccurate) summary of it by Jean Meyer, "Les Français au Mexique au XIXe siècle." pp. 49–51.

21. Levasseur to Department of Foreign Affairs, Mexico, 5 May 1849, AMAE, CC:Mexico City, vol. 6 (1844–50), no. 5. The ministerial instructions of the preceding August are missing from the archives but are mentioned by Levasseur in the above dispatch.

22. Ibid.

23. Doyle to Palmerston, Mexico, 5 May 1851, PRO:FO 50/244, no. 33.

24. Gabriac to French Foreign Ministry, Mexico, 20 Feb. 1860, AMAE,CP:Mexique, vol. 52, f. 345.

25. Doyle to Hammond, private, 17 Sept. 1856, PRO:FO 50/294.

26. See n. 25 for source of British subjects in Mexico. From Francisco López Cámara, Los fundamentos de la economía mexicana en la época de la Reforma y la Intervención, p. 17, one might conclude that German-speaking foreigners in Mexico were the most numerous (eight to nine thousand, according to him). But López Cámara mistranslated his French source of information, Gabriac, minister in Mexico in the 1850s. Gabriac had written eight to nine hundred Germans (Gabriac to French Foreign Ministry, Mexico, 20 Feb. 1860, AMAE,CP:Mexique, vol. 52, f. 345). The scholarly work of Friedrich Katz, Deutschland, Diaz, und die mexikanische Revolution, p. 153, estimates that as late as 1900 only 1,800 Germans were in Mexico.

27. Charles H. Pouthas, La Population française pendant la première moitié du XIXe siècle, p. 122; Abel Chatelain, "Les Migrations françaises vers le Nouveau Monde aux XIXe et XXe siècles," pp. 54–55.

28. Chatelain, "Les Migrations," p. 67.

29. López Cámara, Los fundamentos de la economía, pp. 74–75; Mathieu de Fossey, Le Mexique, p. 273; David M. Pletcher, The Diplomacy of Annexation, pp. 44–46. A large number of claims pressed by the British legation on the Mexican government concerned mining companies, especially the British United Mining Company.

30. Chatelain, "Les Migrations," pp. 62–63.

31. Louis Chevalier, "L'Émigration française au XIXe siècle," p. 142; André Armengaud, La Population française au XIXe siècle, pp. 92–93.

32. Levasseur, Registre, AMAE; Antonio García Cubas, ed., Diccionario geográfico, histórico y biográfico de los Estados Unidos Mexicanos, 3:308 and 4:98.

33. Molé to Deffaudis, Paris, 9 Dec. 1837, AMAE,CP:Mexique, vol. 12, no. 39, f. 62.

34. Levasseur, Registre, AMAE. The French government did not formally recognize Jecker as a French subject until 26 March 1862 in an imperial decree of naturalization, published in the Bulletin des Lois de l'Empire français,21 Aug. 1862, no. 863, p. 218, 11th série, 2e partie supplémentaire, vol. 20.

35. For a demonstration of the connection between Morny and Jecker, see Nancy N. Barker, "The Duke of Morny and the Affair of the Jecker Bonds," pp. 555–61. For later activity of the legation in Mexico in claims, see Nancy N. Barker, "The French Legation in Mexico," pp. 409–26.

36. Deffaudis to Broglie, Mexico, 30 Jan. 1834, AMAE,CC:Mexico, vol. 4, no. 12, ff. 162–65.

37. Alleye de Cyprey to Guizot, Mexico, 1 Nov. 1843, AMAE,CP:Mexique, vol. 25, no. 191; Deffaudis to Molé, Mexico, 26 Feb. 1837, ibid., vol. 11, no. 123, ff. 30–33.

38. Mexique. "1er Mémoire," 22 Nov. 1838, AMAE,CP:Mexique, vol. 13, ff. 213–47. There is no summary exposé of the debt claimed by France of Mexico in

1861, although the conventon of 26 March 1861 negotiated by Dubois de Saligny with the Mexican foreign minister lists the categories into which the claims fell. They represented an accumulation of grievances extending over more than a decade and reported to Paris in the minister's correspondence as they occurred. A large majority of the claimants were small retailers.

39. *Archives du commerce et de l'industrie agricole et manufacturière*, p. 237; Auguste Génin, *Les Français au Mexique du XVIᵉ siècle à nos jours*, pp. 382–90.

40. Gloux to Lamartine, Veracruz, 30 Apr. 1848, AMAE,CC:Veracruz, vol. 2, no. 2, ff. 205–8.

41. Levasseur to French foreign minister, Mexico, 2 Aug. 1850, AMAE,CP:Mexique, vol. 38, no. 46, ff. 150–58.

42. Étienne Micard, *La France au Mexique, étude sur les expéditions militaires, l'influence et le rôle économique de la France au Mexique*, p. 247; Génin, *Les Français au Mexique*, p. 392; F. Arnaud, *Les Barcelonnettes au Mexique*, pp. 21–25.

43. Levasseur to French foreign minister, 14 May 1849, AMAE,CP:Mexique, vol. 37, no. 21, ff. 163–64.

44. Génin, *Les Français au Mexique*, p. 399; for the regulation and membership of the Société in Veracruz, formed in 1839, see AMAE,CC:Veracruz, vol. 2, f. 275. It had 128 founding members and 12 Dames Patronesses. For a critical description of the Société in the capital, see Gabriac to Walewski, confidentielle et réservée, Mexico, 16 July 1856, AMAE,CP:Mexique, vol. 45, ff. 286–91.

45. Micard, *La France au Mexique*, p. 246; Levasseur to French foreign minister, 13 July 1850, AMAE,CP:Mexique, vol. 38, no. 45, ff. 148–50; Dano to Drouyn de Lhuys, Mexico, 19 June 1854, ibid., vol. 42, no. 35, ff. 216–18.

46. Levasseur, *Registre*, AMAE.

47. Examples are legion. See especially Eugène Duflot de Mofras, *Exploration du territoire de l'Orégon, des Californies, et de la mer Vermeille exécutée pendant les années 1840, 1841, et 1842*, 1:21 and 2:67; Fossey, *Le Mexique*, pp. 55, 249; Génin, *Les Français au Mexique*, p. 382; and Margarita Martínez Leal de Helguera, *Posibles antecedentes de la intervención francesa de 1862*, passim.

48. Arnaud, *Les Barcelonnettes*, p. 57.

49. Chatelain, "Les Migrations," p. 69; Arnaud, *Les Barcelonnettes*, p. 25.

50. Cochelet to French foreign minister, Mexico, 15 Jan. 1830, AMAE,CC: Mexico, vol. 2, no. 2, ff. 567–71.

51. Duflot de Mofras, *Exploration*; Rufus Kay Wyllys, *The French in Sonora (1850–1854)*, pp. 1–33, 74–75; Joseph Allen Stout, Jr., *The Liberators*, pp. v–vii, 13–36; *Annuaire des deux mondes*, 1, 1850, 896–97.

52. Chatelain, "Les Migrations," p. 67. n. 4.

53. Wyllys, *The French in Sonora*, pp. 34–47; Daniel Lévy, *Les Français en Californie*, pp. 64–111; Stout, *The Liberators*, pp. 50–51.

54. Hippolyte Du Pasquier de Dommartin, *Les Etats-Unis et le Mexique*, pp. 23–24, 55–60.

55. Ibid., pp. 69–70.

56. Ibid., pp. 70–71.

57. Levasseur to French foreign minister, Mexico, 1 Dec. 1852, AMAE,CP:Mexique, vol. 40, no. 139, ff. 352–55; same to same, 15 Dec. 1852, ibid., no. 141, ff. 364–70; José Aguilar to Levasseur, copy, Ures, 23 May 1850, ibid., f. 371.

58. Levasseur to French foreign minister, Mexico, 1 Aug. 1851, ibid., vol. 39, no. 73, ff. 103–6; same to same, 5 Oct. 1850, ibid., vol. 38, no. 50, ff. 159–60.

59. Same to same, 2 Nov. 1850, ibid., vol. 38, no. 52, ff. 167–71.

60. Levasseur to Bastide, Mexico, 12 Jan. 1849, ibid., vol. 37, no. 8, ff. 108–10.

61. Dommartin, *Les Etats-Unis et le Mexique*, p. 71.

62. Levasseur to French foreign minister, Mexico, 15 Dec. 1852, AMAE,CP:Mexique, vol. 40, no. 141, ff. 364–70.

63. Doyle to Malmesbury, Mexico, 3 Dec. 1852, PRO:FO 50/253, no. 82; Wyllys, *The French in Sonora*, pp. 72–73; Levasseur to Raousset-Boulbon, copy, Mexico, 13 July 1852, AMAE,CP:Mexique, vol. 40, ff. 386–88; Levasseur to governor of Sonora, copy, Mexico, 8 Apr. 1852, ibid., ff. 373–76.

64. Levasseur to French foreign minister, Mexico, 1 Dec. 1852, AMAE,CP:Mexique, vol. 40, no. 139, ff. 352–55; same to same, 15 Dec. 1852, ibid., no. 141, ff. 364–70. Appended to this second report are copies of Levasseur's correspondence with Arista, Aguilar, Calvo, Dillon, Raousset-Boulbon, and Blanco defining and documenting Levasseur's promotional work in behalf of the expedition.

65. The turbulent life of Raousset-Boulbon is described more or less accurately in a number of biographies, among which are Alfred de La Chapelle, *Le Comte Raousset Boulbon et l'expédition du Sonore*; Charles de Lambertie, *Le Drame de la Sonora, l'état de Sonora, M. le Comte de Raousset-Boulbon et M. Charles de Pindray*; and Maurice Soulié, *The Wolf Cub*. See also Fossey, *Le Mexique*, pp. 188–91.

66. Levasseur to Blanco, copy, Mexico, 17 Apr. 1852, AMAE,CP:Mexique, vol. 40, ff. 380; Levasseur to Calvo, copy, Mexico, 19 Apr. 1852, ibid., ff. 383–86; French foreign minister to Levasseur, Paris, 31 Jan. 1852, ibid., vol. 39, n. 1, f. 228.

67. Levasseur to French foreign minister, Mexico, 15 Dec. 1852, AMAE,CP:Mexique, vol. 40, no. 141, ff. 364–70.

68. Levasseur to Ramírez, copy, Mexico, 31 Aug. 1852, AEM, L.XXXI, *RFM*, 2:137, no. 12129; Wyllys, *The French in Sonora*, pp. 87–106.

69. Raousset-Boulbon to Mr. J. Gardet (in Valparaiso), Mazatlán, 14 Dec. 1852, AEM, L.XXXI, *RFM*, 2:144–46, no. 12175. This letter, preserved in the Mexican Embassy, is used here for the first time to the best of my knowledge in a published account of Raousset-Boulbon's first expedition. Raousset-Boulbon had known Gardet earlier when he was organizing his expedition in San Francisco. It is important evidence of his revolutionary aims.

70. Levasseur to French foreign minister, Mexico, June 1852, AMAE,CP:Mexique, vol. 39, no. 112, ff. 364–72; J. F. Ramírez to F. S. Mora, Mexico, 4 June 1852, AEM, L.XXXI, *RFM*, 2:135, no. 12103; Levasseur to Ramírez, copy, Mexico, 26 May 1852, AMAE,CP:Mexique, vol. 39, ff. 339–45; Doyle to Malmesbury, Mexico, 4 June 1852, PRO:FO 50/252, no. 39.

71. Quotations are from Levasseur to French foreign minister, Mexico, 27 June 1852, AMAE,CP:Mexique, vol. 39, no. 116, ff. 448–58; see also same to same, 2 June 1852, ibid., no. 111, ff. 337–38; Levasseur to Dano, 20 June 1852, ibid., ff. 443–45.

72. Levasseur to French foreign minister, Mexico, 26 Aug. 1852, ibid., vol. 40, no. 125, ff. 169–76; Malmesbury to Cowley, copy, Foreign Office, 14 July 1852, ibid., ff. 79–80; J. F. Ramírez to F. S. Mora, Mexico, 4 June 1852, AEM, L.XXXI, *RFM*, 2:135, no. 12103; Mora to Turgot, Paris, 22 July 1852, AMAE,CP:Mexique, vol. 40, ff. 15–16; Ramírez to Mora, res., Mexico, 1 Sept. 1852, AEM, *RFM*, 2:136–37, no. 12128.

73. Levasseur to French foreign minister, Mexico, 20 Sept. 1852, AMAE,CP: Mexique, vol. 40, no. 130, ff. 214–39.

74. Same to same, 5 Mar. 1852, ibid., vol. 39, no. 39, ff. 246–48; Levasseur to Ramírez, copy, Mexico, 26 May 1852, ibid., ff. 339–45; Levasseur to Dano, Mexico, 20 June 1852, ibid., ff. 443–45.

75. Levasseur to Ramírez, copy, Mexico, 31 Aug. 1852, AEM, L.XXXI, *RFM*, 2:137, no. 12129.

76. Wyllys, *The French in Sonora*, p. 112, n. 12.

77. Charles Seignobos, *La Révolution de 1848–Le Second Empire (1848–1859)*, 6:303–4.

78. Drouyn de Lhuys to Mora, Paris, 26 Aug. 1852, AMAE,CP:Mexique, vol. 40, ff. 162–64; Drouyn de Lhuys to Levasseur, Paris, 28 Aug. 1852, ibid., no. 11, ff. 177–78; Arroyo to Mora, res., Paris, 2 Oct. 1852, AEM, L.XXXI, *RFM*, 2:149, no. 12206; Mora to Mexican Foreign Ministry, res., Paris, 20 Oct. 1852, ibid., L.XXX, *RFM*, 2:131, no. 11983; same to same, res., 20 Oct. 1852, ibid., L.XXXI, *RFM*, 2:149, no. 12207.

79. Drouyn de Lhuys to Levasseur, Paris, 31 Dec. 1852, AMAE,CP:Mexique, vol. 40, no. 18, f. 422; dossier personnel of André Nicolas Levasseur, AMAE.

80. All quotations in this paragraph and the preceding one taken from Levasseur to French foreign minister, Mexico, 30 Apr. 1853, AMAE,CP:Mexique, vol. 41, no., 164, ff. 151–60.

81. Pacheco to Mexican Foreign Ministry, Paris, 30 Aug. 1853, AEM, L.XXXIII, *RFM*, 2:165, no. 12956; same to same, 31 Jan. 1854, ibid., 165–66, no. 12955; same to same, 25 May 1854, ibid., 166, no. 12970.

82. Drouyn de Lhuys to Walewski, Paris, 27 Dec. 1852, AMAE,CP:Angleterre, vol. 687, no. 117; Drouyn de Lhuys to Levasseur, Paris, 15 Apr. 1853, AMAE,CP: Mexique, vol. 41, no. 3, ff. 120–21; same to same, 31 May 1853, ibid., no. 4, f. 177; Drouyn de Lhuys to Dano, Paris, 14 Oct. 1853, ibid., no. 8, f. 288; Levasseur to French foreign minister, Mexico, 31 May 1853, ibid., no. 169, ff. 178–89; Pacheco to Mexican Foreign Ministry, Paris, 30 Aug. 1853, AEM, L.XXXIII, *RFM*, 2:165, no. 12956.

83. Pacheco to Drouyn de Lhuys, Reservadíssima, 24 Oct. 1853, AMAE,CP: Mexique, vol. 41, ff. 194–315.

84. Doyle to Clarendon, secret, Mexico, 3 Dec. 1851, PRO:FO 50/261, no. 117; same to same, secret and confidential, 2 Jan. 1854, ibid., 50/266, no. 13; Egon Caesar, Count Corti, *Maximilian and Charlotte of Mexico*, 1:22.

85. Doyle to Clarendon, Mexico, 3 July 1854, PRO:FO 50/268, no. 71.

86. Levasseur to French foreign minister, Mexico, 31 May 1853, AMAE,CP:Mexique, vol. 41. no. 169, ff. 178–79.

87. Dano to Drouyn de Lhuys, Mexico, 1 Aug. 1853, ibid., no. 3, ff. 242–49; same to same, 3 Aug. 1853, ibid., no. 7, ff. 256–58; same to same, 1 Sept. 1853, ibid., no. 9, ff. 265–66; same to same, 31 Oct. 1853, ibid., no. 15, ff. 320–23; same to same, 3 Jan. 1854, ibid., vol. 42, no. 18, ff. 4–13.

88. Dano to French foreign minister, Mexico, 3 Jan. 1854, ibid., vol. 42, no. 18, ff. 4–13; same to same, 18 Jan. 1854, ibid., no. 20, f. 50.

89. Bonilla to Dano, copy, Mexico, 17 Jan. 1854, AEM, L.XXXI, *RFM*, 2:139, no. 12136; Dano to Bonilla, copy, 18 Jan. 1854, ibid., 2:139–40. no. 12137; Bonilla to Pacheco, 31 Jan. 1854, ibid., L.XXIX, *RFM*, 2:109, no. 11208; *Universal*, 22 Jan. 1854; Dano to French foreign minister, Mexico, 1 Feb. 1854, AMAE,CP:Mexique, vol. 42, no. 22, ff. 85–88; Doyle to Clarendon, Mexico, 2 Feb. 1854, PRO:FO 50/266, no. 15; Raousset-Boulbon admitted and even boasted of his conspiracy to Dano (Raousset-Boulbon to Dano, San Francisco, 28 Feb. 1854, AMAE,CP:Mexique, vol. 42, f. 158).

90. Dano to Drouyn de Lhuys, Mexico, 5 Aug. 1854, AMAE,CP:Mexique, vol. 42, no. 42, ff. 282-86; Doyle to Clarendon, Mexico, 5 Aug. 1854, PRO:FO 50/268, no. 92; Dano to Drouyn de Lhuys, Mexico, 19 Aug. 1854, AMAE,CP:Mexique, vol. 42, no. 44, ff. 297-303; same to same, 1 Sept. 1854, ibid., vol. 43, no. 45, ff. 4-22; same to same, 5 Sept. 1854, ibid., confidentielle et très réservée, ff. 68-72; same to same, 19 Sept. 1854, ibid., no. 46, ff. 74-77; same to same, 5 Nov. 1854, no. 49, ff. 174-77; Bonilla to Pacheco, Mexico, 1 Oct. 1854, *RFM*, 2:143, no. 12162.

91. The most thorough and scholarly studies of the French expeditions into Sonora have been made by American historians, who made exhaustive use of sources on this side of the Atlantic. However, because they did not use the archives of the French Foreign Ministry, they could only guess at the degree of involvement of Levasseur and the French government. See Wyllys, *The French in Sonora*, pp. 85-86, and Stout, *The Liberators*, p. 78; also, Helen Broughall Metcalf, "The California French Filibusters in Sonora," pp. 2-21.

92. Dano to French foreign minister, Mexico, 2 Feb. 1854, AMAE,CP:Mexique, vol. 42, no. 23, ff. 103-6; Drouyn de Lhuys to Dano, Paris, 28 Feb. 1854. ibid., no. 3, ff. 137-38; same to same, 15 Mar. 1854, ibid., no. 4, f. 160.

93. Pacheco to Bonilla, Paris, 31 Mar. 1854, AEM, L.XXXI, *RFM*, 2:140-41, no. 12144.

94. Dano to Drouyn de Lhuys, confidentielle et réservée, Mexico, 2 Oct. 1854, AMAE,CP:Mexique, vol. 43, ff. 91-100.

95. A poll of the survivors of Raousset-Boulbon's second expedition taken by the French vice-consul at Guaymas revealed that nearly one-third of them were former soldiers or sailors, another third artisans or unskilled workers. Only 10 were merchants; 22 were clerks; only 3 were members of professions; 18 declared themselves without occupation. There were no women. See AMAE,CP:Mexique, vol. 42, f. 277.

Notes to Chapter 6

1. Drouyn de Lhuys to Gabriac, 19 June 1854, AMAE, dossier personnel of Vicomte de Jean Alexis Gabriac. Virtually all of Gabriac's promotions in the Foreign Ministry occurred when Drouyn de Lhuys held office.

2. Gabriac to Walewski, Mexico, 11 Nov. 1856, AMAE,CP:Mexique, vol. 46, no. 153; same to same, 7 July 1858, AMAE,MD:Mexique, vol. 9, ff. 294-304; with accompanying "Extrait d'Etudes sur l'Amérique," translated and edited by Count de La Londe, secretary of the legation. Gabriac's arguments for intervention are too numerous to cite individually. See, for example, Gabriac to Walewski, Mexico, 9 Aug. 1856, AMAE,CP:Mexique, vol. 46, no. 130; same to same, 1 July 1856, ibid., vol. 45, no. 118; Gabriac to Drouyn de Lhuys, 25 Jan. 1855, ibid., vol. 43, no. 6.

3. Gabriac to Walewski, Mexico, 10 Oct. 1855, AMAE,CP:Mexique, vol. 47, no. 240.

4. Gabriac to Drouyn de Lhuys, Mexico, 25 Jan. 1855, ibid., vol. 43, no. 6; Gabriac to Walewski, 16 July 1855, ibid., vol. 44, no. 41; same to same, confidentielle et réservée, 16 July 1856, ibid., no. 45, ff. 286-91; same to same, 23 Sept. 1856, ibid., vol. 46, no. 140; Luis de la Rosa to Olaguíbel, Mexico, 19 July 1856, AEM, L.XXXIV, *RFM*, 2:178, no. 13678.

5. Otway to Malmesbury, Mexico, confidential, 22 Oct. 1858, PRO:FO 50/324, no. 154.

6. *Le Trait d'Union*, passim. The paper's editor, René Masson, was a troublesome republican agitator. Gabriac to Walewski, Mexico, 1 Nov. 1855, AMAE,CP:Mexi-

que, vol. 44, unnumbered, ff. 220–21; same to same, confidentielle et réservée, 16 July 1856, ibid., vol. 45, ff. 286–91; same to same, 21 July 1856, ibid., vol. 45, no. 124; Lettsom to Clarendon, Mexico, 19 July 1856, PRO:FO 50/292, no. 127; same to same, 31 July 1856, ibid., 50/293, no. 140; Luis de la Rosa to Olaguíbel, Mexico, 19 July 1856, AEM, L.XXXIV, *RFM*, 2:178, no. 13678; Otway to Malmesbury, Mexico, confidential, 22 Oct. 1858, PRO:FO 50/324, no. 154.

7. Luis de la Rosa to Bellangé, copy, Toluca, Sept. 1847, PRO:FO 50/294; Lettsom to Clarendon, confidential, Mexico, 16 Aug. 1856, ibid., no. 156; same to same, 19 Sept. 1856, ibid., no. 184; Gabriac to Walewski, Mexico, 26 July 1856, AMAE,CP: Mexique, vol. 45, no. 125; same to same, 5 Sept. 1856, ibid., vol. 46, no. 136; same to same, 7 Oct. 1856, ibid., no. 144.

8. Lettsom to Clarendon, Mexico, confidential, 19 Sept. 1856, PRO:FO 50/294; "Note remise à Mgr le Duc d'Aumale (à Gibraltar)," 2 Jan. 1857, RP.

9. Radepont to Morny, Mexico, 17 Sept. 1854, RP; for his other connections, see RP, passim.

10. AMAE,CP:Affaires diverses, Mexique, 1847–50. Mission temporaire de Radepont. Radepont's report, entitled "Mémoire sur la guerre entre les Etats Unis du Nord et la République du Mexique," is preserved in AMAE,MD:Mexique, vol. 9, ff. 110–273. He had arrived in Veracruz 30 Sept. 1847.

11. Radepont to Gabriac, copy, Paris, 26 Nov. 1856, Letterbook, RP; "Note remise d'abord à M. le comte Walewsky, communiquée par lui à l'Empereur en octobre 1856, remise à Msgr le Duc d'Aumale . . . , envoyée à Madame la Duchesse d'Orléans," RP; "Mémorandum, Mexique," 1856, AMAE,CP:Mexique, vol. 46, ff. 101–2; Radepont to Walewski, Paris, 4 Oct. 1856, ibid., f. 103, and Radepont, "Projet pour la régénération du Mexique," ibid., ff. 104–21; Daniel Dawson, *The Mexican Adventure*, pp. 50–54; Alfred Jackson Hanna and Kathryn Abbey Hanna, *Napoleon III and Mexico*, pp. 16–20.

12. Gabriac to Walewski, Mexico, 23 May 1857, AMAE,CP:Mexique, vol. 47, no. 203; same to same, 21 June 1857, ibid., no. 210; same to same, confidentielle, 6 July 1857, ibid., no. 214; same to same, 9 July 1857, ibid., no. 215; same to same, 17 Sept. 1857, ibid., no. 232.

13. Same to same, res., 18 Dec. 1857, ibid., no. 257.

14. Same to same, 17 Jan. 1858, ibid., vol. 48, no. 266; same to same, 21 Jan. 1858, ibid., no. 268.

15. Same to same, confidentielle et personnelle, 1 Aug. 1858, ibid., vol. 49, ff. 8–9; see also same to same, 2 July 1858, ibid., vol. 48, no. 302.

16. Walewski to Gabriac, Paris, 28 Aug. 1858, ibid., vol. 49, f. 27; Otway to Malmesbury, Mexico, cypher, 3 Oct. 1858, PRO:FO 50/324, no. 148.

17. Radepont, "Mémoire sur le Mexique," November 1859, RP; "Note remise à S[a] M[ajesté]," Paris, 10 May 1860, RP; see also Radepont to Gabriac, on board the *Féviot*, copy, 8 Oct. 1859, RP.

18. Radepont, "Note remise à S.M.," 10 May 1860, RP. That he was listened to seriously and with respect is evident in Thouvenel's "Note" in the Foreign Ministry on Radepont's mission and French claims (AMAE,CP:Mexique, vol. 53, ff. 103–12).

19. Otway to Malmesbury, Mexico, 2 Jan. 1859, PRO:FO 50/330, no. 1; same to same, 2 Feb. 1859, ibid., no. 26; and same to same, 2 May 1859, ibid., 50/332, no. 71; Gabriac to French Foreign Ministry, Mexico, 1 Jan. 1859, AMAE,CP:Mexique, vol. 50.

20. Otway to Malmesbury, private, Mexico, 2 Aug. 1858, PRO:FO 50/323, unnumbered.

21. Same to same, 1 June 1858, ibid., 50/322, no. 12.

22. See table of exports, p. 193.

23. Report by Mr. Mathews, secretary of the British Legation, Mexico, 20 July 1859, PRO:FO 50/333.

24. "Convención suscrita por Díez de Bonilla y Levasseur," copy, Mexico, 30 June 1853, AEM, L.XXXIV, summarized in RFM, 2:180–81, no. 13811; Dano to Drouyn de Lhuys, Mexico, 2 July 1853, AMAE,CP:Mexique, vol. 41, no. 1, ff. 228–32.

25. Report by Mr. Mathews, secretary of the British Legation, Mexico, 20 July 1859, PRO:FO 50/333.

26. Gabriac to Walewski, Mexico, 1 Feb. 1858, AMAE,CP:Mexique, vol. 48, no. 271.

27. Radepont, "Mémoire sur le Mexique, 1er partie," Nov. 1859, RP; Ralph Roeder, Juarez and His Mexico, p. 189.

28. Otway to Malmesbury, Mexico, 17 Mar. 1858, PRO:FO 50/331, no. 44.

29. Gabriac to Walewski, Mexico, 6 May 1858, AMAE,CP:Mexique, vol. 48, no. 290.

30. Forsyth to Cass, excerpt, quoted by Lettsom to Clarendon, Mexico, confidential, 16 Apr. 1857, PRO:FO 50/308, no. 79; Hanna and Hanna, Napoleon III and Mexico, p. 22.

31. The terms of the treaty are summarized in Hubert Howe Bancroft, History of Mexico, 5:774, n. 24. They are reproduced textually in Spanish and English in Jorge L. Tamayo, ed., Benito Juárez, 3:751–63.

32. Such a message was the gist of Radepont's arguments for intervention, for example, in November 1859. Radepont, "Mémoire sur le Mexique. 2me partie," Nov. 1859, RP.

33. For a summary of the emperor's diplomatic problems in the Italian peninsula in 1859 and 1860, see Nancy Nichols Barker, Distaff Diplomacy, pp. 49–62.

34. Russell to Mathew, London, 26 Jan. 1860, PRO:FO 50/342, no. 4; and same to same, 9 Feb. 1860, PRO:FO 50/342, no. 8.

35. Mathew to Lord John Russell, Mexico, 19 Mar. 1860, ibid., 50/343, no. 23; Jules Doazan to Walewski, Veracruz, 1 Apr. 1860, AMAE,CP des Consuls:Mexique, 1858–60; Hanna and Hanna, Napoleon III and Mexico, p. 26.

36. Mathew to Lord John Russell, Mexico, 1 May 1860, PRO:FO 50/344, no. 37; same to same, confidential, 4 May 1860, ibid., no. 40; Hidalgo to Almonte (in Madrid), Paris, 14 May 1860, AEM, L.XXXVIII, RFM, 2:215, no. 15363.

37. Thouvenel's order is missing in the French archives. Gabriac's acknowledgment of it is in the dossier personnel of Gabriac, AMAE, 28 Apr. 1860.

38. For the career of Dubois de Saligny, see his dossier personnel, AMAE; Nancy N. Barker, "France Disserved," pp. 25–29. The details on the agent's mission in The Hague were supplied mainly by J. G. J. Kuiper, secretary of the embassy of the Kingdom of the Netherlands in Paris.

39. Roeder, Juarez, p. 321; Paul Gaulot, Rêve d'Empire, 1:29.

40. Dubois de Saligny to Radepont, Mexico, 4 Apr. 1861, RP.

41. Radepont to Morny, Mexico, 17 Sept. 1854, RP; and RP passim; Gustave Léon Niox, L'Expédition du Mexique 1861–1867, p. 723; see Nancy N. Barker, "The Duke of Morny and the Affair of the Jecker Bonds," pp. 555–61.

42. During the last months of his mission to Texas he resided on or near Bellechasse, Benjamin's plantation on the Mississippi River. Dubois de Saligny to Guizot, Bellechasse, 20 July 1845, AMAE,CP:Texas, no. 78. All of his subsequent correspondence with the Foreign Ministry until his return to France was dated from

Plaquemines, where Bellechasse was located (6 Aug. 1845 to 30 May 1846, ibid., nos. 79–103).

43. Pierce Butler, *Judah P. Benjamin*, pp. 119–33, 185–90; Robert Douthat Meade, *Judah P. Benjamin, Confederate Statesman*, pp. 121–33.

44. For the various grants of right-of-way across the isthmus by Mexican governments, see Agustín Cué Cánovas, *El Tratado McLane-Ocampo*, pp. 35–38.

45. C. E. Detmold to [Dubois de] Saligny, copy, New York, 6 Dec. 1860, RP. One large bundle in this collection, labeled "Tehuantepec," tells the story of the collusion of Benjamin and Dubois de Saligny, with Radepont as agent, to induce the French government to buy out Benjamin's company.

46. Archives of the County Clerk, Galveston, Texas. On 14 July 1842, one Henry A. Cobb acknowledged indebtedness to Dubois de Saligny for the sum of $20,000 secured by mortgages to 25 scattered lots in the city of Galveston (Book B/2, 326–27). For the sale to Benjamin on 3 October 1859, see Book P, 293–94. After the Tehuantepec affair failed, Benjamin quitclaimed the property back to Dubois de Saligny (Book Z, 182–83). On 10 Dec. 1868, Dubois de Saligny sold the property to J. L. Darragh (Book Z, 224–25) for $20,000, the amount by which he had acquired it. This last transaction proves that the real estate had not appreciated in value and that Benjamin's offer of $40,000 had been far above the going price.

47. Memorandum by Dubois de Saligny, Paris, 7 June 1860, AMAE,CP:Mexique, vol. 53, ff. 312–20. This memorandum has been almost totally ignored by historians, who have been at a loss to explain the connection between the two men. To my knowledge only three scholars have taken note of it. Christian Schefer, in his *La Grande pensée de Napoléon III*, can do no more with it than to label it "curious" (p. 66). Roeder in *Juarez* could describe Benjamin's position as head of the Louisiana-Tehuantepec Company (p. 282), but was unaware of the past association of Benjamin and Dubois de Saligny and the transactions between them. The most recent, Hanna and Hanna, in *Napoleon III and Mexico*, cite the memorandum in another context and make no mention at all of Benjamin and the Tehuantepec affair (p. 32).

48. [Dubois de]Saligny to Benjamin, copy, Paris, 1 Sept. 1860, and Benjamin to Emile Lasère, copy, Washington, D.C., 20 Dec. 1860, RP. Lasère was titular president of the Louisiana-Tehuantepec Company.

49. Radepont to Auguste Martin Duranger, 1 Sept. 1859; duplicate sent 5 Sept. 1859, RP. The letter was a sort of form letter. Appended were the names and addresses of two other individuals to whom similar offers were made.

50. Jecker to Conti, Paris, 8 Dec. 1860, *Papiers et correspondance de la famille impériale*, 1:3; Radepont to Snrs Jecker y Ca, 26 Dec. 1859, RP.

51. Radepont to his sister Louise, New York, 7 Dec. 1860, RP.

52. "Tesoreria general de la Nación. Noticia de los terminos en que recibió esta Tesoreria general el producto de refacción sobre quince millones de pesos, valor de bonos que fueron emitidos por decreto que en 29 del Octobre espidó el llamado Gobierno de la reacción, con garantía de la casa de J. B. Jecker," AEM, L.XXXIX, summarized briefly in *RFM*, 2:230, no. 15935. Léon de Montluc, *Correspondance de Juarez et de Montluc*, pp. 49–50. The account by Émile de Kératry (*La Créance Jecker*) is a partisan attack on the Second Empire. The article by J. B. Jecker, "La Créance Jecker," pp. 129–59, is Jecker's rebuttal of his enemies. One of the clearest explanations of this complicated and usually misunderstood transaction is by Niox, *L'Expédition du Mexique*, pp. 720–23.

53. Xavier Elsesser to Montluc, 1 Oct. 1860, Montluc, *Correspondance de Juarez*, pp. 48–49.

54. The identification of Marpon as Morny's agent and his activity in the affair of the bonds on Morny's behalf have been made only recently through study of documents presented in court on the occasion of an obscure lawsuit against the Morny estate in 1881. See Barker, "Duke of Morny," pp. 555–61. The earlier debate on the role of Morny in the affair was well summarized in app. C, "Morny, Saligny, and the Jecker Bonds," in Carl H. Bock, *Prelude to Tragedy*, pp. 475–84.

55. Correspondence between Jecker and his relatives in Europe intercepted in 1862 reveals the elaborate stratagems to which Morny's agents felt compelled to resort in order to persuade the emperor of the legitimacy of the claim. See especially Luis Elsesser to J. B. Jecker, Paris, 27 Oct. 1862, Niox, *L'Expédition du Mexique*, Appendix, pp. 723–28.

56. Bock, *Prelude to Tragedy*, pp. 391–92.

57. Marpon to Eugène de Pierres, 26 Nov. 1860, "Procès Morny," reported in *Le Temps*, 24 Jan. 1881, p. 2, and *Gazette des tribunaux*, 6 Feb. 1881. See Barker, "Duke of Morny," p. 558.

58. Jecker to Conti, Paris, 8 Dec. 1869, *Papiers et correspondance de la famille impériale*, 1:2; reproduced in part and in English translation by Bock, *Prelude to Tragedy*, app. C, p. 475.

59. Bock (*Prelude to Tragedy*, pp. 94–115) describes his demarches in detail but can give no explanation for them.

60. Thouvenel to Dubois de Saligny, Paris, confidential, 11 Apr. 1861, AMAE, CP:Mexique, vol. 54, no. 4.

61. [Dubois de]Saligny to Radepont, 4 Apr. 1861, RP.

62. Dubois de Saligny to Zarco, particulière, Mexico, 5 Feb. 1861, AMAE,CP: Mexique, vol. 54, ff. 96–97.

63. [Dubois de] Saligny to Radepont, Mexico, 4 Apr. 1861, RP.

64. The convention is reproduced in English translation in Bock, *Prelude to Tragedy*, app. E, pp. 494–95.

65. See Dubois de Saligny's Proposed Ultimatum, Veracruz, 10 Jan. 1862, reproduced in English translation in ibid., app. Q, pp. 539–42.

66. In 1864 a claims commission of mixed nationality (two Mexicans, two Frenchmen, and an American arbitrator) evaluated Mexican indebtedness to France as follows:

Due on Pénaud Convention of 1859 (for claims prior to that year)—$6,000,000
Due on Levasseur Convention of 1853—$190,000, all in bonds then in hands of a
    French banker and speculator
Due on Serment, Fort Convention of 1851—$46,058
Due on a private convention (regarding a claim of 1823)—$80,000
Claims later than Pénaud Convention—$4,000,000
Approximate total—$10,316,058

These figures are taken from Radepont to French foreign minister, copy, Mexico, 18 Apr. 1864, no. 77, RP. Greater precision for the year 1861 is not possible, largely owing to the deviousness and secrecy with which Dubois de Saligny handled French claims. The Treaty of London of October 1861 did not stipulate precisely the demands of the three powers. Dubois de Saligny submitted a list of grievances (see Niox, *Expédition du Mexique*, pp. 731–32), but many of them were not of the kind that should trigger a diplomatic claim. The French government itself estimated its claims in 1861 at $2,000,000 ("Note sur les griefs remise à l'amiral Jurien," ibid., p. 10). Thouvenel later found Dubois de Saligny's estimates "exaggerated" (Thouvenel to Dubois de Saligny, 22 Feb. 1862, ibid., p. 35).

The charge frequently made that Mexican indebtedness to France amounted only to $190,000 in 1861 (see, for example, Jan Bazant, *Historia de la deuda exterior de México*, pp. 88–90; and Edgar Turlington, *Mexico and Her Foreign Creditors*, p. 124) is erroneous. Yet, of course, it would have been absurd for France to have mounted an invasion of Mexico for any of the sums mentioned.

67. Dubois de Saligny to Thouvenel, Mexico, 30 Mar. 1861, AMAE,CP:Mexique, vol. 54, no. 15, ff. 207–9.

68, Mathew to Lord John Russell, Mexico, confidential, 12 May 1861, PRO:FO 50/352, no. 37.

69. Dubois de Saligny to Zarco, copy, confidential, Mexico, 2 May 1861, AMAE, CP:Mexique, f. 198; a copy of this note is also in AEM, L.XXXIX, summarized briefly in *RFM*, 2:229, no. 15931.

70. Dubois de Saligny to Radepont, Mexico, 4 Apr. 1861, RP; Marcel Blanchard, "Le Journal de Michel Chevalier," p. 122.

71. Radepont to Dubois de Saligny, 30 June 1861, RP; Radepont to Lasère, Paris, 2 July 1861, ibid.

72. Dubois de Saligny to Thouvenel, Mexico, 28 Apr. 1861, AMAE,CP:Mexique, vol. 54, no. 19, ff. 266–70.

73. Same to same, 27 May 1861, ibid., no. 27, ff. 316–21.

74. Same to same, 27 July 1861, ibid., vol. 55, no. 35.

75. Same to same, 21 Aug. 1861, ibid., no. 41, ff. 214–20.

76. Same to same, 26 Aug. 1861, ibid., no. 42.

77. Same to same, 29 Sept. 1861, ibid., no. 47.

78. Metternich to Rechberg, Paris, 30 June 1861, HHSA, 9, private letter.

79. The connection between the two questions is worked out in more detail in Nancy Nichols Barker, "France, Austria, and the Mexican Venture, 1861–1864," pp. 224–28.

80. Rechberg to Metternich, Vienna, 28 July 1861, HKM, Carton 1 (1861), no. 2.

81. Napoleon III to Count Flahault, Palais de Compiègne, 9 Oct. 1861, reproduced in English translation in Bock, *Prelude to Tragedy*, app. F, pp. 495–97.

82. Metternich to Rechberg, Compiègne, 16 Nov. 1861, HHSA, 9, no. 67, secret.

83. Rechberg to Metternich, Vienna, 28 July 1862, and Mülinen to Rechberg, Paris, 15 Oct. 1861, ibid., nos. 9, secret and 63C, secret; Mülinen to Rechberg, Paris, 15 Oct. 1861, HKM, Carton 1, no. 11.

84. Barker, "France, Austria, and the Mexican Venture," pp. 226–27.

85. George Maurice Paléologue, *The Tragic Empress*, pp. 92–93.

86. Don José Manuel Hidalgo y Esnaurrizar, "Notes secrètes de M. Hidalgo à développer le jour où il conviendra d'écrire l'histoire de la fondation de l'Empire Mexicain," preserved in HKM, Carton 19 (1865), no. 46. These notes have been used with reservation in the knowledge that Hidalgo always exaggerated his own role and belittled that of his compatriots. Egon Caesar, Count Corti (*Maximilian and Charlotte of Mexico*, 1:35, 78–80) related this incident but was not aware of, or at least did not mention, the Carlist ramification of the intrigue.

87. Hidalgo, "Notes secrètes," HKM, Carton 19 (1965), no. 46. Corti (*Maximilian and Charlotte*, 1:96–97) described the incident but mistakenly placed it in 1860.

88. Extract of a letter from Walewski to Metternich (16 Sept. 1861, HKM, Carton 1 (1861), no. 3) showing that Eugénie advocated the archduke's candidacy in July while visiting the country estate of Walewski at Etiolles. Corti mentions the letter but, probably owing to a mistake of a copying clerk, incorrectly dates it as of 16 November (Corti, *Maximilian and Charlotte*, 1:106, n. 14).

89. Eugénie's letters to Charlotte reveal starkly the French empress's ignorance of

Mexico and Mexicans. See, for example, those of 30 July 1864 and 1 April 1865, reproduced in English translation in Corti, *Maximilian and Charlotte*, 2:844 and 895.

90. Hidalgo to Almonte, Paris, 28 Feb. 1861, AEM, L.XXXVII, excerpted in *RFM*, 2:210, no. 14945; Oseguera to Zarco, Paris, 29 Mar. 1861, no. 13, ibid., L.XXXIX, *RFM*, 2:233, no. 16051.

91. Metternich to Rechberg, Paris, 14 Mar. 1864, private, HHSA, 9, no. 79.

92. Metternich to Beust, Paris, 11 July 1867, HHSA, reproduced in Hermann Oncken, *Die Rheinpolitik Kaiser Napoleons III. von 1863 bis 1870 und der Ursprung des Krieges von 1870/71*, 2:437, no. 499.

93. For a few examples, Corti, *Maximilian and Charlotte*, passim; Pierre de La Gorce, *Histoire du Second Empire*, 4:14-16; Baron Napoléon Beyens, *Le Second Empire vu par un diplomate belge*, 2:227-28; Harold Kurtz, *The Empress Eugénie, 1826-1920*, p. 168; J. P. T. Bury, *Napoleon III and the Second Empire*, p. 136.

94. Hidalgo is often mistakenly assumed to have been a girlhood friend of the empress. See Corti (*Maximilian and Charlotte*, 1:37 and 74) and many others who have followed his lead, including my own *Distaff Diplomacy*, p. 88. Hidalgo's appearance in Europe and his posts held are revealed in Lares to Almonte, Mexico, 28 Sept. 1860, AEM, L.XXXVII, *RFM*, 2:210, no. 14943; Hidalgo to Almonte, Paris, 28 Feb. 1861, ibid., no. 14945; José Manuel Hidalgo, *Un hombre de mundo escribe sus impresiones*, p. 81.

95. Niceto de Zamacois, *Historia de Méjico desde sus tiempos mas remotos hasta nuestros días*, 16:768-69, 777-78.

96. Thouvenel to Flahault, Paris, particulière, September 19, 1861, Louis Thouvenel, ed., *Le Secret de l'Empereur*, 2:167-69.

97. Napoleon III to Count Flahault, Palais de Compiègne, 9 Oct. 1861, reproduced in English translation in Bock, *Prelude to Tragedy*, p. 495.

98. Arthur Louis Dunham, *The Anglo-French Treaty of Commerce of 1860 and the Progress of the Industrial Revolution in France*, pp. 40-63; Camille Jullian, *Histoire de Bordeaux depuis les origines jusqu'en 1895*, pp. 756-57.

99. Schefer, *La Grande pensée*, pp. 3-19.

100. Michel Chevalier, *Le Mexique ancien et moderne*, p. 437. This book, published in 1864, was a compilation of articles published earlier in *Revue des Deux Mondes* to defend and explain the Mexican expedition. It is a full and lofty expression of the *grande pensée* behind the Mexican intervention. See Blanchard Jerrold, *The Life of Napoleon III*, 4:341.

101. Napoleon III to Count Flahault, Palais de Compiègne, 9 Oct. 1861, reproduced in English translation, Bock, *Prelude to Tragedy*, p. 496.

102. Thouvenel to Dubois de Saligny, Paris, 5 Sept. 1861, AMAE,CP:Mexique, vol. 55, no. 12.

103. The text of the convention is published in English translation in Bock, *Prelude to Tragedy*, pp. 517-20.

104. Rechberg to Mülinen, Vienna, 7 Oct. 1861, HHSA, secret, no. 4.

Notes to Chapter 7

1. Karl Marx, "Un Affaire Internacional Mirés," *Die Presse*, 28 Apr. 1862, extract in Spanish translation in José C. Valadés, "Mexico en la obra de Marx y Engels," p. 131.

2. See, for example, Aleksandr Borisovich Belen'Kii, *La intervencición extranjera de 1861-1867 en México*, pp. 48-56, 78-84.

3. Lynn M. Case, ed., *French Opinion on the United States and Mexico 1860–1867*, pp. 309–435.

4. In the autumn of 1858 the chambers of commerce of Le Havre and Bordeaux petitioned the government for intervention. See Almonte to Castillo y Lanzas, Paris, Nov. 1858, AEM, L.XXXI, *RFM*, 2:147, no. 12189; and Oseguera to Ocampo, 29 Nov. 1858, ibid., p. 148, no. 12191.

5. See table of exports, p. 193.

6. Case, *French Opinion on the United States and Mexico*, p. 314.

7. Louis Desgraves and Georges Dupeux, *Bordeaux au XIXe siècle*, p. 272.

8. See, for example, *Archives parlementaires*, Corps législativ, 13 Mar. 1862, 1:156–65; ibid., 25 Jan. 1864, 3:267–77.

9. Gabriac to Walewski, Mexico, 15 Apr. 1859, AMAE,CP:Mexique, vol. 45, no. 100.

10. George Peabody Gooch, *The Second Empire*, p. 77.

11. Christian Schefer, *La Grande pensée de Napoléon III*, p. 261.

12. Otway to Malmesbury, Mexico, private, 2 Aug. 1848, PRO:FO 50/323, un-numbered.

13. Mathew to Lord John Russell, confidential, Mexico, 31 Jan. 1860, ibid., 50/343, no. 16.

14. Margarita Martínez Leal de Helguera (*Posibles antecedentes de la intervención francesa de 1862 a través de las obras de viajeros franceses*) lists a total of 21 travel accounts, 16 in French. I have located 10 more, using the resources of the Nettie Lee Benson Latin American Collection, University of Texas at Austin.

15. J. C. Beltrami, *Le Mexique*.

16. Mathieu de Fossey, *Le Mexique*.

17. Eugène Duflot de Mofras, *Exploration du territoire de l'Orégon, des Californies, et de la mer Vermeille exécutée pendant les années 1840, 1841, et 1842*.

18. These themes are well summarized in an article by Margarita Martínez Leal de Helguera ("Posibles antecedentes de la intervención francesa," pp. 1–24) based on her longer study. She has not noted, as I have done in my reading, the increased tendency to call for intervention after the middle of the century.

19. Thouvenel to Flahault, Paris, particulière, 19 Sept. 1861, in Louis Thouvenel, ed., *Le Secret de l'Empereur*, 1:167–69. See also Lynn M. Case, *Édouard Thouvenel et la diplomatie du Second Empire*, pp. 368–69.

20. For a full statement of this hypothesis, see Michel Chevalier, *Le Mexique ancien et moderne*, pp. 494–508.

21. *Annuaire de deux mondes*, 1 (1850):902.

22. Napoleon to Flahault, Compiègne, 9 Oct. 1861, reproduced in English trans-lation by Carl H. Bock, *Prelude to Tragedy*, pp. 495–97.

23. George M. Fredrickson, *The Black Image in the White Mind*, p. 99.

24. Chevalier, *Le Mexique*, pp. 494–508.

25. Hannah Arendt, *The Origins of Totalitarianism*, p. 160.

26. Among many other things, I am indebted to Professor Nettie Lee Benson, Director of the Latin American Collection, University of Texas, for this line of argument, expressed in her paper, "Mexican Monarchists 1823–1867."

27. Egon Caesar, Count Corti, *Maximilian and Charlotte of Mexico*, 2:586–89.

28. Walewski to Metternich, 16 Sept. 1861, HKM, Carton 1 (1861), no. 3.

29. Bock, *Prelude to Tragedy*, pp. 126–27.

30. Leopold I to Ferdinand Maximilian, 25 Oct. 1861, original in HKM, quoted in Corti, *Maximilian and Charlotte*, 1:117.

31. Rechberg to Mülinen, Vienna, secret, 7 Oct. 1862, HHSA, 9, 79, no. 4.

32. Nancy Nichols Barker, *Distaff Diplomacy*, pp. 88–91.

33. Eugénie to Charlotte, Tuileries, 1 Apr. 1865, original in HKM, reproduced in English translation in Corti, *Maximilian and Charlotte*, 2:895.

34. Prim to Napoleon III, 17 Mar. 1862, in Emeterio Santovenia y Echaide, *Prim*, pp. 109–10.

35. See, for example, Hidalgo to De Pont, Paris, 21 Feb. 1863, HKM, Carton 3 (1863), no. 450; Rechberg to Ferdinand Maximilian, Vienna, 7 Mar. 1863, ibid., no. 449; Ferdinand Maximilian to Metternich, Miramar, 13 June 1863, ibid., no. 431; Metternich to Ferdinand Maximilian, Paris, 26 June 1863, ibid., no. 560.

36. Stefan Herzfeld to De Pont, London, 12 Dec. 1863, HKM, Carton 6, no. 80s. Wyke gave a frank account of his conversation with the emperor to Herzfeld, confidant to the archduke.

37. Alfred Jackson Hanna and Kathryn Abbey Hanna, *Napoleon III and Mexico*, pp. 169–77.

38. Nancy Nichols Barker, "France, Austria, and the Mexican Venture," pp. 234–38; and Barker, *Distaff Diplomacy*, pp. 126–27.

Bibliography

Unpublished Materials

Archives de la Mairie du VIe Arrondissement. Paris.
   Etat-Civil. Registre 68. de Saligny 170.
      Informative record of civil marriage in Mexico of Dubois de Saligny.
Archives de la Mairie. Saint Martin-du-Vieux-Bellême, Normandy.
      Contain an informative death certificate of Dubois de Saligny. The present
      mayor is the owner there of Le Prieuré, the former residence of Dubois de
      Saligny in retirement.
Archives du Consulat de France à Mexico. Mexico, D.F.
      Informative marriage contract, 19 December 1863, of Dubois de Saligny.
Archives du Ministère des Affaires Étrangères. Paris.
   Correspondance commerciale.
      Archives des postes
      Austin, 1 vol., 1840–46
      Mexico, D.F., vols. 1–7, 1817–61
      Paquebots, 1 folder, 1827–40
      Veracruz, vols. 1–3, 1826–63
   Correspondance politique.
      Affaires diverses, Mexique, 1847–50. Mission temporaire de Radepont.
      Angleterre, vol. 687, 1852
      Correspondance politique des consuls. Mexique, 1858–60, 1861–62.
         The political dispatches of the consuls before 1858 are classed with the corre-
         spondence of the Legation.
      Espagne, vols. 714–24, 1821–24
      Etats Unis, vols. 105–12, 1848–52
      Mexique, vols. 3–60, 1827–64
      Texas, vols. 1–9, 1839–46
   Dossiers personnels
      Alleye de Cyprey, Baron Isidore Elisabeth Jean-Baptiste
      Cochelet, Adrien Louis
      Dano, Alphonse François Marie
      Deffaudis, Baron Antoine Louis
      Dubois de Saligny, Alphonse
      Gabriac, Jean Alexis, Vicomte de
      Goury du Roslan, Célian Louis Anne-Marie
      Gros, Baron Jean-Baptiste Louis
      Levasseur, André Nicolas
      Martin, Alexandre Victor

Mémoires et documents.
  Amérique, vol. 41, 1830–32
  Mexique, vol. 9, 1837–59; vol. 7, 1849
  Papiers Desages
Archives Nationales. Paris.
  AB XIX 171–72, Papiers des Tuileries and dossiers du Mexique
Archives of the County Clerk. Galveston, Texas.
  Books B/2, P, and Z
    Records of real estate transaction between Dubois de Saligny and Judah P.
    Benjamin.
Archives of the County Clerk, Travis County. Austin, Texas.
    Contain legal documents on the house known as the French Legation built by
    Dubois de Saligny.
Archivo Histórico de la Secretaría de las Relaciones Exteriores. Mexico, D.F.
    This archive as a whole is less rewarding on Franco-Mexican relations than the
    archives of the Mexican Embassy in Paris. In some cases, as would be expected,
    the contents of the two archives duplicate each other, the one containing either
    the original or a copy of the document in the other.
  Camacho, Sebastián. L-E-385. Su expedienta personal, 1823–66
  Francia. Expediente H/112.4 (44–0), 1826–31, 6-20-1 to 6-20-6.
    Correspondence of Murphy with Mexican commercial agent in Bordeaux.
  Francia. Relaciones con México, 2-5-2635, 1825–26
    Contains reports of Rocafuerte to Mexican Foreign Ministry and copies of
    Murphy's reports, some of much interest, to Rocafuerte.
  Francia-Mexico. Primera Intervención de. L-E-1917 to L-E-1931, 1836–1841.
  Incidentes y diversos sucesos motivados por dicha Intervención.
    Fifteen bound volumes of documents of great diversity and some of high
    interest (a number have been published in the *AHDM* series).
  Garro, Máximo. Su expediente, 1829–46. L-E-395.
Archivos de la Embaja Mexicana. Paris.
    A very important but unwieldy collection of correspondence and documents of
    great diversity giving the Mexican side of Franco-Mexican relations. Nearly as rich
    on this subject as the French Foreign Ministry archives but not as well or-
    ganized. It is preserved in the basement storeroom of the embassy where,
    unfortunately, it is not easily accessible. The excellent two-volume guide by
    Luis Weckmann (*RFM*) greatly facilitates its use.
  Legajos I–XXXIX, 1823–61.
Benson, Nettie Lee. "Mexican Monarchists, 1823–1867."
    An unpublished paper read in Dallas, Texas, 23 March 1973 to a meeting of the
    Southwest Social Science Association.
Bibliothèque Nationale. Salle des Manuscrits. Paris.
  Papers of Léonce Angrand (N.A. France, 22072)
Haus-, Hof-, und Staatsarchiv. Vienna.
  Politisches Archiv, Frankreich, 1856–61.
Hausarchiv Kaiser Maximilians von Mexico. MSS in the HHSA.
  Photostatic copies in the Library of Congress, Washington, D.C.
    Ferdinand Maximilian's papers on the Mexican expedition and the Mexican
    empire.
Paredes Papers. Nettie Lee Benson Latin American Colllection, Austin, Texas.
  Contain hundreds of letters to Mariano Paredes y Arillaga.

Public Record Office. London. Microfilm copies in the Nettie Lee Benson Latin American Collection, Austin, Texas.

FO 50/28 to FO 50/361, 1826–61

Correspondence between the British secretary of foreign affairs and the British legation and consulates in Mexico. A very full and valuable source of information on diplomacy and commerce, very useful to this study of the French in Mexico, since it revealed how the agents of another European maritime power reacted to the same set of circumstances and provided a kind of control for the French reports emanating from Mexico.

Radepont Papers. Harvard College Library. Boston.

Miscellaneous collection of papers of Aimé Louis Victor du Bosc, Marquis of Radepont, that includes his passports, letterbooks, letters received, and a diary. Important, among other things, for information on the financial combinations of Dubois de Saligny, Judah P. Benjamin, and Radepont.

Published Materials

Adams, Ephraim Douglass, ed. *British Diplomatic Correspondence concerning the Republic of Texas, 1838–1846.* Austin: Texas State Historical Association, 1917.

Alamán, Lucas. *Historia de Méjico desde los primeros movimientos que prepararon su independencia en el año de 1808, hasta la época presente.* 5 vols. Mexico: Impr. de J. M. Lara, 1849–52.

Annales du commerce extérieur, France. Faits commerciaux. Nos. 46 à 59, 1861–1866. Publiées par le Ministère de l'Agriculture, du Commerce, et des Travaux publics. Paris: Paul Dupont, 1866.

Important source for statistics on French commerce. Although the title refers only to the 1860s, many of the tables go back to 1847.

Annuaire des deux mondes: histoire générale des divers états. Paris: Bureau de l'Annuaire des deux mondes, 1850–66.

A useful summary of informed opinion on public affairs of the day. Revelatory of contemporary attitudes and prejudices.

Archives du commerce, recueil de tous les documents officiels, renseignements, faits et avis, pouvant intéresser les négocians, fondé et dirigé par M. P. Henrichs. 39 vols. Paris: Bureau de Recueil, 1833–47.

A vast collection of documents and commercial information designed for use by embassies, consulates, chambers of commerce, etc.

Arendt, Hannah. *The Origins of Totalitarianism.* New York: Harcourt Brace, 1951.

Armengaud, André. *La Population française au XIXe siècle. (Que sais-je? Le point des connaissances actuelles.* No. 1420). Paris: Presses universitaires de France, 1971.

Arnaud, F. *Les Barcelonnettes au Mexique. Extrait des documents et notions historiques sur la vallée de Barcelonnette.* Digne: Imprimerie Chaspoul, Constans et Barbaroux, 1891.

Bancroft, Hubert Howe. *History of Mexico.* 6 vols. San Francisco: A. L. Bancroft and Co., 1883–88.

Barker, Nancy Nichols. *Distaff Diplomacy: The Empress Eugénie and the Foreign Policy of the Second Empire.* Austin and London: University of Texas Press, 1967.

———. "The Duke of Morny and the Affair of the Jecker Bonds." *French Historical Studies* 6 (1970): 555–61.

———. "France, Austria, and the Mexican Venture, 1861–1864." *French Historical Studies* 3 (1963): 224–45.

———. "France Disserved: The Dishonorable Career of Dubois de Saligny." In *Diplomacy in an Age of Nationalism: Essays in Honor of Lynn Marshall Case*, edited by Nancy N. Barker and Marvin L. Brown, Jr., pp. 25–43. The Hague: Martinus Nijhoff, 1971.

———. "The French Colony in Mexico, 1821–1861: Generator of Intervention." *French Historical Studies* 9 (1976): 596–618.

———. "The French Legation in Mexico: Nexus of Interventionists." *French Historical Studies* 8 (1974): 409–26.

———. ed. and trans. *The French Legation in Texas*. 2 vols. Vol. 1, *Recognition, Rupture, and Reconciliation*. Vol. 2, *Mission Miscarried*. Austin: Texas State Historical Association, 1971–73.

   Edited and translated copies of the correspondence between the French Foreign Ministry and their agents in Texas from 1838 to 1846. The originals are in the archives of the French Foreign Ministry.

———. "From Texas to Mexico: An *Affairiste* at Work." *Southwestern Historical Quarterly* 76 (1972): 15–37.

———. "In Quest of the Golden Fleece: Dubois de Saligny and French Intervention in the New World." *Western Historical Quarterly* 3 (1972): 253–68.

———. "Monarchy in Mexico: Harebrained Scheme or Well-Considered Prospect?" *Journal of Modern History* 48 (1976): 51–68.

———. "Voyageurs Français au Mexique, fourriers de l'intervention (1830–1860)." *Revue d'histoire diplomatique*. Janvier–Juin 1972, Nos. 1–2, pp. 1–19.

Bazant, Jan. *Historia de la deuda exterior de México (1823–1946)*. Mexico: El Colegio de México, 1968.

Beck, Thomas D. *French Legislators, 1800–1834: A Study in Quantitative History*. Berkeley: University of California Press, 1974.

Belen'kiĭ, Aleksandr Borisovich. *La intervención extranjera de 1861–1867 en México*. Mexico, D.F.: Fondo de Cultura Popular, 1966. Translated from the Russian by María Teresa Frances. Originally published by the Academy of Sciences of the USSR, Moscow, 1959.

   A Marxist account of the intervention.

Beltrami, J. C. *Le Mexique*. 2 vols. Paris: Crevot, 1830.

Bertier de Sauvigny, Guillaume de. *The Bourbon Restoration*. Translated by Lynn M. Case. Philadelphia: University of Pennsylvania Press, 1966.

Beyens, Baron Napoléon. *Le Second Empire vu par un diplomate belge*. 2 vols. Paris: Plon-Nourrit, 1925–26.

Blanchard, Marcel. "Le Journal de Michel Chevalier." *Revue historique*. 171 (1933): 115–42.

Blanchard, P., and Dauzats, A. *San Juan de Ulùa* [sic], *ou relation de l'expédition française au Mexique, sous les ordres de M. le contre-amiral Baudin*. Paris: Gide, 1839.

   The official French version of the Franco-Mexican war of 1838–39, published by order of the king and based on French documents.

Blumenthal, Henry. *A Reappraisal of Franco-American Relations, 1830–1871*. Chapel Hill: University of North Carolina Press, 1959.

Bock, Carl H. *Prelude to Tragedy: The Negotiation and Breakdown of the Tripartite Convention of London, October 31, 1861*. Philadelphia: University of Pennsylvania Press, 1966.

Brissot, M. A. *Voyage au Goazacoalcos* [sic], *aux Antilles, et aux Etats-Unis*. Paris: Arthus Bertran, 1857.

Bulletin des Lois de l'Empire français.

Bury, J. P. T. *Napoleon III and the Second Empire*. London: English Universities Press, 1964. Reprinted by Harper and Row, New York, 1968.

Bustamante, Carlos María. *El Gabinete mexicano durante el segundo periódo de la administración de exmo. señor presidente D. Anastasio Bustamante, hasta la entrega del mando al exmo. señor presidente interino, D. Antonio López de Santa Anna*. 2 vols. Mexico: J. M. Lara, 1842.

Butler, Pierce. *Judah P. Benjamin*. Philadelphia: Geo. W. Jacobs and Co., 1907.

Cady, John F. *Foreign Intervention in the Río de la Plata, 1838–1850: A Study of French, British, and American Policy in Relation to the Dictator Juan Manuel Rosas*. Philadelphia: University of Pennsylvania Press, 1929.

Calderón de la Barca, Fanny. *Life in Mexico: The Letters of Fanny Calderón de la Barca. With New Material from the Author's Private Journals*. Edited and annotated by Howard T. Fisher and Marion Hall Fisher. New York: Doubleday and Co., 1966.
    The author was the wife of Angel Calderón de la Barca, the first Spanish minister to Mexico.

Cambas, Manuel Rivera. See Rivera Cambas, Manuel.

Cameron, Rondo. *France and the Economic Development of Europe, 1800–1914: Conquests of Peace and Seeds of War*. 2d ed. Revised and abridged with the collaboration of Max E. Fletcher. Chicago: Rand McNally and Co., 1961.

Case, Lynn M. *Édouard Thouvenel et la diplomatie du Second Empire*. Translated by Guillaume de Bertier de Sauvigny. Paris: Editions A. Pedone, 1976.

————, ed. *French Opinion on the United States and Mexico 1860–1867: Extracts from the Reports of the Procureurs Généraux*. Copyright 1936, by the American Historical Association. Reprinted 1969 by Archon Books.

————, and Spencer, Warren F. *The United States and France: Civil War Diplomacy*. Philadelphia: University of Pennsylvania Press, 1970.

Castillo, Ignacio B. *El rompimiento de las relaciones diplomáticas entre Francia y Mexico en 1845*. Mexico, 1913.
    Only five copies printed. No publisher given.

Chabrand, Émile. *De Barcelonnette à Mexico*. Paris: E. Plon, Nourrit and Co., 1892.

Charléty, S. *La Monarchie de juillet (1830–1848)*. Vol. 5, *Histoire de France contemporaine depuis la révolution jusqu'à la paix de 1919*. Edited by Ernest Lavisse. Paris: Hachette, 1921.

Charnay, Désiré. *Cités et ruines Américaines*. Paris: Guide éditeur, 1963.
    The author was sent by Napoleon III in 1857 to Mexico to study ancient Mexican cultures.

Chateaubriand, François Auguste René, Vicomte de. *Voyages en Amérique, en Italie, au Mont-Blanc*. Vol. 6, *Oeuvres complètes*. Paris: Garnier frères, 1859–60.

Chatelain, Abel. "Les Migrations françaises vers le Nouveau Monde aux XIXe et XXe siècles." *Annales: économies, sociétés, civilisations* 1 (1947): 54–70.

Chevalier, E., capitaine de vaisseau. *Histoire de la marine française de 1815 à 1870*. Paris: Hachette, 1900.

Chevalier, Louis. *Classes laborieuses et classes dangereuses à Paris pendant la première moitié du XIXe siècle*. Paris: Librairie Plon, 1958.

————. "L'Emigration française au XIXe siècle." *Études d'histoire moderne et contemporaine* 1 (1947): 127–71.

Chevalier, Michel. *Lettres sur l'Amérique du Nord* (Petite Bibliothèque Américaine: Institut Français de Washington). Princeton, N.J.: Princeton University Press for Institut Français de Washington, 1944.

————. *Le Mexique ancien et moderne*. 2d ed. Paris: Hachette, 1864.

Christophe, Robert. *Le Duc de Morny. "Empereur" des Français sous Napoléon III.* Paris: Hachette, 1951.

Clercq, Alexandre Jehan Henri de, ed. *Recueil des traités de la France.* 17 vols. Paris: Ministère des Affaires Étrangères, 1864–91.

Cluseret, Gustave. *Mexico and the Solidarity of Nations.* New York: Blackwell, Printer, 1866.

Le Constitutionnel.

Contamine, Henri. *Diplomatie et diplomates sous la restauration 1814–1830.* Paris: Hachette, 1970.

Corti, Egon Caesar, Count. *Maximilian and Charlotte of Mexico.* Translated by Catherine Alison Phillips. 2 vols. New York: Alfred A. Knopf, 1928.
    Based entirely on European sources, mostly Austrian.

Cosío Villegas, Daniel. "La riqueza legendaria de México." *El Trimestre Económico* 6 (1939): 58–83.

Cubas, Antonio García. See García Cubas, Antonio.

Cué, Cánovas, Agustín. *Historia social y económica de México.* 2 vols. Mexico: Editorial América, 1946.

———. *El tratado McLane-Ocampo: Juárez, los Estados Unidos y Europa.* México: Editorial América Nueva, 1956.

Cuevas, Luis Gonzaga. *Exposición del Ex-Ministro que la suscribe, sobre las diferencias con Francia.* Mexico: Ignacio Cumplido, 1839.

Daumard, Adeline. *La Bourgeoisie parisienne de 1815 à 1848.* Paris: S.E.V.P.E.N., 1963.

Dawson, Daniel. *The Mexican Adventure.* London: G. Bell and Sons, 1935.

Deffaudis, Baron Antoine Louis. *Questions diplomatiques et particulièrement des travaux et de l'organisation du ministère des affaires étrangères.* Paris: Goujon et Milon, 1849.

Desgraves, Louis, and Dupeux, Georges. *Bordeaux au XIXe siècle. Histoire de Bordeaux,* vol. 6. Edited by Charles Higounet. Bordeaux: Fédération historique du Sud-Ouest, 1969.

Diario del Gobierno de la República Mexicana.

Díaz-López, Lilia, ed. and trans. *Versión francesa de México. Informes diplomático.* 4 vols. Vol. 1, 1853–58. Vol. 2, 1858–62. Mexico: El Colegio de México, 1963–64.
    Translations of selected correspondence between the French Foreign Ministry and its agents in Mexico. Originals are in the archives of the French Foreign Ministry.

Domenech, Emmanuel Henri Dieudonné. *Histoire du Mexique. Juarez et Maximilien. Correspondances inédites des présidents, ministres et généraux Almonte, Santa-Anna, Gutierrez, Miramon, Marquez, Mejia, Woll, etc. de Juarez, de l'empereur Maximilien et de l'impératrice Charlotte.* 2 vols. Paris: Librairie internationale, 1868.

Dommartin, Hippolyte Du Pasquier de. *Les Etats-Unis et le Mexique: l'intérêt européen dans l'Amérique du nord.* Paris: Librairie Guillaumin, 1852.

Don Juan Prim y su labor diplomática en Mexico. With an Introduction by Genaro Estrada. *AHDM.* No. 25. Mexico: Secretaría de Relaciones Exteriores, 1928.

Douanes. Administration des. *Tableau général du commerce de la France avec ses colonies et les puissances étrangères (Années 1829–1858).* After 1851 the title is *Direction générale des douanes et des contributions indirectes.* Paris: Imprimerie nationale, 1830–63. 1830–63.
    Published annually by the government, this series gives the official figures for French commerce.

Duflot de Mofras, Eugène. *Exploration du territoire de l'Orégon, des Californies, et de la mer Vermeille, exécutée pendant les années 1840, 1841, et 1842.* 2 vols. Paris: Arthus Bertrand, 1844.

Dunham, Arthur Louis. *The Anglo-French Treaty of Commerce of 1860 and the Progress of the Industrial Revolution in France*. Ann Arbor: University of Michigan Press, 1930.

Farragut, Loyall. *The Life of David Glasgow Farragut: First Admiral of the United States Navy, Embodying his Journal and Letters*. New York: D. Appleton and Co., 1879.

Ferry, Gabriel. *Scènes de la vie mexicaine*. Paris: Lecon éditeur, 1855.
> Ferry is a pen name for E. G. L. de Bellemare, a popular novelist whose works on Mexico went through several editions.

Flores, Jorge. *Lorenzo de Zavala y su misión diplomática en Francia (1834–1835)*. AHDM. 2d ser. Vol. 8. Mexico: Secretaría de Relaciones Exteriores, 1951.

Fossey, Mathieu de. *Le Mexique*. Paris: Plon, 1857.

France. *Archives parlementaires. Recueil complet des débats législatifs et politiques des Chambres françaises, imprimé par ordre du Sénat et de la Chambre des députés*. 2d ser. Paris: Libraire administrative Paul Dupont, 1867–1913.

Frank, André Gunder. See Gunder Frank, André.

Fredrickson, George M. *The Black Image in the White Mind: The Debate on Afro-American Character and Destiny*. New York: Harper and Row, 1971.

Gaillardet, Frédéric. *Sketches of Early Texas and Louisiana*. Translated and edited by James L. Shepherd III. Austin: University of Texas Press, 1966.

García Cubas, Antonio, ed. *Diccionario geográfico, histórico y biográfico de los Estados Unidos Mexicanos*. 5 vols. Mexico: Oficina Tipográfica de la Secretaría de Fomento, 1888–91.

Gaulot, Paul. *Rêve d'Empire. La Vérité sur l'expédition du Mexique d'après les documents inédits de Ernest Louet, Payeur en Chef du Corps Expéditionnaire*. 4th ed. Vol. 1, 1861–64. Paris: Paul Ollendorff, 1890.

Gazette des Tribunaux.

Génin, Auguste. *Les Français au Mexique du XVIᵉ siècle à nos jours*. Paris: Nouvelles éditions Argo, 1933.
> Written by a patriotic French businessman established in Mexico. Impressionistic and sometimes inaccurate, but valuable for many individual case histories.

Gooch, George Peabody. *The Second Empire*. London: Longmans, 1960.

Gravière, Jurien de la. *Les Gloires maritimes de la France: L'Amiral Baudin*. Paris: Plon, Nourrit et Cie, 1888.
> A eulogy.

Guérard, Albert. *Napoleon III*. Cambridge, Mass.: Harvard University Press, 1943.

Gunder Frank, André. *Lumpenbourgeoisie: Lumpendevelopment*. New York: Monthly Review Press, 1972.

Hale, Charles. *Mexican Liberalism in the Age of Mora, 1821–1853*. New Haven: Yale University Press, 1968.

Hanna, Alfred Jackson, and Hanna, Kathryn Abbey. *Napoleon III and Mexico: American Triumph over Monarchy*. Chapel Hill: University of North Carolina Press, 1971.

Haslip, Joan. *Imperial Adventurer: Emperor Maximilian of Mexico*. London: Weidenfeld and Nicolson, 1971.
> A popular account.

Hidalgo, José Manuel. *Apuntes para escribir la historia de los proyectos de monarquía en México desde el reinado de Carlos III hasta la instalación del Emperador Maximiliano*. Paris: Garnier Hermanos, 1868.
> An apology for the failure of the empire.

————. *Un hombre de mundo escribe sus impresiones; cartas*. edited by Sofía Verea de Bernal. Mexico: Editorial Porrúa, 1960.

Higonnet, Patrick-Bernard. "La Composition de la Chambre des Députés de 1827 à 1831." *Revue historique* 239 (1968): 351–79.

Houdaille, J. "Les Français au Mexique et leur influence politique et sociale (1760–1800)." *Revue française d'histoire d'outre-mer* 48 (1961): 143–233.

Howarth, Thomas E. B. *Citizen-King: The Life of Louis-Philippe King of the French.* London: Eyre and Spottiswoode, 1961.

Huber, Michel; Bunle, Henri; and Boverat, Fernand. *La Population de la France: son évolution et ses perspectives.* Preface by P. Haury. 4th ed. Paris: Librairie Hachette, 1965.

Hufton, Olwen H. *The Poor of Eighteenth-Century France 1750–1789.* Oxford: Clarendon Press, 1974.

Humboldt, Alexander von. *Political Essay on the Kingdom of New Spain.* Translated by J. Black. 4 vols. London: Longman, Hurst, Rees, Orme, and Brown, 1811.

Hyde, Harford Montgomery. *Mexican Empire: The History of Maximilian and Carlota of Mexico.* London: Macmillan, 1946.

Jecker, J. B. "La Créance Jecker." *Revue contemporaine,* 10 Jan. 1868, pp. 129–49.

Jenkins, E. H. *A History of the French Navy from Its Beginnings to the Present Day.* London: Macdonald and Jane's, 1973.

Jerrold, Blanchard. *The Life of Napoleon III.* 4 vols. London: Longmans, Green, and Co., 1882.

Johnson, Douglas. *Guizot. Aspects of French History 1787–1874.* London: Routledge and Kegan Paul, 1963.

Joinville, François Ferdinand Philippe Louis Marie d'Orléans, Prince de. *Notes sur l'état des forces navales de la France.* Paris: P. Masgana, 1844.
   The sailor son of Louis Philippe pleads for an increase in the size of the French navy.

———. *Vieux souvenirs, 1818–1848.* Paris: Calmann Lévy, 1894.
   The prince reminisces about (among other things) his part in the bombardment of Veracruz in 1839.

Le Journal des débats.

Jullian, Camille. *Histoire de Bordeaux depuis les origines jusqu'en 1895.* Bordeaux: Feret et Fils, 1895.

Katz, Friedrich. *Deutschland, Diaz, und die mexikanische Revolution: die deutsche Politik in Mexico 1870–1920.* Berlin: Deutscher Verlag der Wissenschaften. 1964.

Kératry, Émile de. *La Créance Jecker: les indemnités françaises et les emprunts mexicains.* Paris: Librairie internationale, 1868.

Kohl, Clayton Charles. *Claims as a Cause of the Mexican War.* New York: The Faculty of the Graduate School, New York University, 1914.

Kurtz, Harold. *The Empress Eugénie, 1826–1920.* London: Hamish Hamilton, 1964.

Labracherie, Pierre. *Michel Chevalier et ses idées économiques.* Paris: Picart, 1929.

La Chapelle, Alfred de. *Le Comte Raousset Boulbon et l'expédition du Sonore.* Paris: E. Dentu, 1859.

Lacour-Gayet, Jacques. *Histoire du commerce.* 5 vols. Paris: SPID, 1952.

Lafayette, Marie, Marquis de. *Mémoires, correspondance et manuscrits.* 6 vols. Paris: H. Fournier Ainé, 1837–38.

Lafond, Georges. *Le Mexique.* Paris: J. Dumoulin, 1928.

La Gorce, Pierre de. *Histoire du Second Empire.* 7 vols. Paris: Plon-Nourrit, 1894–1905.

Lambertie, Charles de. *Le Drame de la Sonora, l'état de Sonora, M. le Comte de Raousset-Boulbon et M. Charles de Pindray.* Paris: Ledoyen, Libraire-Éditeur, 1855.

Larenaudière, M. de. *Mexique et Guatemala*. Paris: Didot frères, 1843.

Lefèvre, D. *Documents officiels recueillis dans la secrétairerie privée de Maximilien. Histoire de l'intervention française au Mexique*. 2 vols. Brussels and London: n.p., 1869.

Léonardon, Henri. *Prim*. Paris: F. Alcan, 1901.

Levasseur, E. *Histoire du commerce de la France: de 1789 à nos jours*. Paris: Arthur Rousseau, 1912.

Lévy, Daniel. *Les Français en Californie*. San Francisco: Grégoire, Tauzy et Cie, 1884.

López Cámara, Francisco. *Los fundamentos de la economía mexicana en la época de la Reforma y la Intervención*. Mexico: Sociedad Mexicana de Geografía y Estadística, sección Historia, 1962.

Madelène, Henri de. *Le Comte Gaston Raousset Boulbon. Sa vie et ses aventures d'après ses papiers et sa correspondance*. Paris: Charpentier, 1876.

Maissin, Eugène. *The French in Mexico and Texas (1838–1839)*. Translated, with introduction and notes by James L. Shepherd III. Salado: Anson Jones Press, 1961.
    Maissin was Baudin's aide-de-camp and later chief of staff. He kept a diary while serving on the admiral's flagship off Veracruz in 1838–39.

Martínez Leal de Helguera, Margarita. "Posibles antecedentes de la intervención francesa." *Historia Mexicana* 15 (1956): 1–24.

———. *Posibles antecedentes de la intervención francesa de 1862 (a través de las obras de viajeros franceses)*. Mexico: Universidad Nacional Autonoma de Mexico, 1963.

Meade, Robert Douthat. *Judah P. Benjamin, Confederate Statesman*. New York and London: Oxford University Press, 1943.

Metcalf, Helen Broughall. "The California French Filibusters in Sonora." *California Historical Society Quarterly* 18 (1934): 3–21.

Mexico. *Memoria del Ministerio de Guerra y Marina. Años 1850–1857*. Mexico: Vicente G. Torres. 1850–57.
    Reports of the minister of war read in the Mexican Chambers. Important source of Mexican military history.

Meyer, Jean. "Les Français au Mexique au XIX e siècle." *Cahiers des Amériques latines* 9–10 (1974): 43–86.

Micard, Étienne. *La France au Mexique, étude sur les expéditions militaires, l'influence et le rôle économique de la France au Mexique*. Paris: Editions du Monde Moderne, 1927.
    An impressionistic work based mostly on travelers' accounts.

Miller, Robert Ryal, trans. and ed. "New Mexico in Mid-Eighteenth Century: A Report Based on Governor Velez Capuchín's Inspection." *Southwestern Historical Quarterly* 79 (1975): 168–81.

Le Moniteur Universel.

Montluc, Léon de. *Correspondance de Juarez et de Montluc*. Paris: G. Charpentier et Cie, 1885.

Morelet, Arthur. *Voyage dans l'Amérique centrale et le Yucatan*. Paris: Gide éditeur. 1857.

Muñoz Oraá, Carlos E. "Pronóstico de la independencia de América, y un proyecto de monarquías en 1781." *Revista de Historia de América* 50 (1960): 439–73.

Niox. Gustave Léon. *L'Expédition du Mexique 1861–1867: récit politique et militaire*. 2 vols. Paris: Librairie Militaire de J. Dumaine, 1874.

Noailles, H. G. H., Marquis de. *Le Comte Molé, 1781–1885. Sa vie, ses mémoires*. 6 vols. Paris: E. Champion, 1922–30.

Noël, Octave. *Histoire du commerce du monde depuis les temps les plus reculés*. 8 vols. Vol. 3, *Depuis la Révolution française jusqu'à la guerre franco-allemande 1870–1871*. Paris: Plon-Nourrit et Cie, 1906.

Nouvelle biographie générale depuis les temps les plus reculés jusqu'à nos jours. 46 vols. Publiée par M. M. Firmin Didot frères, sous la direction de M. le Dr. Hoefer. Paris: Firmin Didot, 1855–67.

Oncken, Hermann. *Die Rheinpolitik Kaiser Napoleons III, von 1863 bis 1870 und der Ursprung des Krieges von 1870/71.* 3 vols. Stuttgart: Deutsche Verlags-Anstalt, 1926.

Palacio, Vicente Riva. See Riva Palacio, Vicente.

Paléologue, George Maurice. *The Tragic Empress: A Record of Intimate Talks with the Empress Eugénie, 1901–1919.* Translated by Hamish Miles. New York: Harper and Brothers, 1928.

Papiers et correspondance de la famille impériale. 2 vols. Paris: Imprimerie nationale, 1870.

Parkes, Henry Bamford. *A History of Mexico,* 3d ed. Boston: Houghton Mifflin, 1966.

Peña y Reyes, Antonio de la, ed. *El Baron Alleye de Cyprey y el Baño de las Delicias.* AHDM. No. 18. Mexico: Secretaría de Relaciones Exteriores, 1926.

————,ed. *La labor diplomática de D. Manuel María Zamacona como Secretario de Relaciones Exteriores.* AHDM. 2d ser. Vol. 28. Mexico: Secretaría de Relaciones Exteriores, 1928.

————, ed. *La primera guerra entre México y Francia.* AHDM. 2d ser. Vol. 23. Mexico: Secretaría de Relaciones Exteriores, 1927.

Penot, Jacques. "L'Expansion commerciale française au Mexique et les causes du conflit franco-mexicain de 1838–1839." *Bulletin Hispanique* 75 (1973): 169–201.

Pereyra, Carlos. *De Barradas á Baudin: un libro de polémica historial.* Mexico: Tipografía económica, 1904.

Pike, Frederick B. *Hispanismo, 1898–1936: Spanish Conservatives and Liberals and their Relations with Spanish America.* Notre Dame: University of Notre Dame Press, 1971.

Pinkney, David. *The French Revolution of 1830.* Princeton: Princeton University Press, 1972.

Pletcher, David M. *The Diplomacy of Annexation: Texas, Oregon, and the Mexican War.* Columbia, Mo.: University of Missouri Press, 1973.

Pouthas, Charles H. "Les Ministères de Louis-Philippe." *Revue d'histoire moderne et contemporaine* (1954): 102–30.

————. *La Population française pendant la première moitié du XIXe siècle.* Institut nacional d'études démograhique. Travaux et Documents, Cahier No. 25. Paris: Presses Universitaires de France, 1956.

Quirarte, Martín. *Historiografía sobre el imperio de Maximiliano.* Mexico: Universidad Nacional Autónoma de México, Instituto de investigaciones históricas, 1970.

Reinach Foussemagne, Comtesse de. *Charlotte de Belgique: Impératrice du Mexique.* 5th ed. Paris: Plon-Nourrit, n.d.

Relaciones diplomáticas hispano-mexicanas (1838–1898). Documentos procedentes del Archivo de la Embajado de España en México. 1st ser. Despachos generales. Vol. 1, 1839–41. Mexico: El Colegio de México, 1949.
   This series is comprised of correspondence between the Spanish foreign ministers and Spanish ministers in Mexico drawn from the archives of the Spanish legation in Mexico. A valuable source of nineteenth-century diplomatic history.

Rémond, René. *The Right Wing in France from 1815 to de Gaulle.* Translated by James M. Laux. Philadelphia: University of Pennsylvania Press, 1966.

Richards, Edward W. "Louis Napoleon and Central America." *Journal of Modern History* 34 (1962): 178–84.

Rippy, James Fred. *The United States and Mexico*. New York: A. A. Knopf, 1931.

Riva Palacio, Vicente, ed. *México a través de los siglos. Historia general y completa del desenvolvimiento social, político, religioso, militar, artístico, científico y literario de México desde la antigüidad más remota hasta la época actual*. 5 vols. Barcelona: Espasa y compañia, 1888–89.

Rivera Cambas, Manuel. *Historia de la intervención Europea y Norte-Americana en México y del imperio de Maximiliano de Hapsburgo*. 3 vols. Mexico: Tip. de Aguilar é Hijos, 1888–95.

Roberts, W. Adolphe. *The French in the West Indies*. Indianapolis: Bobbs-Merrill Co., 1942.

Robertson, William Spence. *France and Latin-American Independence*. Baltimore: Johns Hopkins Press, 1939.

    A pioneering work on diplomatic relations of France with the Latin American republics in the 1820s.

————. "French Intervention in Mexico in 1838." *Hispanic American Historical Review* 24 (1944): 222–52.

————. *The Rise of Spanish American Republics as Told in the Lives of Their Liberators*. New York, London: D. Appleton and Co., 1921.

Roeder, Ralph. *Juarez and His Mexico*. New York: Viking Press, 1947.

Romero, Sr Matias. *Historia de las intrigas Europeas que ocasionaron la intervención francesa en Mexico. Nota del Sr Romero á Mr. Seward, el 2 de octubre de 1862*. Mexico: Imprenta del Gobierno, 1868.

Santovenia y Echaide, Emeterio. *Prim: el Caudillo estadista*. Madrid: Espasa-Calpe, S.A., 1933.

Schefer, Christian. *La Grande pensée de Napoléon III: les origines de l'expédition du Mexique (1858–1862)*. Paris: Librairie Marcel Rivière, 1939.

    A respected French authority on the origin of the Maximilian affair. Quite sympathetic to Napoleon III. Based almost exclusively on European sources.

Seignobos, Charles. *La Révolution de 1848–Le Second Empire (1848–1859)*. Vol. 6, *Histoire de France contemporaine depuis la révolution jusqu'à la paix de 1919*. Edited by Ernest Lavisse. Paris: Hachette, 1920–22.

El Siglo XIX.

Smith, Ashbel. *Reminiscences of the Texas Republic. Annual address delivered before the Historical Society of Galveston, December 15, 1871*. Galveston: Published by the Society, 1876.

Soulié, Maurice. *The Wolf Cub: The Great Adventure of Count Gaston de Raousset-Boulbon in California and Sonora, 1850–1854*. Translated by Farrell Symons. Indianapolis: Bobbs-Merrill Co., 1927.

Statistique de la France: Commerce exterieur. 2 vols. Paris: Imprimerie royale, 1825–48.

Stout, Joseph Allen, Jr. *The Liberators: Filibustering Expeditions into Mexico 1848–1862 and the Last Thrust of Manifest Destiny*. Los Angeles: Westernlore Press, 1973.

Tamayo, Jorge L., ed. *Benito Juárez: documentos, discursos y correspondencia*. Mexico: Secretaría del Patrimonio Nacional, 1964–

Temperley, Harold. "French Designs on Spanish America in 1820–1825." *English Historical Review* 40 (1925): 34–53.

Le Temps.

Tenenbaum, Barbara A. "Straightening Out Some of the Lumpen in the Development." *Latin American Perspectives* 2 (1975): 3–14.

Thouvenel, Louis, ed. *Le Secret de l'Empereur: correspondance confidentielle et inédite échangée entre M. Thouvenel, le Duc de Gramont, et le général Comte de Flahault, 1860–1863*. 2 vols. Paris: Calmann Lévy, 1889.

El Tiempo.

Tornel, José María. *Breve reseña histórica de los acontecimientos más notables de la Nación Mexicana desde el año de 1821 hasta nuestras días.* Mexico: Imprenta de Cumplido, 1852.

Torre Villar, Ernesto de la. *Correspondencia diplomática franco-mexicana 1808–1839.* Vol. 1. Mexico: El Colegio de Mexico, 1957.

A guide to French diplomatic correspondence preserved in the archives of the French Foreign Ministry. It also contains translations of two long French memoranda on Mexico in vol. 1 of those archives.

———. *Las fuentes francesas para la historia de México y la guerra de intervención.* Colección del Congreso Nacional de Historia para el estudio de la Guerra de Intervención. No. 10. Mexico: Sociedad Mexicana de Geografía y Estadística, Sección de Historia, 1962.

A guide to French archives for history of Mexico from the sixteenth century to the present. Unfortunately, all archives and collections are listed in Spanish translation.

———, ed. *Labor diplomática de Tadeo Ortiz. AHDM.* Mexico, D.F.: Secretaría de Relaciones Exteriores, 1974.

Le Trait d'Union.

French language newspaper published in Mexico, D.F. At mid-century its editor, René Masson, was republican and often hostile to the French minister in Mexico.

Tratados y convenciones celebrados y no ratificados por la República Mexicana. In *Derecho internacional mexicano.* Pt. 2. Mexico: Gonzolo A. Esteva, 1878.

Tratados y convenciones concluidos y ratificados por la República Mexicana desde su independencia hasta el año actual, acompañados de varios documentos que les son referentes. Edición oficial. Mexico: Gonzalo A. Esteva, 1878.

Turlington, Edgar. *Mexico and Her Foreign Creditors.* New York: Columbia University Press, 1930.

El Universal.

Valadés, José C. *José María Gutiérrez de Estrada. Diplomático e historiador, 1800–1867, Enciclopedia yucatenense.* Mexico: Edic. oficial del Gobierno de Yucatán, 1944.

———, ed. "Mexico en la obra de Marx y Engels." *El Trimestre Económico* 6 (1939): 84–140.

Valle, Rafael Heliodoro, ed. *Un diplomático mexicano en Paris (Don Fernando Mangino, 1848–1851). AHDM.* 2d ser. No. 6. Mexico: Secretaría de Relaciones Exteriores, 1947.

La verdad desnuda sobre la guerra de Tejás o sea contestación al folleto titulado: La Guerra de Téjas sin máscara. Mexico: Calle de la Palma, Número 4, 1845.

Villegas, Daniel Cosío. See Cosío Villegas, Daniel.

Villèle, Jean-Baptiste Guillaume Joseph, Comte de. *Mémoires et correspondance du Comte de Villèle.* 5 vols. Paris: Perrin et Cie, 1904.

Weckmann, Luis, ed. *Las relaciones Franco-Mexicanas 1823–1867. AHDM: Guías para la Historia Diplomática de México.* No. 1. 2 vols. Mexico: Secretaría de Relaciones Exteriores, 1961.

An excellent guide to the archives of the Mexican Embassy in Paris. The editor has affixed a number to each document and has summarized or partially quoted from some of the most significant papers.

Wellesley, Victor, and Sencourt, Robert, eds. *Conversations with Napoleon III. A Collection of Documents Mostly Unpublished and Almost Entirely Diplomatic, Selected and Arranged with Introductions.* London: E. Benn, 1934.

Weymuller, F. *Histoire du Mexique*. Paris: Presses Universitaires de France, 1953.

Wise, H. A. *Seven Decades of the Union. The Humanities and Materialism Illustrated by a Memoir of John Tyler, with Reminiscences of Some of his Great Contemporaries*. Philadelphia: J. B. Lippincott, 1872.

Wolf, L'Intendant-Général. *Mes Souvenirs militaires*. Paris: 39, rue de Grenell-Saint-Germain, 1886.

Wyllys, Rufus Kay. *The French in Sonora (1850–1854): The Story of French Adventurers from California into Mexico*. Berkeley: University of California Press, 1932.

Zamacois, Niceto de. *Historia de Méjico desde sus tiempos mas remotos hasta nuestros días*. 18 vols. Mexico: Párres y Compania, 1876–82.

Zavala, Lorenzo de. *Ensayo histórico de las revoluciones de México*. 2 vols. Mexico: Imprenta de M. N. de la Vega, 1855.

Index

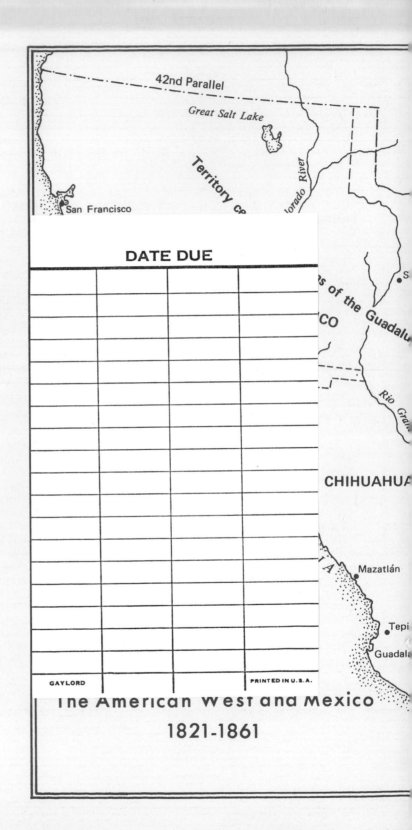

42nd Parallel

Great Salt Lake

Territory

Colorado River

San Francisco

s of the Guadalu

CO

S

CHIHUAHUA

Rio Gra

Mazatlán

Tepi

Guadala

The American West and Mexico

1821-1861

DATE DUE

GAYLORD			PRINTED IN U.S.A.